Christopher Marlowe
DR FAUSTUS: THE A-TEXT

Doctor Fauſtus.

Come Helen, come giue mee my ſoule againe.
Here wil I dwel, for heauen be in theſe lips,
And all is droſſe that is not Helena: *enter old man*
I wil be Pacis, and for loue of thee,
Inſteede of *Troy* ſhal *Wertenberge* be ſackt,
And I wil combate with weake Menelaus,
And weare thy colours on my plumed Creſt:
Yea I wil wound Achillis in the heele,
And then returne to Helen for a kiſſe.
O thou art fairer then the euening aire,
Clad in the beauty of a thouſand ſtarres,
Brighter art thou then flaming Iupiter,
when he appeard to hapleſſe Semele,
More louely then the monarke of the ſkie
In wanton Arethuſaes azurde armes,
And none but thou ſhalt be my paramour.   *Exeunt.*

   Old man Accurſed Fauſtus, miſerable man,
That from thy ſoule excludſt the grace of heauen,
And flieſt the throne of his tribunall ſeate,
           Enter the Diuelles.
Sathan begins to ſift me with his pride,
As in this furnace God ſhal try my faith,
My faith, vile hel, ſhal triumph ouer thee,
Ambitious fiends, ſee how the heauens ſmiles
At your repulſe, and laughs your ſtate to ſcorne,
Hence hel, for hence I flie vnto my God.   *Exeunt.*

   Enter Fauſtus with the Schollers.

   Fau: Ah Gentlemen!
   1. Schr what ailes Fauſtus?
   Fau: Ah my ſweete chamber-fellow! had I liued with
thee, then had I liued ſtil, but now I die eternally: looke,
comes he not? comes he not?
   2. Sch: what meanes Fauſtus?
   3. Scholler Belike he is growne into ſome ſickenıſſe, by
                  F   being

Doctor Faustus: the 1604 Edition.

Signature F1ʳ, original size, from Bodleian Mal. 233(3), the unique surviving copy. Reproduced from the Scolar Press Limited facsimile edition (Menston, 1970).

See lines 1381–1412 of the text of this edition.

Christopher Marlowe
DR FAUSTUS: THE A-TEXT

Edited by

DAVID ORMEROD and **CHRISTOPHER WORTHAM**

UNIVERSITY OF WESTERN AUSTRALIA PRESS

First published in 1985
by the University of Western Australia Press
Nedlands, W.A. 6009

Reprinted with amendments 1989
Open University Set Book edition

Agents: Eastern States of Australia, New Zealand and Papua New Guinea: Melbourne University Press, Carlton South, Vic. 3053; U.K., Europe, Africa and Middle East: Peter Moore, P.O. Box 66, 200a Perne Road, Cambridge CB1 3PD, England; U.S.A., Canada and the Caribbean: International Specialized Book Service Inc., 5602 N.E. Hassalo Street, Portland, Oregon 97213, U.S.A.; Singapore and Malaysia: National University of Singapore Multi-Purpose Co-operative Society Ltd, Ground Floor, Central Library, Kent Ridge, Singapore 0511.

Phototypeset by the University of Western Australia Press, printed and bound in Singapore by Chong Moh Offset Printing Pte. Ltd.

National Library of Australia Cataloguing-in-Publication data

Marlowe, Christopher, 1564-1593.
[Doctor Faustus] Dr. Faustus, the A-text.
Bibliography.
ISBN 0 85564 232 7.

I. Omerod, David, 1935- . II. Wortham, Christopher, 1940- . III. Title.

822'.3

Preface

We first conceived the project of producing a modern edition of the A-text of Marlowe's *Doctor Faustus* early in 1980, largely as a result of re-reading and approving the cogent arguments put forward by Constance Brown Kuriyama and Fredson Bowers. The views of these scholars on the primacy of the 1604 A-text over the 1616 B-text are discussed in Section 4 of the Introduction, together with the later findings of Michael J. Warren and Michael H. Keefer, which were published opportunely at staggered intervals and served to revive our periodically flagging sense of purpose. We had originally decided to produce a text with explanatory notes after the fashion adopted by the editors of the text of *Everyman* which had appeared under the imprint of the University of Western Australia Press in 1980. In the Cooper and Wortham *Everyman* the text is printed on the recto leaf, and the notes appear *en regard* on the facing verso. In that edition, major importance was attached to the explanatory notes, and the amount of text per page is in direct proportion to the necessity to include, amplify or moderate the facing explanatory material. We were soon compelled to abandon this methodology for the A-text of *Doctor Faustus*, for the sheer volume of critical elucidation which we initially thought was necessary — especially for the opening and closing episodes of the play — produced a play-text so skewed that it grotesquely distorted the speed, homogeneity and integrity of Marlowe's play. We eventually decided that the major goal of the project should be the production of a modernised but faithful text, and this has had three important results: we have cut down very considerably on the amount of material printed *en regard*, we have considerably enlarged the Introduction, and we have regretfully resisted the temptation to relineate the closing episode of the play. In this edition, as in the original, Faustus' final hour lasts for only 57 minutes.

We hope, therefore, that we have achieved our initial aim: to produce, for the modern reader of Marlowe's play, whether he or she be undergraduate, actor, or literary scholar, a version which will be arguably closer to the play as it was probably envisaged by Marlowe, and which will hence provide the first real opportunity for Marlowe's twentieth century audience to come to grips with whatever it is we invoke when we allude to such logically vexed issues as the 'meaning' of the play or the nature of the playwright's 'intentions'.

Technically, this has not been an easy book to produce, and we are enormously grateful to the University of Western Australia Press, and especially to Mr Vic Greaves, Mr Ray Firkin, and Mr Bryan Lewis, for the skill and patience they have employed in decoding a manuscript, of joint authorship, which sometimes must have presented bibliographical and exegetical problems akin to the decipherment of the most mangled of Elizabethan prompt books, the grossest of foul papers, and the worst of bad quartos. If the welding of the innumerable joints and integuments is anywhere apparent, the blame rests solely with the editors.

PREFACE

During the four years which it took to produce a finished version of this edition, we have had a great deal of help from many quarters. Our main debt of thanks is to the University of Western Australia for providing us with the opportunity to take study leave in 1980 and 1983, to our colleagues in the English Department who undertook the resultant extra teaching loads, and to Professor John Hay and the English Department Budget Committee for a grant-in-hand to initiate the publication of the work. Research for the edition has been undertaken in several libraries in Australia and abroad. We are most grateful to the librarians of the Reid Library of the University of Western Australia for their invariably cheerful and highly professional assistance, and especially to Mrs En Kho, to Mrs Audrey Black, and to the late Miss Mary Alexander, for the way in which they always provided such efficient I.L.L. and computer search facilities. Our thanks are also due to the librarians of the Warburg Institute of the University of London, the Cambridge University Library, the Cambridge English Faculty Library, and the British Library, together with the Master and Fellows of Winchester College and Mr Paul Yeats-Edwards, Fellows' Librarian.

Many individual friends and scholars have provided noble assistance. Our special thanks are due to Dr Richard Douglas Jordan, of the University of Melbourne, and Dr David J. Lake, of the University of Queensland, who both read the work in its entirety, and offered myriad suggestions for revision and improvement. Human nature being what it is, we sometimes mulishly rejected their excellent advice; they are hence to be held responsible for some of the improvements but none of the remaining errors and solecisms. Our thanks, too, to Dr Philip Tyler, of the University of Western Australia, for sharing with us his expert and disturbing knowledge of witchcraft in Reformation England, to Dr Robert van Pelt, of the Sir Thomas Browne Institute, University of Leyden, for several discussions regarding Renaissance number systems, to Professor Antony Price, formerly of the University of Malaya, for reading sections of the Introduction in their original inchoate state and making just the right suggestions for improvement, to Miss Roma Gill, of the University of Sheffield, for sharing with us her experiences as a Marlowe editor, to the members of the Marlowe Society of America for their advice at the 1983 Marlowe Conference in Sheffield, to the late Dame Frances Yates, of the Warburg Institute, for enthusiastically endorsing the critical rationale which underlies our reading of the story of Faustus' life and death, and to the late Emeritus Professor Max Jones, of the University of Western Australia, for advice on the patrology of the play which we did not sufficiently value at the time. To Professor John Hill, too, who, although distant, is always present, and to Anne and Bev, who are unable to escape and who have had a lot to put up with over the last quadrennium.

Nedlands, 1985

For this revised edition, we wish to record our thanks to those reviewers who have pointed out errors and omissions, and especially to Bruce McClintock for his painstaking and scholarly scrutiny of the first edition. Our thanks are due, too, to the Marlowe Society of America, who, at the beginning of 1988, honoured the first edition of *Doctor Faustus: the A-Text* by awarding it the Roma Gill Prize.

Nedlands, 1988

CONTENTS

INTRODUCTION

SELECT BIBLIOGRAPHY

INTRODUCTION

1. Christopher Marlowe

On 26 February, 1564 Christopher Marlowe was baptized in Canterbury, where he had been born a few days before. He was older by about two months than another child of 1564 who would become famous as a poet and dramatist — William Shakespeare. The Marlowe family was modestly respectable, Christopher's father being a shoemaker of at least moderate means, but it was a contentious household. Marlowe senior was known to be extremely aggressive, and somewhat feckless; two of Christopher's sisters acquired unenviable reputations for uncouth and vexatious behaviour in the town of Canterbury. There were two other boys apart from Christopher, but both died young.[1]

Both Marlowe and the young Shakespeare benefitted from the surge of humanistic education which marked the high Renaissance in England. The "humanities", so called, derived from the *studia humanitatis*, or studies of humanity, which became increasingly influential towards the close of the Middle Ages. The Latin classics, and more gradually the Greek, gained increasing attention in a curriculum which sought to rediscover those elements of classical education which had been lost and to develop yet further those which had been maintained through the predominantly religious education of the Middle Ages. Throughout Europe, Christianity remained immensely influential and it was an abiding preoccupation of the humanists (from Sir Thomas More early in the sixteenth century to John Milton late in the seventeenth) to reconcile the immediate demands of true revealed religion, as Christianity was generally acknowledged to be, with pagan cultures which had been graced only with dim glimmerings of the truth. Even though education had become thoroughly secularized by Marlowe's time, most dons at Cambridge were still members of the clergy.

The schooling received by Marlowe and Shakespeare would have been very similar in scope. Their great contemporary, Ben Jonson, was also educated in the humanistic tradition and his famous phrase "small Latin and less Greek" in describing Shakespeare's academic attainments has often been grossly distorted by being quoted out of context. In fact, Jonson was not denigrating Shakespeare but rather praising his native genius as far surpassing Jonson's own achievements through studied emulation of the classics. All three — Marlowe, Shakespeare, and Jonson — would have had a grounding in the classical literatures and ancillary disciplines which no twentieth-century school-boy or schoolgirl could hope to have.

Although the name of the King's School, which Marlowe attended in Canterbury, was as recent as 1541, it had been part of the cathedral precinct. At the dissolution of the monasteries the ancient school continued, under new patronage and government.

Marlowe had probably attended the school for several years when, in 1579, he won a scholarship to pay for his last two years there. By the time he finished his schooling he had won a further scholarship, which took him to Corpus Christi College, Cambridge. The scholarship was endowed by Matthew Parker, Archbishop of Canterbury, who was himself a former scholar, Fellow and Master of Corpus.

University studies continued the strongly classical education of the schools. At the King's School Marlowe would have studied Latin grammar from Lily's *Rudiments* in his first year; in the second form he would have encountered Cato's *Disticha*, Aesop's *Fables*, and works by Erasmus, together with more advanced grammar; in the third form, the comedies of Terence and the *Eclogues* of Mantuan; in the fourth form, yet more syntax, with exercises in Latin on models of Latin poetry, and the letters of Cicero; in the fifth form, rhetoric and translation, putting Latin verse and prose into English; in the sixth, more studies from Erasmus, together with more advanced exercises in composition within a variety of literary genres. Once at Cambridge, Marlowe would have given most of the first year to rhetoric, to which he had already been introduced at school; the second year to logic; and the third year to philosophy.[2]

In terms of religious thought, the Cambridge of Marlowe's day was a controversial place. Extremes of opinion were widespread: on the one hand, several of the colleges had Puritan leanings strong enough to cause disquiet at the court of Queen Elizabeth; on the other hand, the university was producing a number of defectors to Roman Catholicism. Marlowe seems to have become involved, possibly through circumstance rather than any act of deliberate commitment, in spying on defectors who had gone to join the English college at Rheims, where Catholic priests were being trained and ordained before returning to practise their secret ministry in England. Since 1570, when Pope Pius V had excommunicated Queen Elizabeth and dissolved her subjects' oath of allegiance to her, Papism had become a matter of treason: the penalty for priests who were discovered was generally death, preceded by some of the nastier forms of torture.

During his Cambridge years Marlowe was taken up and befriended by one of the richest and most powerful families in England. The relationship with Thomas Walsingham, nephew of Sir Francis Walsingham (Secretary of State to Queen Elizabeth), was probably genuinely grounded in mutual admiration: the shoemaker's son may have been as deeply impressed by the sophisticated manners and social prestige of the rich young gentleman as the rich young gentleman evidently was by the astonishing intellectual powers of the shoemaker's son. Unfortunately for Marlowe, in the long run, his association with the Walsinghams led, indirectly at least, to his own violent death, for Sir Francis Walsingham was also head of the Queen's espionage service and through his nephew he recruited spies to infiltrate the seminaries for English Catholics on the continent. To the mysterious and uncertain circumstances surrounding Marlowe's death we shall return.

Instead of leaving Cambridge after earning his B.A., Marlowe stayed another three years for his M.A. Those who remained were usually, though not invariably, candidates for Holy Orders in the Church of England. Students who intended to defect to Roman Catholicism generally made the most of their post-graduate studies at Cambridge and then left, quietly and suddenly, shortly before taking their M.A. At such a moment Marlowe himself left, but he returned to present himself for his higher degree. Evidently the University authorities were suspicious, for it took a directive from the Privy Council to satisfy them that he should graduate. The Privy Council's resolution read:

> Whereas it was reported that Christopher Morley [Marlowe's name was variously spelt] was determined to have gone beyond the seas to Reames [Rheims] and there to remain Their Lordships thought good to certefie that he had no such intent, but that in all his accions he had behaued himselfe orderlie and discreetelie wherebie he had done her Majestie good seruice, and deserued to be rewarded for his faithfull dealinge: Their Lordships request was that the rumor thereof should be allaied by all possible meanes, and that he should be furthered in the degree he was to take this next Commencement [Graduation]: Because it was not her Majesties pleasure that anie one emploied as he had been in matters touching the benefitt of his Countrie should be defamed by those that are ignorant in th'affaires he went about.[3]

The resolution does not say whether Marlowe in fact went to Rheims during his absence from Cambridge, or what precisely the "rumor" was, or what form the "good seruice" which he had performed so "discreetelie" actually took. But the moment of his departure and his connection with the Walsingham famiiy make for a clear enough inference: Marlowe was spying on candidates for the Catholic priesthood by pretending to be one of them.

When Marlowe went down from Cambridge to London in 1587, with his M.A. safely awarded and a career as professional dramatist in prospect, he seems to have put his dangerous liaisons behind him — for the time being. Whatever company Marlowe kept during the six remaining years of his short life, he must have committed himself wholeheartedly to his work: his output was astonishing, even by Elizabethan standards of literary industriousness. Those few years yielded seven plays and the long, though unfinished, poem *Hero and Leander*. He probably wrote *Hero and Leander* while the theatres were closed indefinitely following a terrible outbreak of plague early in 1592.

Although there is no certainty that Marlowe and Shakespeare ever met, it is highly probable that they did. It is possible, though not certain, that Shakespeare and Marlowe were briefly members of the same company, for Pembroke's Men performed Marlowe's *Edward II* and two early Shakespeare plays, *3 Henry VI* and *Titus Andronicus*. In his younger days, Shakespeare was considerably influenced by Marlowe who, by the time of his death, had achieved more works of stature than had Shakespeare. It is generally agreed that Shakespeare's *Richard II* owes much to Marlowe's *Edward II*, which advanced the evolving form of the history play. Similarities in form, theme, and treatment between Marlowe's *Hero and Leander* and Shakespeare's *Venus and Adonis*, both written round about 1592, have led some critics to think that Shakespeare saw Marlowe's poem in manuscript, but a case can also be made for mutual influence: it is possible that the two poets exchanged drafts or read portions aloud in the same company. Nine of Shakespeare's 154 sonnets allude to a rival poet; while the rival poet may have been Marlowe, George Chapman is generally regarded as a more likely contender.

Unfortunately, most of what we know about Marlowe's last few years can be pieced together only by conjecture, through the second-hand evidence of other people who all had their own axes to grind. An example is Marlowe's alleged association with an alleged School of Night, or atheism. One Robert Parsons speaks of "Sir Walter Rawleys school of Atheisme . . . & of the Conjurer that is Master thereto, and of the diligence used to get yong gentlemen of this schoole."[4] The conjurer is almost certainly Sir Thomas Herriot, whose valid scientific and mathematical discoveries were meeting with suspicion from the ignorant and the conservative. Assuming for the moment that he was associated with Raleigh, one can well imagine that Marlowe would have been a prime catch for their circle. Parsons further declares that within this School "both Moyses & our Savior, the olde and the new Testamente, are iested at", which fits in with a deposition by one Richard Baines as the basis for a charge of blasphemy against Marlowe: Baines accuses Marlowe of saying "that Moyses was but a Jugler & that one Heriots, being Sir W. Raleighs man, Can do more than he."[5] In corroboration of Baines' testimony, Thomas Kyd, the dramatist and Marlowe's erstwhile room-mate, wrote that Marlowe would "iest at the devine scriptures, gybe at praiers, & stryue in argument to frustrate & confute what hath byn spoke or wrytt by prophets & such holie men."[6] Baines and Kyd make many more allegations in similar vein. The only person to link Marlowe directly with Sir Walter Raleigh was one Richard Chomley, who remarked in a passing reference that "one Marlowe is able to show more sound reasons for atheism than any divine in England is able to give to prove divinity: and that Marlowe told him that he hath read the atheist lecture to Sir Walter Ralegh and others."[7] Just what this atheist lecture contained, if it was ever given, is impossible to say, for there is no other allusion to it and no copy of its text survives.

While it is quite possible that Marlowe became antagonistic to all forms of religion, not just Catholicism, after leaving Cambridge, the evidence being assembled against him was of extremely doubtful provenance: much of it was hearsay, and the witnesses were biased. The only one favourably disposed towards Marlowe was Chomley, who was himself involved in trouble-stirring against the government in undercover activities. Baines was a Catholic priest, trained and ordained at Rheims; having fallen foul of the Rector there he returned to England, where he worked for Walsingham by informing on the Rheims community. We do not know where his true loyalties, if any, lay; he may have had a personal motive for revenge against Marlowe, dating back to Marlowe's own spying exploit, and in any case it would have strengthened his own position in England to denounce an anti-establishment blasphemer. Kyd was not a spy, but when he incriminated Marlowe he was a very frightened man who had broken down under torture. He had been arrested on political grounds and a heretical document had been found in his possession. Kyd's way out was to blame Marlowe, saying that Marlowe had left it behind when he moved out of their shared accommodation. To prove his innocence, Kyd sent two letters to his torturers in which he accused Marlowe of saying all sorts of outrageous things. Robert Parsons' allegations concerning a "school of Atheisme", on which Baines was clearly building, are the voice of protest against ungodly times: Parsons was also a Catholic priest and was actively promoting the Counter-Reformation in England by insinuating (his own word) priests into England; he was probably genuinely shocked by the licentiousness which he would have perceived to have followed in the wake of Protestantism. In those times of exceptionally paranoid religious politics he would have been quick to discern a "school of Atheisme" where only a loose-knit group of individualists, connected only by their propensity for unconventional thought, actually existed.

The times were very dangerous. Whoever Marlowe's real friends and associates may have been, he should have chosen his enemies more judiciously. Kyd's confession saw Marlowe arrested within a week. The trial was never to take place, however, and

Baines' testimony was never to be used: ten days after his arrest, Marlowe was dead. He had been freed on licence pending trial and was stabbed to death in a tavern brawl. He died on 30 May, 1593, aged only twenty-nine.

The circumstances of Marlowe's death, according to the coroner's findings, were straightforward. He had spent the day of 30 May with three men at a tavern in Deptford; in the evening there had been a quarrel over the bill and Marlowe drew his dagger, wounding one of the others. This man, by name Ingram Frizer, turned the weapon back on Marlowe and "in defence of his life . . . gave the said Christopher then and there a mortal wound over his right eye . . . of which mortal wound the aforesaid Christopher Morley then & there instantly died."[8] The Privy Council accepted the coroner's findings at the inquest and a month later Frizer was free on a royal pardon.

Perhaps what happened on that fateful day was not as straightforward as the coroner's findings indicated. Who were those three companions? Frizer was a Walsingham agent. What of the other two? One of them, Robert Poley, was another Walsingham agent, who had helped to uncover the Babington plot by posing as a conspirator in the plan to assassinate Queen Elizabeth; the other, Nicholas Skeres, was an associate of Poley's at the time of the Babington plot and later worked as a courier for the Earl of Essex, who was married to Frances Walsingham. The recurrence of the name of Walsingham with Marlowe's last days has not quite ended: the warrant for Marlowe's arrest directed the messenger of the court to look for him at the house of Thomas Walsingham in Kent; it is not certain that that was where Marlowe was found, but it seems probable that he spent his last few days there since the Deptford tavern where Marlowe died was only a few miles from Walsingham's country house.[9]

In Corpus Christi College there hangs a portrait of a self-possessed young man with good, if rather soft, features rather too youthful for the downy moustache between his assertive nose and delicate mouth. His arms are folded with confidence and his dark eyes bespeak a piercing intellect. He looks a little awkward, unaccustomed perhaps, to his finery. The subject is unknown, but is widely thought to be Marlowe; certainly the date fits, for 1585 is written beneath the caption *aetatis suae 21* (at the age of 21). And beneath the date is written the motto: *Quod me nutrit, me destruit* — what nourishes me, destroys me. Not a highly original thought, but if, as is also commonly believed, the portrait was commissioned by Thomas Walsingham, it bears a terrible proleptic irony.

Whether Thomas Walsingham had any deliberate or willing part in a plot to kill Marlowe before he could give any damaging evidence in court concerning members of the Walsingham spy ring, we shall never know. While the circumstantial evidence points to the existence of such a plot, it is by no means as likely that Walsingham was party to it. After Marlowe's death *Hero and Leander* was published by Edward Blount, one of Marlowe's London friends. Blount speaks affectionately of the dead poet in his dedication, which is to the man who had been Marlowe's friend — Thomas Walsingham.

2. The Date of *Doctor Faustus*

Several chronologies have been suggested for Marlowe's seven plays, but none of the plays can be dated with precision. It is generally agreed that *Dido, Queen of Carthage* and the two *Tamburlaine* plays are earlier works and that *The Jew of Malta* and *Ed-*

ward II are somewhat later in his all-too-short career. *Doctor Faustus*, as in other respects, is more controversial: some scholars think it is a relatively early play, probably coming immediately after Part II of *Tamburlaine*; others conclude that it is Marlowe's last work.

Arguments concerning the date are necessarily linked with the appearance of another work, a lengthy prose tract entitled, in its English version, *The History of the Damnable Life and Deserved Death of Doctor John Faustus*. This work has come to be known by the shorter title of *The English Faust Book*, commonly abbreviated yet further (as hereinafter) to *EFB*. This work is a translation, with some degree of adaptation, from the German *Historia von D. Iohann Fausten*, which was first published in 1587. Undoubtedly *EFB* was a major source for Marlowe, rather than the German original, for even if he knew German he made use of some passages in *EFB* which do not occur in the parent text. Unfortunately the date of the translation, which would provide a *terminus a quo*, i.e. an earliest possible date, for Marlowe's *Doctor Faustus*, is not known.

The sole surviving printed copy of *EFB*, dated 1592, is evidently a second edition, for it claims to have "imperfeect matter amended: according to the true Copie printed at Franckfort." Such claims are not uncommon on Elizabethan title pages and usually occur when a later edition claiming textual and legal authority sets out to displace an earlier pirated edition. Indeed, there had been a dispute over copyright in *EFB*: the Court Book of the Stationers' Company, which was the body responsible for safeguarding copyright, records on 18 December, 1592 that Abel Jeffes had successfully challenged the claim of Thomas Orwin, the publisher of the supposedly amended edition. The court found that Jeffes had registered his copyright "about May" that year and that Jeffes would retain copyright unless Orwin could substantiate his allegation of having made an earlier entry in the Stationers' Register. Orwin was unable to prove an entry earlier than Jeffes', so presumably *EFB* first appeared in print in or after May, 1592.

To some modern scholars, these facts concerning *EFB* establish a presumption that Marlowe's source does not date from before mid-1592 and that *Doctor Faustus* must be later. However, dates of printing and publication do not always mean much: in Elizabethan times, as now, books would often pass in manuscript through the hands of a number of like-minded readers prior to publication or before a publisher could be found. Furthermore, transmission by manuscript was then a process by which wider demand was established; dissemination of a work in manuscript could often lead to demand for a printed version. In the specific case of *EFB*, there is evidence to suggest that it was circulating in manuscript among Cambridge men as early as 1590.[10]

More positive evidence pointing to the existence of *Doctor Faustus* before 1592 has been found in works which seem to allude directly to Marlowe's play or to draw upon it. Three plays of the early 1590s are indicative. *A Knack to Know a Knave*, a poorly written play of unknown authorship, seems to imitate Marlowe's style and to borrow from its subject matter.[11] In this play, a wicked old bailiff faces death with certainty of being carted off to hell; his vision of God's judgement is reminiscent of Faustus' last speech and contains what looks very like a direct borrowing from an earlier monologue. Another incident in *A Knack* finds an archbishop conjuring a devil in terms remarkably similar to Faustus' conjuration of Mephostophiles. *A Knack* is recorded as having been first performed on 10 June, 1592.

Thomas Lodge and Robert Greene collaborated in writing *A Looking-Glass for London and England*. The glass they offered reflected many lines from writers other than themselves: *A Looking-Glass* is heavily plagiarised, containing numerous borrowings from Marlowe's *Tamburlaine*, and has many passages which are too close to *Doctor Faustus* for the similarities to be coincidental. Arguments for Marlowe as the borrower cannot be wholly discounted, but seem improbable. *A Looking-Glass* is a little earlier than *A Knack*; it must have been written by August, 1591.[12]

The third play to be considered as containing borrowings from Marlowe's *Doctor Faustus* is *The Taming of a Shrew*. This anonymous work is probably better known as being a source for Shakespeare's *The Taming of the Shrew*. It was published in 1594, but was probably written about 1590. Like *A Looking-Glass*, it abounds in plagiarisms. One passage in *A Shrew* which runs closely parallel to *Doctor Faustus* is particularly significant because it confirms the earliness of the version of *Doctor Faustus* on which this edition is based.[13]

Although the evidence of the three plays mentioned above all points to the years 1590 or 1591 as being the date of composition of *Doctor Faustus*, there is still no absolute certainty.[14] Inter-textual evidence is always tricky and may often be interpreted in a variety of ways. Nevertheless, the inference to be drawn from these other Elizabethan plays seems strong enough.

Henslowe's *Diary*, which commences in 1592, makes no mention of *Doctor Faustus* until 30 September, 1594. He does not record the play as a new one, however, in 1594.[15] There seems to be an allusion which would substantiate the early date for Marlowe's play in another work, *The Blacke Booke* (1604) by T. M. (Thomas Middleton?). Here a villainous person is described as possessing "a head of hayre like one of my Divells in Dr. Faustus when the old Theatre crackt and frighted the audience."[16] The Admiral's Men, who had performed *Tamburlaine* and would later perform *Doctor Faustus* for Henslowe, were only at the old "Theatre", the first public playhouse to be established in London and so called because it was in its early days the only one of its kind, for the season of 1590–91.

For the time being, and in the absence of stronger evidence to the contrary, the present editors are of the opinion that Marlowe had access to *EFB*, either in manuscript or printed edition before 1592; that the combined weight of borrowings in other plays constitute a case for an early date; and that the allusion in *The Blacke Booke* reinforces what those plays together indicate.

3.   The Source

There probably was an historical Faustus to whom the protagonist of Marlowe's play bears some relation. The matriculation records of Heidelberg University mention one Johann Faust in 1509. This Faustus, or possibly another, was referred to in correspondence between two educated churchmen as "a certain soothsayer by the name of George Faust, the demigod of Heidelberg, a mere braggart and fool."[17] The letter containing this reference is dated 3 October, 1513. At all events, the Faustus of later legend has something in common with both the Johann Faust and George Faust of these early references and it may well be that two strands of historical truth have become intertwined. (See also Section 8 of this Introduction.)

In 1587 the *Historia von D. Johann Fausten* brought together some sixty years of accreted legend. It purports to be a true history, but it is almost pure fiction.[18] In this work, Faustus has become the central figure in a cautionary tale which warns the presumptuous not to seek beyond the limits of divinely-allowed knowledge. The *Historia* begins with Faustus' intellectual restlessness, but only in order to present him as a sinful reprobate from his earliest days.

Far more significant than similarities in *Doctor Faustus* with the *Historia* and its English progeny, the *EFB*, are the differences. There is a wealth of incident in the *Historia* and *EFB* which Marlowe completely ignores as being irrelevant to his conception of Faustus or in contradiction of it. The ponderous and insistent moralising of the *Historia*, lightened somewhat in *EFB*, is absent from Marlowe's play. There is also a world of difference between the subtle stylistic elegance of Marlowe and the suety prose from which he extracts his subject matter.

The precise relationship between *EFB* and *Doctor Faustus* has been much debated, but despite the amount of discussion which has accrued, the whole subject is still extremely confused. The reasons for this are several. The first and most obvious is the difficulty inherent in our partial access to the text of *EFB*. Even if we assume that *Doctor Faustus* existed in Marlowe's own lifetime only in the form of foul papers, or perhaps a prompt-book, we are still compelled to acknowledge that the first draft, in whatever form it existed, must have been worked up from a manuscript or from the first edition of *EFB*, an edition of which no copy has survived and from which the surviving edition of 1592 probably diverges.

The 1592 edition is available to the modern reader in a facsimile edition published in Amsterdam by Theatrum Orbis Terrarum in 1969 as item 173 in the English Experience series. This is a blackletter publication, as was the text of Marlowe's play, and it has been argued that the gothic forms of blackletter were "a form of printing designed to appeal to the lower classes," so that works appearing in this format tend to be of an inflammatory and sensationalist character.[19] For those who find blackletter difficult to decipher, the 1592 *Damnable Life*, together with the 1594 *Second Report of Faustus, Containing His Appearances and the Deeds of Wagner*, has been edited by William Rose (London: Routledge, n.d. [1925]). Citations to *EFB* in the ensuing discussion will be by chapter and page reference to the Rose edition in the absence of a more modern critical edition of the work.

Discussion of Marlowe's use of *EFB* has been further confused by the offhand and cavalier attitude which even eminent scholars have taken to the issue of the legitimacy and transmission of the text of Marlowe's play. The tendency has been to employ either the B-text, or one of the many hypothetical eclectic constructs. In one of the most professional discussions to date, Sara Munson Deats admits the problem in her initial discussion but then weakly opts for the eclectic Jump version, although, interestingly, the most stimulating parts of the discussion seem often to be concerned with those passages common to both playtexts.[20] A close comparison of the present text with the 1592 *EFB* produces the strong impression that much of Marlowe's play was written at high speed with the objective of dramatising a prose work which was enjoying at the moment a considerable public success. It is hard to resist the impression that Marlowe was engaged in an undertaking remarkably similar to the modern film-of-the-book enterprise, and his work was doubtlessly as difficult of achievement as that of the modern entrepreneur. Whilst the *EFB* translator, who is named only as P. F. (Gent), makes a fairly workmanlike fist of his task and produces a volume which intrigues the reader in a plainly sensationalist way, *EFB* does not at any point contain an element which Marlowe, no matter what the circumstances of the composition, was able to supply; that is, the presence of a genuine metaphysical dread.

We may imagine how Marlowe, with a copy of the now lost first impression of *EFB* (or MS version) on the desk before him, addresses himself to the problem, step by step, of transforming an episodic prose narrative into a verse drama. How does he go about it?

EFB opens with a short account of the parentage and birth of Faustus, with a brief description of his decision to study magic (I, pp. 65-66). Marlowe compresses this into lines 1-28, the opening choric speech of the play, but then reverts to it and amplifies it in the form of the magnificent opening soliloquy, incorporating several dramatic devices, such as the ironic invocation of typological parallelisms, which Faustus himself evidently does not understand, and the machinery of the *sortes virgilianae*. This passage ends at line 92; Marlowe has compressed the somewhat diffuse narrative of *EFB* into the situation which was exemplified by Renaissance emblem writers as *occasio* — a particularly important and significant moment of time where a dramatic choice binds a protagonist for good or ill.

The passage from line 93-238 is not in *EFB*, and constitutes Marlowe's attempt, through the intrusion of the two angels and the badinage between Wagner and the scholars, to represent the process of time necessary for Faustus' re-education in magic. It elaborates dramatically on a single sentence in *EFB*:

> For he accompanied himself with divers that were seen in those Devilish Arts, and that had the Chaldean Persian, Hebrew, Arabian and Greek tongues, using Figures, Characters, Conjurations, Incantations, with any other ceremonies belonging to these infernal Arts, as Necromancy, Charms, Soothsaying, Witchcraft, Enchantment, being delighted with their books, words, and names so well, that he studied day and night therein. (I, pp. 66-67. See lines 77-81)

Faustus' first attempt at conjuration now ensues at lines 239-62 and is a very *piano* rendition of *EFB*'s second chapter, which is highly pyrotechnical in manner, for the Mephostophiles of *EFB* is determined to give the neophyte necromancer his money's worth: 'This pleasant beast [*sc.* a fiery man] ran about the Circle a great while and lastly appeared in manner of a grey Friar' (II, p. 69). Later, in the contract, Faustus charges Mephostophiles that 'he should always come to him like a Friar, after the order of St Francis, with a bell in his hand like St Anthony . . .' (V, p. 74). Lines 275-342 are a considerably expanded version of *EFB*, which at this point contains no theological speculation, and is merely to the effect that Mephostophiles must consult his employer before he can provide Faustus with an estimate for the proposed contract. 'Then Faustus demanded the Spirit, what was his name? The Spirit answered, my name is as thou sayest, Mephostophiles, and I am a prince, but servant to Lucifer: and all the circuit from Septentrio to the Meridian, I rule under him' (V, p. 74). In Marlowe's version of the potency of Faustus' 'conjuring speeches,' Mephostophiles carefully equivocates, but *EFB* is intriguingly dogmatic: '. . . so soon as we saw thy heart, how thou didst despise thy degree taken in Divinity, and didst study to search and know the secrets of our Kingdom; even then did we enter unto thee, giving thee divers foul and filthy cogitations, pricking thee forward in thine intent, and persuading thee that thou couldst never attain thy desire, until thou hast the help of some

Devil' (XV, pp. 91-92). Faustus' query at line 305 — 'Was not that Lucifer an angel once?' — inaugurates, in *EFB*, an account of the hierarchy of the angels in Heaven (X, p. 85). Faustus' query at line 316, which elicits one of the most moving speeches in the play from Mephostophiles, should be set against *EFB*'s account (XV, pp. 92-98) of Hell purely as *poena sensus* (physical punishment) devoid of the pains of emotional longing as Marlowe envisages them. Interestingly, in view of Faustus' plea in his last great speech for an end to the sufferings of the damned, *EFB* emphatically denies the doctrine of *apocatastasis*, asserting that 'the damned have neither end nor time appointed in the which they may hope to be released' (XV, p. 97).

The colloquy of Marlowe's Faustus with the demon he has raised ends at line 342, and has lasted a little over 60 lines. The ensuing section in the play, lines 343-470, marks the passage of time between the two consultations with Mephostophiles, and incorporates two episodes, in the first of which Wagner enacts the role of Faustus' zany and recruits the starving clown as his apprentice, and in the second of which Faustus stands torn between resolution and contrition as exemplified in the psychomachia involving his Bad and Good Angels. This has no counterpart in *EFB*, which moves immediately into the ensuing episodes for the negotiation of the pact. The 'deed of gift' which Marlowe's Faustus must sign with his own blood is an important occasion in *EFB* too, to such an extent that some form of narrative authentication is offered: for 'certainly this letter of Obligation was found in his house after his lamentable end' (V, p. 75). The blood pact, the congealing of the blood, and the message *Homo fuge*, all appear in *EFB*, and Marlowe seems at pains to transpose the episode accurately. The pact is almost verbatim from *EFB* IV and VI, pp. 73 and 76; in addition, in *EFB* Mephostophiles demands a detailed and itemised repudiation of Christianity.

The conclusion of the pact leads immediately, in *Doctor Faustus*, to the protagonist's quizzing of Mephostophiles on the nature of Hell, as Marlowe omits *EFB*'s lengthy account of the brigandage carried out by Faustus, Wagner, and Mephostophiles, together with the details of their housekeeping arrangements. Chapters X-XV of *EFB*, however, concentrate for the most part on an elaborate discussion of the nature of Hell, with the interpolation of the 'wife in the devil's name' episode of line 595ff of *Doctor Faustus*, which receives short shrift in Marlowe's work but is more extensively treated in pp. 82-84 of *EFB*. *EFB*'s underworld courier is tendentiously moralistic on the subject of matrimony, for 'thou can'st not marry; thou can'st not serve two masters, God, and my Prince; for wedlock is a chief Institution ordained of God' (p. 81). His attitude to Hell is literalistic, and largely limited to the concept of *poena sensus*; he is tactfully and lyrically agnostic where topographical detail is concerned. '. . . we Devils know not what substance it is of, but a confused thing. For as a bubble of water flieth before the wind, so doth hell before the breath of God. Further we devils know not how God hath laid the foundation of our hell, nor where it is: but to be short with thee Faustus, we know that hell hath neither bottom nor end' (XI, pp. 86-87).[21] Mephostophiles describes the kingdoms and political structure of Hell in Chapter XII of *EFB*.

The astronomical and astrological speculations of the protagonist are as central to *EFB*, of course, as they are to Marlowe's play. Faustus' delighted reversion to the subject at 662-63 ('. . . let us dispute again/And argue of divine astrology'), has its counterpart in *EFB* in frequent animadversions about Faustus' immense learning in this field, which is viewed as antithetical in nature to true knowledge:

Doctor Faustus . . . forgot all good works, and fell to be a Calendar maker by help of his spirit; and also in a short time to be a good Astronomer or Astrologin: he had learned so perfectly of his Spirit the course of the Sun, Moon, and Stars, that he had the most famous name of all the Mathematicks that lived in his time; as may well appear by his works dedicated unto sundry Dukes and Lords: for he did nothing without the advice of his Spirit, which learned him to presage of matters to come, which have come to pass since his death. The like praise won he with his Calendars, and Almanacs making, for when he presaged upon any change, Operation, or alteration of the weather, or Elements; as wind, rain, fogs, snow, hail, moist, dry, warm, cold, thunder, lightning: it fell so duly out, as if an Angel of heaven had forewarned it . . . If anything wonderful were at hand, as death, famine, plague, or wars, he could set the time and place in true and just order, when it should come to pass. (*EFB* XVII, pp. 100–101)

Later in *EFB*, however, Faustus' letter to 'a Physician named John Victor' (XXI, pp. 115–121) is less astrological (in the modern sense of the word), and provides a cosmo-logical commentary which combines Copernican heliocentrism with an impassioned dithyramb in praise of the Book of Genesis.

The conversation concerning astronomy is pettishly terminated with Faustus' dis-missive remark that Mephostophiles' information is mere 'freshmen's suppositions' (686); in a huff, the demon declines to answer the obvious question on the nature of the Prime Mover, Faustus is again subjected to the psychomachia of the Good and Bad Angels, and terrified by the visitation of no less than the Devil and his infernal entour-age, who entertain him with the masque of the Seven Deadly Sins (in all, 708–815). The pageant of the Sins is Marlowe's own archaising version of *EFB* XIX, pp. 104–109, where Faustus asks after the Creator and is answered by an antimasque of outlandish diabolical monsters paraded as the aristocracy of Hell. *EFB* concentrates the bestiary on 'seven of the principal devils,' and the scene ends with Faustus' own acquisition of the power to change his shape at will, an element present only hurriedly in Marlowe's version at line 810.

After the Deadly Sins depart at 802.1, Marlowe's Faustus longs to visit Hell and view its delights for himself. This motif is probably a weak echo, at several removes, of the epic hero's traditional journey to the underworld; the A-text omits Faustus' protracted tour of the regions of Hell as described in *EFB* XX, pp. 110–114. In *EFB*, Faustus' tour of Hell is balanced by a complementary tour of the heavens (XXI, pp. 115–121). The A-text compresses this into seven lines, and leads immediately into Faustus' third, terrestrial, tour. The original passage in *EFB*, which views the cosmos from a Coperni-can and heliocentric vantage point, is of great interest for lines 662–97.

Faustus' Grand Tour, mounted upon an equine Mephostophiles, occupies the longest chapter in *EFB* — XXII, pp. 121–144. Marlowe's own rendition follows *EFB* very closely in 827–848, and one should hence treat with caution the attempts of the play's editors to wrench thematic meaning and relevance from the allusions. Faustus' desire to view the city of Trier (French Trèves) has puzzled most modern readers, and neither *EFB* nor the play itself provide any reason other than a passion for tourism. This, in an age when British moralists inveighed constantly against the moral corrup-tion endemic upon the Grand Tour, may be enough. Neither *EFB* nor *Doctor Faustus* mentions the real significance of Trier for the medieval mind — that is, that it was the repository of a famous relic, the Holy Coat of Trier, Christ's seamless robe, symbolic of the perfection of Christ's mortal body and hence of the unity of Christendom; it had been discovered and presented to the city by the Empress Helena, mother of Constantine the Great. Marlowe's 'sumptuous temple' is *EFB*'s 'sumptuous Church standing therein called the Saint Mark's,' and his description of Rome, down to the detail of the 365 cannon, follows *EFB* closely (XXII, pp. 126-27). The section in which Faustus participates in the Pope's banquet 'for the Cardinal of Pavia' closely follows *EFB* XXII, pp. 127-30.

At the conclusion to the slapstick episode of the Pope's banquet, the writer of *EFB* — and Marlowe with him — is faced with a problem which can now no longer be postponed, the narrative problem of entertaining an invisible and all-powerful magician for sixteen years. *EFB*'s solution is to resort, helplessly, to tourism on the grand scale, and *EFB*'s Faustus is an indefatigable seer of sights. Marlowe wearies of it all before the *EFB*'s rapturous chronicle of Renaissance Italy, and omits the ensuing descriptions of Milan, Florence and Siena, together with the topographical, architectural and hagiological delights of nearly thirty cities in Europe and the Near East (XXII, pp. 131-144). In *EFB*, Faustus only very rarely ceases to be the passive spectator — only long enough to spend six days and nights in the Grand Turk's harem, or to snigger at the Tomb of the Magi in Cologne.

The ensuing scene — that of the comic knock-about magic with Ralph and Robin and the Vintner — is not in *EFB*, but Marlowe reverts to his source at line 1047, relying upon *EFB* XXIX, pp. 150-153. Note, for instance, that Faustus' proviso at 1092-1103, which is theologically and dramatically of great importance, is carefully transposed from *EFB* XXIX, p. 152. However, a rather less significant detail, the 'great wart or wen' of *EFB* XXIX, p. 153, is also duly transposed by Marlowe — to the lady's 'wart or mole' at line 1116.

The transformation of the knight, via the motif which *EFB* borrows in part from the myth of Actaeon, receives large-scale treatment in the B-text, but the A-text's treatment of the incident is more cursory. In *EFB*, the knight's transformation occurs without provocation, as a mere whim on Faustus' part. See chapter XXX, pp. 154-155. The A-text omits all reference to the knight's attempt at revenge, but the B-text incorporates it from *EFB* XXXI, pp. 155-56, together with the reprise at LII, pp. 190-192. The ensuing episode, that of the gulling of the horse-courser, is not Marlowe's invention, but has been adapted from *EFB* XXXIV, pp. 162-163, where it occurs in the context of a large number of other trivial practical jokes which are plainly intended to pad out the material available to the writer. The ensuing highlife episode, that of the Duke and Duchess of Anholt and the winter grapes, is from *EFB* XXXIX, pp. 167-68. Wagner terminates the down-market buffoonery at line 1240 with the announcement of the summons from the Duke. The Anholt (Vanholt) episode, which extends until line 1286, marks the last of the long series of incidents which serve simultaneously to satisfy the audience's demands for farce as a necessary element in this mixed dramatic mode, pad the central void of Faustus' career, and illustrate eloquently, to the more pensive viewer, the boredom and spiritual wasteland of all attempts to live exclusively in, and for, the world of Adamic fallen time. Marlowe does not choose to develop the Anholt (Vanholt) episode, but in *EFB* it provides, potentially, the material for considerable poignancy in the symbolism of the bunch of grapes and the description, later, of Faustus' miraculous garden in Wittenberg, blooming in its summer splendour, while 'without in the streets, and all over the country, it lay full of Snow and Ice' (*EFB*, LI, pp. 189-90).

The concluding episodes of the play, from line 1287 onwards, revert to the main tragic action in a variety of modes, and illustrate the playwright's energetic and perceptive handling of the variety of material at his disposal in *EFB* XLV-LXIII, pp. 177-208. For the original of the Helen episode, one should study closely *EFB* XLV, pp. 177-180, where it bears little thematic importance. Marlowe heightens its pungency, glamour and horror in several ways, not least by omitting its bathetic sequel at LV, pp. 193-94. The crucial episode of the Old Man, inaugurated at line 1322, is enormously simplified, and given a brilliant chiaroscuro character, by Marlowe; in *EFB* much of the dramatic juxtaposition between Helen and the Old Man is dissipated by two intervening practical joke chapters and the Old Man's loquacity, incorporating a vigorous sermon against necromancers (XLVIII, pp. 183-185), citing Acts 8.9-13, Matthew 11.28, and Ezekiel 18.32, as was only proper in the circumstances. Lines 1397-1405, brief though the episode may be, are remarkably telling; the ordeal of the good Old Man prepares for the death of the wicked *vetus homo*, or Old Adam, in the person of Faustus. In *EFB*, Faustus himself attempts to take the Old Man's life, but is powerless to harm him, as are the devils. 'Thus doth God defend the hearts of all honest Christians, that betake themselves under his tuition' (XLIX, p. 187).

In the final two episodes of *Doctor Faustus*, Marlowe has abbreviated *EFB* very considerably, and always with immense tact. In *EFB*, Faustus' farewell to the students is a prolix and wordy sermon, preceded by several bombastic literary 'complaints,' and provides a protracted passage from LVIII to LXIII, pp. 197-206. In the A-text, this is reproduced as the swift incisive exchange of lines 1407-70. In contrast, the actual death of Faustus, which Marlowe renders powerfully as a parodic version of the traditional deathbed soliloquy, is enacted offstage in *EFB*, in a bathetic half-dozen lines. The students in the antechamber recoil when 'the hall door flew open wherein Doctor Faustus was, then he began to cry for help, saying: murther, murther, but it came forth with half a voice hollowly: shortly after they heard him no more' (*EFB*, LXIII, p. 206). In a hurry to tidy up, the author of *EFB* takes a final page and a half to describe the dismembered remains of Faustus, discovered on the morrow, their decent interment, the suddenly remembered offspring of the Faustus-Helen union, the postmortem reappearance of Faustus to Wagner to attend to a number of unfinished undertakings, and the parting observation that it all served Faustus right.

4.   The Text of *Doctor Faustus*

No manuscript of *Doctor Faustus* has survived. Nor was the play published in Marlowe's lifetime. The first known edition appeared in 1604, eleven years after the playwright's death. There is an entry in the Stationers' Register on 7 January, 1601 which records "A booke called the plaie of *Doctor Faustus*", but this may have been a holding entry, i.e. the owner's attempt to preserve his copyright pending publication, rather than the date of printing. There may have been an edition published round about then, however, of which the 1604 text is a reprint: the title page of the 1604 edition proclaims that the play "hath bene Acted by the Right Honorable the Earle of Nottingham his servants" and since the Earl's players passed into new patronage in 1603 the title page would seem to antedate the change, though not necessarily so. Of the 1604 edition only one copy survives; indeed, from the first three editions only a total of five copies are extant: so it is quite likely that an entire edition has perished entirely.

Doctor Faustus exists in two widely-divergent forms. The 1604 version, reprinted with some editorial changes in 1609 and 1611, has become known as the A-text. In 1616 a very different version appeared, about one-third longer, and containing episodes not found in the A-text as well as episodes similar in outline to those of the A-text but substantially independent of the A-text version. The 1616 version and its progeny have become known as the B-text. Further editions of B followed in 1619, 1620, 1624, 1628, and 1631. Recensions of A and B have no greater authority than their original, but the emendations of seventeenth-century editors in the second and later editions of both versions have been influential in the efforts of modern editors to account for difficulties in both A1 and B1.

For almost two hundred years after this flurry of early editions, *Doctor Faustus* — and with it a great deal of Renaissance drama outside Shakespeare — lay almost forgotten. There was to be one more edition in the seventeenth century, a bowdlerised issue of the B-text, with a new episode added.[22] A century later, Marlowe's play came to Goethe's attention, however, and he admired it enough to use it as a source for his *Faust*. Early in the nineteenth century three new editions of *Doctor Faustus* appeared, all based on the B-version. There was a general revival of interest in Marlowe as a result of the Romantic movement, which acclaimed his protagonists as Promethean challengers to the gods. The Romantic interpretation persists in much twentieth-century writing on *Doctor Faustus*.

The later nineteenth century saw a number of editions, in which editorial favour oscillated between the A- and B-versions. But it was not until F. S. Boas' edition of 1932 that the B-version found a whole-hearted modern supporter. From 1932 until 1973 the B-text was almost universally preferred by editors and textual critics. Only within the last decade has it been fully realised to what extent even the most informed and balanced textual studies hitherto have been grounded on doubtful analogies and false assumptions. A case in point is Leo Kirschbaum's influential essay, "The Good and Bad Quartos of *Dr Faustus*."[23]

Kirschbaum, writing in 1946, approved Boas' choice of the B-text. Arguing by analogy with other Elizabethan dramatic texts, Shakespeare's especially, Kirschbaum concluded that "the 1604 text of *Dr Faustus* is a bad quarto; and that this bad quarto reports the 1616 text, which is a good quarto . . . very close to Marlowe's original." Theoretically a bad quarto is a reported text of some kind, sometimes pirated. It may be culled from memory by actors putting their parts together, or "reported" by a short-hand writer, whereas a good quarto is authentic and is generally, although not invariably, published with the author's approval. Good quartos are often printed from the holding company's prized prompt-book copy. Quarto simply indicates the common form in which Elizabethan play-texts appeared, i.e. on a moderate-sized sheet of paper achieved by folding a very large sheet twice to make four leaves (hence quarto).

The distinction which Kirschbaum makes between good and bad quartos is not clear-cut in reality: what may be true of Shakespeare, writing somewhat later in a more settled phase of theatre history, does not as readily apply to *Doctor Faustus*. If Marlowe's play first appeared in 1590–91 (see previous section of Introduction), it is more than likely that the precious prompt-book copy may have been destroyed or even sold to pay expenses in the disastrous plague years of 1592 and 1593. There are signs enough that the 1604 text is a memorial reconstruction, e.g. in the transliterated Greek words and phrases which are reproduced phonetically but without their sense by someone who evidently did not understand Greek, presumably an actor who had previously played the part (see note to 40 and 1512); and the topical allusion to Dr Lopez who only rose to public notoriety in 1594 (see note to 1194–95) affirms that the copy used for the A-text was assembled well after Marlowe's death. Nevertheless, the 1604 text's claim to represent the play "As it hath bene Acted by the Right Honorable the Earle of Nottingham his servants", who had performed the play in Marlowe's lifetime, offers some consolation in the search for a pure text; and the characteristics of the stage directions (see note to 618.1) further indicate that, however memorially-based, the A-text of 1604 was printed from the reconstructed prompt-book copy owned by the company. In short, the A-text of *Doctor Faustus* comprises characteristics both of good quarto and bad quarto, all because of the particular circumstances of its transmission.

More astonishing to the modern reader than Kirschbaum's doubtful analogy is his false assumption concerning the structure of Marlowe's play. It is now well known and widely accepted that *Doctor Faustus* owes far more to the native English form of the morality play than to any neo-classical precepts which were circulating in Marlowe's time. Neo-classical drama had very little to do with the public playhouse until Ben Jonson, who wrote from 1598 onwards. It followed Roman precepts, which had in turn sought to recover the principles of the Greek drama of earlier centuries. One neo-classical idea was that plays, whether comedy or tragedy, should be written in five acts and neo-classically minded editors imposed such divisions where they had never been: almost all the act-divisions in Shakespeare's plays, for example, are posthumously imposed, for none of the quartos published in his own lifetime bears such divisions, save a few indications in three bad quartos. As to Marlowe's *Doctor Faustus*, Kirschbaum, accepting Boas' division into five acts, takes it as axiomatic that the B-text is superior and more complete: he says "surely we can assume that the original *Doctor Faustus* contained five acts." At no point does he come to terms with the fact that the division of the B-text into five acts dates back no further than the nineteenth century. All the early editions of *Doctor Faustus*, both A- and B-texts, are without any act or scene division. This lack of act-scene division is a very common, though not invariable, characteristic of English drama written in the morality tradition. It must be admitted, though, that not all scholars would allow this reasoning, contending rather that a university wit like Marlowe *would* write in acts, but that the players would ignore them. Hence their absence from the A-text.

In its time, Kirschbaum's argument was impressive enough to convince the great textual scholar of the mid-twentieth century, W. W. Greg. In his *Doctor Faustus 1604–1616: Parallel Texts*, published in 1950, Greg built upon the Kirschbaum hypothesis. It is to be regretted that he did so, not only because the false hypothesis derogates from the value of an otherwise-great piece of scholarship, but also because Greg's great reputation was enough to quell contrary opinion for a quarter of a century afterwards. The essence of Greg's argument is that the additional material exclusive to the B-text derives from an authorial manuscript which was available to the B-text editor but which has since been lost. This manuscript, Greg maintains, restores material excluded from the A-text. Despite the enormous length of his argument and the detail in which it is presented, Greg allows that his findings are provisional. He admits that his principal hypothesis has to be sustained by a secondary, and less likely one. Greg admits that where the A- and B-versions run parallel B1 is indebted to A, and to A3 rather than A1, and so he hypothesises that the manuscript was mutilated or only partially legible. This would explain, he says, why the manuscript "was only occasionally available or was only occasionally consulted."[24] It is the present editors' view that lost manuscript theories must always be treated with caution, especially where hedged about with qualifications and sub-speculations. The fact that the supposed manuscript was collated with A3 rather than A1 is enough to make one doubt its provenance: an editor concerned with restoring a text to its pristine state would hardly have contented himself with the manifestly corrupt A3. It is highly probable that there was a manuscript of some kind from which the editor of B1 worked, for how else would he have come by his additional material? Is it at all likely that the manuscript was Marlowe's?

While Greg never quite commits himself to declaring that the lost manuscript was Marlowe's, he attempts to establish a relatively early date for it as an indication of authenticity. He also seeks to refute a separate piece of evidence which is damaging to his case. The damaging evidence is the record which Philip Henslowe, the theatre manager and impresario, made in his diary of having paid £4 (a handsome sum in those days) to two hack writers, William Birde and Samuel Rowley, for "ther adicyiones in doctor fostes".[25] We know that Henslowe was not the sort of man to part with money lightly, so presumably the additions were very substantial, substantial enough to account for the six hundred new lines found in the B-version, which also tinkers with and expands some of the existing material in A. The money changed hands in 1602, by which time the work was presumably completed, so one could enquire whether the additions are not already in the A-text of 1604. Against this possibility, it seems unlikely in the extreme that a very short play by Elizabethan standards, such as the A-version of *Doctor Faustus* was, could incorporate a substantial body of new material, and furthermore, there is the likelihood that the 1604 text is a reprint of a 1601 edition, which would ante-date an arrangement between Henslowe and Birde and Rowley. Greg, looking for an early date for the exclusive B-version material which would place it before the Birde-Rowley collaboration, cites a passage in Shakespeare's *Merry Wives of Windsor* (1600–01) which seems to contain a passing reference to an incident in *Doctor Faustus* found only in the B-version. Greg says: "it follows that the scene in question was at any rate no part of the Rowley-Birde additions of 1602." But, as Greg's critics have not been slow to point out, the vital reference in *The Merry Wives* does not appear in the first quarto edition of 1602. The reference to *Doctor Faustus* does not occur until the First Folio text of 1623.

In many respects Greg's monumental *Parallel Texts* remains a most valuable work, but it had the unfortunate effect of setting up the B-version. Arguments which to Greg had been tentative and provisional became prescriptive to his followers. In consequence, a generation of scholarly interpretive writing on *Doctor Faustus* has been debased by widespread recourse to the B-version. Several editions, single-text editions intended for students in schools and universities, appeared in the 1960s and all of them present the B-version. Their editors mutter darkly about some of Greg's findings, but without departing from his overall judgements.[26]

The first scholar to disagree radically was Fredson Bowers. Having previously accepted Greg, albeit with reservations, Bowers reversed his position in 1973.[27] Returning to the textual problems of *Doctor Faustus*, Bowers, in his later opinion, finds that B is indeed later than A, as the *prima facie* evidence of the clusters of dates surrounding publication clearly indicates. The extra length of B he finds to be accounted for by a late tampering with the original, the extended form of pre-existing scenes and the entirely new scenes being the "adicyones" for which Henslowe paid Birde and Rowley.

In the same year that he published his revised opinion, Bowers also presented his edition of Marlowe's *Complete Works*.[28] In it he gave the B-version of *Doctor Faustus*! The apparent inconsistency is explained by his attitude towards A as a reported text. Still under the influence of the Kirschbaum-Greg rejection of A as a "bad quarto", he preferred the manifest imperfections of B. His decision will seem odd to many: surely it is better to follow a bad quarto than a worse one. He himself describes A "as representing the form of the original play even though in a memorially corrupted version." As we have already indicated, and as we shall argue further, the status of the A-version is superior to what is normally meant by the term "bad quarto." The situation persisting since 1973 is aptly summarised by a recent commentator on the state of the debate: "Readers are thus informed that the A-version is more authentic — and are given the B-version to read."[29]

Following the new direction given by Bowers, Constance Brown Kuriyama has put a strong case for the A-version in her article "Dr Greg and *Doctor Faustus*: The Supposed Originality of the 1616 Text."[30] Centrally, she confirms that the extra material in B is not Marlowe's but Rowley's. She detects Rowley's part through his unconscious mannerisms of style, his literary fingerprints, rather than through his lapses in pseudo-Marlovian prosody. She is unable to account for any part by Birde, however, because there is no surviving work known to be his with which the B-material can be compared. Kuriyama also notices that the B-version is confused thematically, the changes to it conforming to a popularised view of magic which "credits Faustus with more power than he possesses in A." Though farther-reaching than Bowers, she does not pursue the implications of her findings to their conclusion: she allows that while "the A-text is preferable for critical purposes or general reading" an eclectic text of "passages and meanings which the two extant versions share" would be a reasonable compromise for purposes of interpretation.

Neither Bowers nor Kuriyama proposes to eliminate the B-version entirely. Granted that neither A1 nor B1 is perfect at the level of type-setting, and granted that in parallel passages B has some superior readings, some such compromise as suggested by Kuriyama would seem to provide a solution. On closer examination, however, one finds that a broadly eclectic approach is not practicable. This is because the two versions, even where they run parallel, often differ in ways that vitally affect interpretation. A more recent contributor to the textual debate, Michael J. Warren, has singled out a pair of passages which exemplify the difficulty. In "*Dr Faustus*: The Old Man and the Text", Warren shows that one cannot put together an eclectic text that is more coherent or otherwise better than the sum of its two variant parts: on examining the two variants of the Old Man scene, he finds that there is an "unsurprising, radical dissimilarity" which militates against conflation. The A-version, says Warren, "maintains a consistent Christian context," whereas the B-version "appears to reflect a Christianity which is less intellectual, more homely, more timid, superstitious even."[31] A closer investigation of Christian writings on witchcraft than Warren offers would have confirmed that the A-version is orthodox rather than merely consistent, whereas the B-version is startlingly heterodox in relation to the intellectual tradition, though only at a level of vulgar superstition.

Yet more recent contributions to the textual debate are David J. Lake's "Three Seventeenth-Century Revisions: *Thomas of Woodstock, The Jew of Malta,* and *Faustus B*"[32] and Michael H. Keefer's "Verbal Magic and the Problem of the A and B Texts of *Doctor Faustus.*"[33]

Making a linguistic-stylistic analysis based on the presence or absence of certain colloquialisms and contractions which were changing late in the sixteenth-century, Lake argues that *"Doctor Faustus* (Q1616) must have been revised after c. 1600," whereas *"Faustus A* is a more authentic text." The A-text, says Lake, has features which should "suggest a date in the late 1590s" and he concludes that *"Faustus A* is nearer to Marlowe's autograph than *Faustus B."* This is an important corroborative view, for it concurs with the date indicated by topical allusions in A1 of 1604 but takes an entirely separate route towards the same conclusion.

Keefer further pursues the line of attack taken by Kuriyama and Warren, which finds the material exclusive to the B-version thematically inconsistent with the rest of the play. Concerned principally with the question of magic, Keefer sees Faustus as a man who fails. Common Renaissance attitudes ascribe a magical power to language, and hence the importance in the play of incantatory formulae, but Faustus achieves nothing through such formulae. A signal instance of his failure is the very first conjuration, following which Mephostophiles manifests himself, but only *"per accidens"*: as Mephostophiles points out, there is no force in Faustus "conjuring speeches" beyond their revelation that Faustus' soul is sufficiently in danger to be worth Mephostophiles' personal attention. For Keefer, "the B-version is fundamentally incoherent" as a result of alterations and additions to the A-version, or to the original which the A-version quite closely represents. Because the B-version intrudes scenes wherein verbal magic is successful, presumably for their sensational value, Keefer finds "a second, conflicting attitude towards verbal magic" through which "one of the central patterns of the play is disrupted." He ends with a plea for "a new edition of *Dr Faustus* based upon the A-version of the play."

Doctor Faustus was a very popular play in the 1590s, as the large amounts of the takings and the frequency of performance show. However, takings tailed off in 1597, so badly evidently that the play was dropped thereafter. It is not hard to see why: the plot of the play would by then have been too well known to retain any element of shock or surprise to theatre-goers; the growing taste for larger and more sensational works would have demanded more for what the audience felt to be its money's-worth; and the towering figure of Shakespeare, by now very well established, would have put pressure on rival companies to offer in excitement what they could not emulate in dramatic quality. Henslowe's decision to commission Birde and Rowley to re-vamp *Doctor Faustus*, when seen in this context, makes as much sound business sense as everything else he did. His dealings with the players testify that Henslowe would have given no thought to aesthetic or intellectual sensibility, at least not where money was involved. From the circumstances of the commission that resulted in the B-version of *Doctor Faustus*, no great degree of conjecture is required to deduce what the brief he gave to Birde and Rowley was: more magic, effective magic to astonish the vulgar; more knock-about farce; and some anti-Catholic stuff to appeal to growing antipathy. Within these terms, Birde and Rowley succeeded admirably, but they did violence to Marlowe's play.

Whoever edited the B-version for publication made an honest effort to rid his edition of errors and misreadings which occurred in the successive editions of the A-text. Unfortunately, he did not have before him a copy of the 1604 or the putative 1601 text, for he perpetuated some of the specific errors of A3, to which he added a few of his own. For example, from A3 he took "*Oeconomy*", which is meaningless in its context, whereas A1's "*Oncaymaeon*" at least preserves the sound of the Greek phrase "on kai me on" even if it does not comprehend the sense of the phrase; and on his own account, the B-version editor twice emends "erring stars", which is correct Renaissance terminology for the planets, to "evening stars." The B-version editor also bowdlerises, leaving out the name of God many times and excising some of Faustus' more anguished lines, presumably in deference to the more stringent controls on blasphemy, or what was though to be blasphemy, in operation after 1605. The worst that can be said of the B-version's editor is that he either did not know or did not care that his incorporation of the Birde-Rowley material violated the integrity of Marlowe's *Doctor Faustus*. The only remaining mystery concerning the B-version is that it took so long to get into print.

The A-text of 1604 is by no means perfect. Signs that it has been memorially reconstructed are incontestable, but textual scholars have too easily dismissed it as another reported text without due regard for its special characteristics or the circumstances of its transmission. An exhaustive analysis of the A-text would occupy many pages and would require an intensive point-for-point commentary on Greg and others. Now that the A-version is once more generally accepted as being closer to Marlowe's original, it seems less important to vindicate it against B than to describe more precisely its characteristics so that its merits and limitations can be assessed.

Given that *Doctor Faustus* was in existence by 1590-91, possibly a little earlier, how closely does the 1604 quarto represent the play as it had been given some thirteen years before? While a complete answer cannot be made unless and until *Doctor Faustus* in its original playhouse form comes to light, there are grounds for cautious optimism.

The structure of the A-version as we know it is corroborated by the early allusions to it, but only now is it possible to assert that the comic scenes are Marlowe's own. Greg, working on the fact that the B-version's comic scenes are manifestly corrupt, deduced that the A-version must be doubly so; but since we now know that B derives from A, and not the other way around, Greg's conclusion is invalidated. Greg and the critics of his time share an assumption that comic scenes upset the decorum of tragedy and they are therefore disposed to suspect the comic scenes in *Doctor Faustus*. This neo-classical assumption does not take into account Marlowe's use of the morality play structure and conventions, very well established in Marlowe's day, whereby the tragic and the comic intermingle freely.[34] In the morality tradition, comic and tragic episodes are harmonised by themes shared in common; at its best this structuring technique leads to work of exquisite and subtle irony — it was used to advantage, if sparingly, by Shakespeare. Outside *Doctor Faustus* there is no prose writing or comic dramaturgy known to be Marlowe's, so no stylistic comparison is possible as a means of establishing authorship, but the large extent to which the matter of the comic scenes echoes the more elevated scenes generally recognised to be Marlowe's must create a presumption that the comic scenes are also by Marlowe or at worst by a collaborator writing under Marlowe's general direction.[35]

The status of the 1604 text as a reported text or "bad quarto" has already been discussed. If we accept that the A-version is memorially reconstructed rather than "memorially corrupted", as Bowers describes it, then our entire perception of it is altered. It remains to be asked how soon after the original prompt-book copy was lost the text was re-established. Champions of the B-version have never tired of pointing out that A's allusion to the death of Dr Lopez, the former physician to the Queen who was executed in 1594, proves that the A-text is contaminated. This challenge to A can easily be turned the other way: the quick throw-away reference, "Dr Lopus was never such a doctor", alluding only momentarily to a man who enjoyed only a brief notoriety, suggests that the Lopez affair was still highly topical. Nothing in the public theatre tires more quickly than a joke which has lost its topicality. Besides, within a few years it would have become necessary to explain the joke. The reason for the removal in the B-version of the obvious intruder into Marlowe's text was surely not on purist grounds but simply because the joke had long since ceased to be funny. In 1985 a reference to Christine Keeler would be as remote as a reference to Dr Lopez would have been in 1616. Similarly the excision from B of the guilders-gridirons-French crowns joke can be attributed less to editorial scruple than to the simple fact that the time for good Englishmen to knock holes in debased French coins had long since passed. But the problem with French coinage was still very much an issue in 1594-95.

These topical allusions strongly suggest that the 1604 text represents the play as it was reconstituted in the mid-1590s. There is one indication that the text dates from no later than 1598. An allusion to Philip II's American source of wealth speaks of "the golden fleece,/That yearly stuffs old Philip's treasury." Since old Philip died in 1598, the present tense "stuffs" puts the text as recorded in A1 as being in existence before his death; B1, interestingly, emends "stuffs" to "stuff'd", which is a further sign of its general lateness.

To what extent the text of *Doctor Faustus* became contaminated by non-Marlovian intrusions in the process of being reconstituted for performance by the Admiral's Men in 1594, (September 30 of that year being recorded by Henslowe as the first date for its performance) it is impossible to say with any certainty. To what extent it may have become further corrupted in the years between 1594 and 1604 is no easier to determine. There is enough in favour of the A-version in general terms, however, to create a presumption in favour of authenticity and it is now up to its opponents to prove the contrary for every line and every reading which is questioned. In closely parallel passages B has some superior readings, but these can be put down to intelligent editorial emendation rather than access to a supposed manuscript by Marlowe. One whole scene in the A-version, distantly parallelled in B, is problematical enough to ground suspicion, but there is no reason to prefer the B-version here. It is the scene which immediately follows a Chorus speech that promises an interview with the Emperor, and it is questionable in two ways. Instead of following the Chorus, the promised interview is deferred in favour of a conjuring scene between Robin the ostler and Ralph, his fellow-worker at an inn where Faustus is apparently staying. Though there is something to be said for the comic bathos achieved in having Robin appear at the moment when the Emperor is expected, it seems more likely that the Robin-Ralph scene originally followed the scene at the imperial court. Like the two earlier comic scenes involving servants (Wagner-scholars, 196-238, and Wagner-Clown, 356-441), the Robin-Ralph scene may be seen to ape or *zany* the main action. In the two earlier scenes the comic action gains its effectiveness from following more elevated action, upon which it comments thematically. The Robin-Ralph scene is quite funny in itself

and certainly bears upon one of the major motifs of *Doctor Faustus* — conjuring supernatural forces for petty and morally dubious purposes — but it bears especially upon
the Faustus-Emperor scene in its blend of curiosity and credulity with sexual pruri-
ence. It is possible that in the printing of the text the two scenes have become reversed:
if the Robin-Ralph scene follows the Faustus-Emperor scene, it has a pointed ironic
immediacy which is otherwise lost. Furthermore, the awkward transition at the end of
the Faustus-Emperor scene from court to open road — though it can be justified within
the stage practice of the morality tradition — would disappear if the clownage scene
intervened.

The second doubt we have concerning the Robin-Ralph scene is that the text seems
contaminated in precisely the same way that very much larger tracts of the B-version
are contaminated: the effectiveness of magic is over-played. Only a few lines are
suspect, however, and they contradict the drift of the scene, in which magic is lam-
pooned.[36] Mephostophiles appears after Robin's preposterous conjuring in nonsense-
Latin and pseudo-Greek, in a parody of his earlier attendance upon Faustus' conjuring, but he says:

> How am I vexed with these villains' charms!
> From Constantinople am I hither come,
> Only for pleasure of these damned slaves. (1032-34)

These lines do not sound like Marlowe's verse and they are at odds with the A-version
as a whole. Nevertheless, they do not invalidate the scene in its entirety.

In this edition of the A-version of *Doctor Faustus*, we have aimed at presenting a
consistent and honest rendering of the 1604 text with as few anomalies as possible. B-
version readings have been introduced as sparingly as possible, and only when the A-
version is manifestly deficient. All departures from A are recorded in the facing-page
notes. Having weighed the sets of advantages and disadvantages attendant upon
choice between an old-spelling edition and a modernised text, we have adopted the
latter as being more suited to the needs of the majority of likely readers. Modernising
always has its problems; in this as in other respects, we have done our best to keep
editorial intrusion to a minimum. The notes may be read or ignored, according to the
reader's preferences, and in format our priority has been a sequence of right-hand
pages consistent in length: we wish to render, as faithfully as possible without resorting
to the strictures of a facsimile edition, the unbroken text without act or scene division
of the A-text of 1604. The notes are offered as an explicatory and by no means exhaustive guide to the modern student of Christopher Marlowe's play.

5.   Magic in the Renaissance

The presence of the phenomenon of magic in a drama which provides many moments
of high tragic dignity is a considerable stumbling block for a modern audience, which
brings to the subject a number of highly unsuitable and misleading associations — the
conjuror's white rabbits, the Toytown Magician's packets of Red Fire, the comic-book
Mad Scientist's stinks and bangs, or, at only a very slightly more sophisticated level,
seedy backstreet shops displaying A. E. Waite's books on the Tarot, and the alternative
culture's resurrection of Blavatsky and Ouspensky. A distinguished authority on the

subject of Renaissance magic concludes an excellent discussion of its characteristics with the verdict that it "appears sometimes to be simply misunderstood physics and chemistry and botany and zoology, sometimes to be identical with astrology, and sometimes to be like elaborately ceremonialised prayer."[37] But this conclusion is not as dismissive as it may seem; it represents the outcome of a complex investigation, and to understand what Faustus believes himself to be doing at lines 239-62, and why he can be intellectually drunk with excitement at the prospect of learning the arts of magic, is an essential ingredient in our understanding of *Doctor Faustus*. In the following few pages we will attempt to indicate the nature of the world which Faustus believes himself to inhabit, the apparent intellectual justification for the practice of magic, and the actual mechanics of its implementation.

As moderns, we live in an overwhelmingly nominalist world, and our way of understanding it consists usually of an attempt to describe its physical characteristics as accurately as we can. We describe it principally in terms of our own numeracy; that is, we measure it, by determining how much its individual parts weigh, how long, high, and wide they are, at what speed they travel, and so forth. Our analogy, often unspoken, is with a machine. We understand our world by taking it to pieces, scrutinising its components, describing them, and putting them all together again with the hope that we will have nothing left over and that we will now understand how the whole coheres. We murder to dissect, and we dissect in order to know.

The world which the Renaissance thinker inherited from the Middle Ages was quite different. As a great biblical scholar has remarked, modern man looks at the world, but medieval man looked through it. His attempt was not to describe the world, but to determine its meaning, and this meaning was to be fathomed in terms of the extent to which the world contained messages confirming and elaborating the revelation of divine scripture. The Renaissance thinker finds himself at a half-way house between the medieval and modern world views. He believes, for reasons which will appear below, that the world is an ordered and planned manifestation, and that all its component parts lock together and gear, but he believes that this plan cannot be located immediately at a literal level. The relationships between things constitute a mechanical order just below the surface appearance of things, and it is the task of the scholar to penetrate through the outward husk of reality, its *cortex* or "exoteric" aspect, and to locate its *nucleus*, its inner or "esoteric" nature. This distinction between the outer literal meaning—the letter—and the inner spiritual meaning, is, of course, basic to Christianity, and was most usually manifested in the need not simply to read Holy Scripture, but to interpret it as one read. Perused literally, the Old Testament was largely a narrative of Middle Eastern military history; read spiritually, it was a repository of images which foretold mystically their own fulfilment in the incidents of Christ's redemption of man in the New Testament. For the Renaissance magus, true knowledge consists in rejecting the literal surface of things, and attempting to understand the hidden logic which supports and impels the whole cosmos. Once this logic has been understood, it can be harnessed, and hence translated into a power system which the magus can employ for practical ends. The most obvious way of doing this is through an attempt to understand the nature of number itself.

Since the time of the Greek philosopher Pythagoras, number has often been thought of as in some way the basic building block of the material world. The only Platonic dialogue to survive relatively intact throughout the Middle Ages, the *Timaeus*, regards the universe as compounded of a limited number of categories of three-dimensional solids whose polygonal surfaces interlock together in complex ways reminiscent of the methods employed in the twentieth century by cubist painters. This view is derived from the basic tenet of Platonic philosophy, viz., that the mutable world of experience and sense data is only a shadowy representation, at one or more removes, of an ideally real world which we can know by induction and intellection. It seemed obvious, given this view of the world, that numbers, and mathematical propositions were somehow more real and more eternal because they maintained an unchanging truth and applicability outside space and time. Numbers, therefore, were deemed to have two meanings and uses; there was their ordinary, everyday function in commerce and technology (i.e. their exoteric aspect), and an inner, arcane, or occult aspect which was viewed as an additional dimension. This aspect can be illustrated by something as banal as the nine times multiplication table. At the literal level, it gives us a series of statements like this: $2 \times 9 = 18$, $3 \times 9 = 27$, $4 \times 9 = 36$, and so on, up to, say, $12 \times 9 = 108$. The added dimension, the esoteric aspect, of this sequence was thought to lie in the fact that the sum of the digits of each product reverted to the original number, 9. So, $4 \times 9 = 36$, and $3 + 6 = 9$. For a mind anxious, in the terminology we have already employed, to look not at but through things, the accumulation of such phenomena suggested a continuous systematic order lying behind the usually perceived sense data of the passing day, an order which, it was Platonically supposed, constituted the *real* meaning of the world lurking just behind the curtain or façade of the immediately visible and apprehensible world. The nine times multipliation table provides another refinement, too. The sums of the digits of the products from 2×9 to 12×9 add up to 9, but with one exception: 11×9 results in a number, 99, the sum of whose elements is not 9 but twice 9. That is, it is an exception to the pattern, but an exception which seems to hint at an additional scheme.[38] It is the location and unravelling of such hypothetical schemes which is seen, in certain contexts, as the ultimate reward of the life of scholarship. 'Lines, circles, scenes, letters, and characters . . .' (80). If we were searching for a Tourneuresque subtitle for *Doctor Faustus*, we might dub it *The Intellectual's Tragedy*. The protagonist's academic erudition is stressed from the very inception, and the necromantic books to which he turns towards the conclusion of the exemplum are represented, by their dramatic position, as the apogee or culmination of a lifetime's study.[39]

Our own numbers, from one to nine, are of course Arabic in origin, and, importantly, they incorporate the concept of zero, but the Greeks did not have such a system of notation, and, naturally, tended to think of numbers as spatial in nature, rather like dots on a piece of paper or pebbles on an expanse of sand. A number is therefore a sort of diagram, and there comes to light a similarity between certain numbers which is not otherwise apparent. Some numbers are seen as triangular, viz:

In a similar way, other numbers can be laid out in squares and combinations of squares, and are thought of as square numbers. So, numbers are viewed as geometrical entities that denote physical objects, and hence there came into being the idea that things essentially *were* number and were caused or defined by number. This idea gained support when it was realised that the first four numbers (1, 2, 3, 4) could represent a progression from a single point (1), through an extended line (2), to a two-dimensional surface (3, a triangle) and finally to a solid, three-dimensional object (4, a tetrahedron, i.e. a three-sided pyramid complete with its base). The more the subject was pondered, the more internal logic it seemed to have, and the more it seemed to deserve a religious veneration. For instance, a category of perfect numbers was created—that is, numbers which are the sum of all the numbers with which they can be divided, like 6, which is the sum total of 1 + 2 + 3, or 28, which is the sum total of 1 + 2 + 4 + 7 + 14. Not all numbers are like this; there are some where the dividing constituents add up to less (deficient numbers, like 14 − 1 + 2 + 7), and others where the dividers add up to more than the final number which they are thought of as compounding (abundant numbers, like 12 − 1 + 2 + 3 + 4 + 6). Again, there are circular numbers which, when multiplied by themselves, contain themselves in the answer (e.g. 5 and 6).

In the *Timaeus*, Plato demonstrated, to the satisfaction of ensuing generations, that the cosmos was essentially a compound of number. Starting with the postulate of the four elements, he selected two as basic: earth, to give a solid location in space, and fire, to confer visibility upon objects. Objects would, he thought, be best envisaged as cohering by virtue of their numerical proportion, and the basic elements should be envisaged as cubes, because the cube was the most solid and stable form of matter. Given this assumption, the result was logical enough, and reminiscent of certain modern children's play kits. Material forms were held together by intermediary elements which could be located in the cube sequence, so that one could say that objects cohered together through relationships which might be mathematically described as 2:4::4:8, or that 8:4::4:2, or that 4:2::8:4. This seems ludicrous to us, but it is not ludicrous if we once make some allowance for the way in which much pre-scientific thought is qualitative rather than quantitative. Plato was not grappling with the problem of how much substance was present; he was concerned with relationships, not with the mass, weight or measurement of objects, and his thought was somewhat analogous to the way in which, say, Watson and Crick discovered the DNA molecule through the construction of hypothetical models. Finally, Plato allotted a particular solid geometrical figure to each element, so that the cube is earth, the pyramid is fire, the octahedron is air, and the twenty-sided icosahedron is water. For a modern person trying to understand the thought of a past age, these individual details are less important than the eventual conclusion which one commentator has made: "thus we are given an extended description of a mathematically planned universe, of the eternal model, whose mere changing likeness we actually experience."[40]

For the reader of the play, three issues present themselves, viz., what is the intellectual basis of Renaissance magic, how does one effect a magical operation, and what does Faustus make of all this?[41]

The Renaissance magical world view springs from the following assumptions:

(a) The theory of a shared middle ground between otherwise distinct and unrelated entities, such as, for instance, an *anima* or *spiritus mundi* which connects God (or the Creative Principle) and the material world. Such a shared common ground impinges upon both levels of existence, and affords a bridge from lower to higher.

(**b**) The theory of correspondences—that is, that all creation is linked in a series of elaborate parallelisms, analogies which are believed to have an objective and physical validity, and are not mere verbal forms. So, as the entire Ptolemaic cosmos produces a divine if inaudible music, it must in a real sense *be* a musical instrument, and the various theories as to the number of its component spheres (usually seven or nine) must be mirrored in the numbers of strings appropriate to a musical instrument. The most important correspondence, which was often illustrated in elaborate diagrams, was that between the body of the individual man and the "body" of the cosmos.[42] To produce an effect on one of these entities, therefore, is, by means of a ripple phenomenon, to produce, simultaneously, that same effect on the other entity as well.

(**c**) A pervasive animism—that is, the belief that in order to provide a mirror or parallel for human life, the cosmos itself must also, in a real sense, be alive, and must therefore incorporate sexual differentiation. Such a sexual and animate universe provides much of the intellectual underpinning for Renaissance alchemy and the fashionable alchemical/medical theories of Paracelsus.

(**d**) From the theory of correspondences under (b) above, it allegedly follows that the powers inherent in the various parts or aspects of the macrocosm may be guided or captured by eating or (where, as in the case of indigestible metals, this is impossible) by wearing objects which participate in the powers required. The importance of astrology/astronomy both here and in the preceding category is obvious, and Faustus' questions to Mephostophiles at lines 662–706, have, for the would-be magus, an extremely important practical aspect. In an example which is often cited by writers on the subject, Ficino relates how, in his youth, he desired to exploit the powers of the constellation Ursa Major, and so he engraved a bear on a magnet and hung this contraption around his neck by means of an iron thread. To his alarm, however, he found that he had miscalculated, and was attracting the sinister and baleful attentions of the planet Saturn.

(**e**) The principle of *pars pro toto* (viz., 'the part signifies the whole') results in the belief that both numbers and words are not simply descriptive modes of calculation and illustration, but that they have an objective, Platonic existence, and inhere in objects, so that to invoke the part, and to tamper with it or entrap it is to gain power over the whole of which it is an ingredient. This is a familiar enough phenomenon today in many cultures, where one is careful to conserve parts of one's body (locks of hair, nail-parings) lest they fall into vengeful hands, and to conceal one's real, baptismal name under the cloak of a calling-name or nickname, and to be on one's guard against the theft of one's photograph or reflection. A practice which is alluded to on several occasions in *Faustus* is that of 'racking' and anagrammatising a name. This springs indirectly from traditional Hebrew ways of interpreting the scriptures, where it is believed that, since the Old Testament is the inspired word of God, any meaning which can be extracted from it by any consistent methodology must itself contain metaphysical power. Such methods include *gematria*, based upon the fact that in languages such as Latin and Hebrew the same symbols function as both letters and numbers and can therefore be seen, at least theoretically, as interchangeable, *notarikon*, an acrostic system where words are run on to form new compounds, and *themurah*, the transposition of code values for Hebrew letters by means of anagrams.[43]

How does one effect a magical operation? The method is outlined with great clarity (albeit complexity) in Agrippa's *De Occulta Philosophia*.[44] Basically, one constructs an object which, by its mathematical — that is, numerological — form resembles the planetary force one desires to capture, and this resemblance is itself deemed to be a participation in the form of the force in question. In other words, the control of distant things is guaranteed by the control of their immediate manifestations. Faustus evidently has a grasp of this methodology when the play opens, for he has constructed "bills hung up as monuments,/Whereby whole cities have escaped the plague" (48–49). In his first encounter with the peripatetic magicians Valdes and Cornelius, who are evidently intended to represent the sort of gnostic brotherhood which Agrippa founded in order to protect his knowledge from the vulgar (see Nauert, chapter 2, 'The Making of a Scholar'), Faustus is urged to utilise "Albanus' works" (183). Albanus (*sc.*, Peter of Abano, also known as Peter of Padua) was a fourteenth century scholar and magus whose best-known work, *The Conciliator* of 1310, contains much discussion on the making and employment of astrological images and amulets, as well as discussions of incantation, number mysticism, and poisons — both how to administer them, and how to safeguard oneself against them. A work attributed to Peter, but probably spurious, the *Heptameron* or *Elements of Magic*, "consists entirely of specific directions how to invoke demons . . . The reader is instructed in the construction of the magic circle, in the names of the angels, and concerning benedictions, fumigations, exorcisms, prayers to God, visions, apparitions, and conjurations for each day of the week."[45]

Agrippa stresses number as the basic building block of the universe; numbers are purer, more formal, than physical objects. The character and power of objects is therefore derived from their numerical components. For example, a plant known as the cinquefoil was thought to have curative properties not because of the chemistry of its juices but because of the number of its leaves, so that it participated in the power of the quinary. To formulate such a law was to approach closer to divine truth than if one remained with the physical manifestation. "Symbols, whether numbers, words, or figures, if they truly designated things, did not therefore only represent them, but were themselves more nearly the 'reality' of which the natural object imperfectly partook" (Calder, p. 197). Anything which is a sign of another object is also a part of it, and has power over it. An alchemical function follows, for conventional chemical elements are flawed, as their names merely allude to their perfected forms, which can be obtained by subjecting the actual metals and chemicals to purifying treatments.

The old Arab systems had assigned a number, in the form of a magic square, to each planet in the order of its distance from the earth.[46] Agrippa uses a reverse system, numbering inwards from Saturn down to the earth, and this became general. The Arabic name for Saturn had a number value of 45, equalling the sum of the numbers used in the magic square of three. The magic square of four was appropriate to Jupiter, because of the tetragrammaton, and so on.

Let us undertake a simple piece of Renaissance magic, and suppose that we wish to

capture, direct, or participate in the influence of Saturn, whose number is 3. We
accordingly construct this square

4	9	2
3	5	7
8	1	6

Figure 1

which is derived from the following natural square, numbered from left to right (as in
the construction of all uneven squares) by a turn of 45° to the right, and the insertion
of the numerals thus left on the opposite sides. The seal of Saturn represents this shift
in diagrammatic form, as the seal of Jupiter represents diagrammatically the shifts
necessary in creating the magic square of 4 by leaving in place one half of the numerals
of the natural square and turning the other half by 180°.

The process by which the natural square is transposed into the magic square and
then into the appropriate *signaculum* may be represented diagrammatically in the
following way.

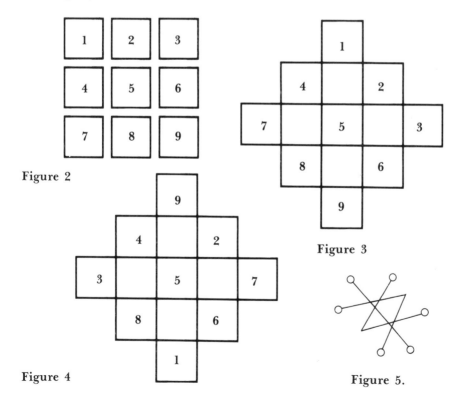

Figure 2

Figure 3

Figure 4

Figure 5.

LIBER SECVNDVS.

Nomina respondentia numeris Lunæ.

9	Hod	דוד
81	Elim	אלים
369	Hasmodai, Dæmonium Lunæ.	השמוראי
3321	Schedbarschemoth Schartathan, Dæmonium dæmoniorum Lunæ.	שרברשהמעתשרתתן
	Intelligentia intelligentiarum Lunæ.	
3321	Malcha betharsisim hed beruah schehakim,	מלכא בתרשיתים ער ברוח שהקים

Tabula Saturni in abaco.

In notis Hebraicis.

4	9	2
3	5	7
8	1	6

ד	ט	ב
ג	ה	ז
ח	א	ו

Saturni.

Signacula siue characteres,
Intelligentiæ Saturni.

Dæmonij Saturni.

Tabula Iouis in abaco.

In notis Hebraicis.

4	14	15	1
9	7	6	12
5	11	10	8
16	2	3	13

ד	יד	טו	א
ט	ז	ו	יב
ה	יא	י	ח
יו	ב	ג	יג

Iouis.

Signacula siue characteres
Intelligentiæ Iouis.

Dæmonij Iouis.

Figure 2 is the natural square of 3, and has 9 cells. Figure 3 represents the natural square turned 45° to the right, and Figure 4 is deduced by transposing the numbers at the opposite ends of the vertical and horizontal axes, viz., 1 and 9 in the vertical axis and 7 and 3 in the horizontal.

Figure 5 represents the *signaculum* or seal of the nine-cell magic square of Saturn, and is merely an attempt to represent diagrammatically, on a plane surface, the 45° shift via the diagonal stroke from top left to bottom right and the two transpositions of Figure 4 via the intersecting V's. The atmosphere of Agrippa's work, and of much of Renaissance occultism, may be gleaned from the full-page reproduction (p. xxxvi) of signature niii of the *De Occulta*, which features the magic square of Saturn, its equivalent in Hebrew letters by means of a gematric transposition, and the resultant *signaculum*, together with the *signacula* and names of Saturn's attendant daemons. It will be noted, therefore, that all this information has been allegedly uncovered by following apparently objective mathematical procedures. As Nowotny remarks, "these numbers and lines seem to reveal the laws of the harmony of the spheres. The construction of this harmony is on rational lines. To a contemporary observer it would appear that only the absence of a key to the harmony of these squares conceals from him a knowledge of the final solution" (p. 57).

Beneath the figures for the seal of Saturn, Agrippa provides the appropriate symbols for the dialectical antithesis to the gloomy saturnine temperament, that is, the impedimenta for the jovial temperament of Jupiter. The modern student of the subject may gain a considerable insight into the mind of the Renaissance magus by studying Durer's engraving *Melencolia I* (p. xxxviii), which is replete with Agrippan erudition. The figure of Melancholy is placed beneath the counteractive magic square of Jupiter (bearing, incidentally, the date of the engraving's execution), and, if the latest research is to be credited, the giant polyhedron balancing the magic square on the opposite side of the composition has been derived by a series of three-dimensional mathematical transpositions from the magic square.[47] In addition to the magic square and its attendant solid, Durer's Melancholy should be wearing about her person an amulet inscribed with the Jovian seal depicting a circle upon which two intersecting diagonal lines have been imposed (see the bottom left diagram in the reproduction from the *De Occulta*). This seal will, in theory, combat the scholar's solitary proclivity to the Saturnian mood. The modern student of Renaissance magic will find the construction of magic squares easier to follow if he employs numbered index cards, whereupon he will find himself engaged upon a pastime located somewhere between Patience and Rubik's cube. The editors of this text assume no responsibility for any untoward occult manifestations.

The employment of magic squares, and the sometimes exacting mathematical operations involved in designing them, for they were often enormous and of great complexity, is fundamental to an understanding of the apparently irrefragable reasoning of the Renaissance magician. He saw himself as a man engaged in an exacting intellectual undertaking which was designed to uncover and analyse the inner working of matter: ". . . four-letter names of God (in Hebrew) can be written in a square on the front of a round medal in such a way as to produce four additional names or seals read vertically, the square being circled by other Hebrew letters which express the names' 'intention' . . . Each such square is accompanied by another containing Hebrew letters instead of numbers, these presumably having equivalent values. A tablet representing

Albrecht Durer, *Melencolia I*

Saturn, thus engraved on a lead plate—lead being the metal associated with Saturn—helps in childbirth, confers safety and power, and causes requests made of princes and other men of authority to be granted, provided only the tablet is dedicated to the planet's beneficent aspect. If the planet's maleficent powers are invoked, the tablet will be inimical to buildings and plantings, destructive of honors and dignities, provocative of quarrels, and dispersive of armies" (Shumaker, pp. 149 and 143).

Whether such knowledge, and its practical application, was widely regarded as malevolent and forbidden (black magic or *goetia*) or as permissible and salutary (*magia*) is an issue hard to decide, and probably impossible of resolution. As Thorndike repeatedly points out in his monumental study, the authors of individual magical tomes seem themselves unclear on the subject, and there seems to be a large penumbral area in between the two moral activities. It is precisely in this area that we first encounter Faustus, and his dilemma is in a sense an inevitable outcome of the predicament of the humanist scholar of his age, imbued with an animistic view of the universe and not equipped with the benefit of our own hindsight in his attempts to distinguish between the main highway of European intellectual development and its culs-de-sac, blind-alleys and one-way streets. "Nature and nature's laws lay hid in night," Alexander Pope dogmatically remarked; "God said, Let Newton be, and all was light." This reflects a typical post-Royal Society attitude, to which we still subscribe. Before the breaking of the circle and the irruption of the Enlightenment, all knowledge was barbarous, all science pseudo-science or mumbo-jumbo. But it was not so obvious at the time. Harvey, discoverer of the circulation of the blood, was an intimate friend of the magus Robert Fludd, and Agrippa was widely regarded as a great mind in the vanguard of human knowledge. The mighty Newton himself attached enormous importance to his own researches into alchemy and biblical typology. The authorities to which Faustus alludes, the necromantic books which he craves, are, for many of his contemporaries, advanced works whose applicability is theoretically perfectly sound provided their premises are accepted. And this was to demand nothing more than what the age subscribed to almost universally—a Platonic view of the universe.

6.   A Note on Witchcraft

"Magic and Witchcraft are far differing Sciences," declares one Robert Turner in his introduction to a translation (published in 1655) of Peter of Abano's *Heptameron*.[48] Turner's more famous contemporary, Sir Thomas Browne, holds the opposite opinion, speaking of "witches, or as we term them, magicians".[49] This difference is largely explained by their respective points of view: those who seek to defend some forms of magic as the permissible practice of *theurgia* (working with beneficent spirits) make a distinction between white magic and the hellish arts of *goetia* (working with evil spirits) and necromancy (communicating with the dead for prophetic and other purposes). Cornelius Agrippa, as one might expect, was one who endorsed the distinction. The age was deeply confused, however, on the issue of the legitimacy of the operations we have been describing in the last few pages. Authorities differed as to the possibility of there being a true form of white magic by which the scholar might participate in the powers of Christ and the saints, or utilise the morally neutral *daemons* (spirits rather than demons in the modern sense) which were thought to be resident in natural forces and physical forms.

Most people in Marlowe's time believed in the existence of black magic, and many believed in its efficacy. For a Christian, belief in witchcraft — as the practice of black magic in collusion with diabolical forces — was necessitated by the Old Testament, especially Exodus 22.18, which uncompromisingly insisted: "Thou shalt not suffer a witch to live." The New Testament stress on the casting out of devils reinforced earlier beliefs and attitudes. From the fourteenth to the seventeenth century there were many outbreaks of persecution in which the senile, the retarded, the mildly eccentric, and many quite ordinary citizens were done to death in hundreds upon accusations of witchcraft. Sometimes the accusers and the judicial authorities in charge of witchcraft trials were in good faith, sometimes not. At all events, wherever inexplicable disasters, large or small, from famine to still-birth, were interpreted in a spirit of suspicious or hysterical malevolence, witch-hunting was always likely to break out. Levels of tolerance and persecution varied throughout late medieval and Renaissance Europe, depending on time, place, and prevailing circumstances.

Groundless as many of the allegations of witchcraft must have been, there were some who sought to practise the black arts. Whether they achieved any measure of success is another matter, but in any society there will always be people who thrive on the expectation of easily-gained advantage garnished with the spice of danger. There is a grim *double entendre* in Wagner's jest to the scholars about "the place of execution" (221).

In the sixteenth century there was a spate of treatises on the subject of witchcraft, to match the number of trials. The base text was the *Malleus Maleficarum* (hammer against evil-doers) of 1486, compiled by two Dominican members of the Inquisition. This text and those that followed it were compounded of scripture, patristic and medieval commentaries, and the body of folklore which had become absorbed into ideas about witchcraft through centuries of accretion. Notable later works include Nicholas Remy's *Demonolatry* (1595), which incorporates its author's experience as judge in many witchcraft trials in Lorraine from 1576 to 1591, the Italian Guazzo's *Compendium Maleficarum* (1608) and the German Godelmann's *Tractatus de Magis* (1591), the *Demonomanie des Sorciers* (1580) and the *De Republica* (1591) of the great jurist and political theorist, Jean Bodin, and, of course, King James I's own *Daemonologie* (1597). One of the few writers to be openly sceptical about the reality of witchcraft as a working arrangement between man and devil was Reginald Scot, in *The Discoverie of Witchcraft* (1584).[50]

The reader of Marlowe's *Doctor Faustus* is provided with two sorts of magical activity within the framework of the play. In the main plot, which deals with Faustus' scholarship and erudition, we are in the presence of a man who in spite of his humble birth is a scholar and a gentleman. The conjurational methods Faustus imbibes from his necromantic books, and the authorities he cites, all denote a man who is learned in the methods we have been describing. Some of his activities are consonant with *theurgia*, but he has also crossed far into the forbidden ground of *goetia*. White or black, his magic is the intellectual's.

There is a second order of magic in the subplot of the play. Its magicians are the low-life figures of Wagner and the comic ostlers, its conjurations are a series of demotic practical jokes and folk-beliefs rooted in folklore rather than the books they cannot read. The two worlds are linked structurally, partly by the *commedia dell'arte* concept of the *zany* (the servant who apes his master), partly by the intrusion of ignorant hucksters like the Horse-courser into the increasingly petty life of Faustus the magus, and partly by the very pact towards which the early action of the play advances and from which the later action recedes.

The pact is at the heart of the play. "Witchcraft . . . was everywhere and always understood to involve a pact with the Devil. The pact, indeed, was its defining characteristic" (Shumaker, p. 72). That Faustus, the great scholar, binds himself to the powers of darkness by such a popular concept as the pact provides a profound current of irony throughout the play, an irony which is scarcely present in the *Historia* or *EFB*. The irony consists, ultimately, in a motif central to much medieval drama and to most of Shakespeare's mature theatre — the Christian theme that those who are wise in the ways of this world are foolish in terms of the world of the spirit, and that naive simpletons will eventually inherit the earth.

7. The Pact with the Devil

On the occasion when Mephostophiles first materialises, the conjured devil speaks with commendable honesty, but his honesty is in keeping with well-established tradition about the tactics of demons in gathering human disciples. Such tactics are well understood by Banquo in *Macbeth*, for after the three witches have uttered their prophecies, Banquo muses:

> . . . oftentimes, to win us to our harm,
> The instruments of darkness tell us truths,
> Win us with honest trifles, to betray's
> In deepest consequence.

I. iii. 123-26

Faustus, on learning that Lucifer alone is Mephostophiles' master, nevertheless pursues his desire for affirmation by asking: "Did not my conjuring speeches raise thee?" (285). To which Mephostophiles returns: "That was the cause, but yet *per accidens*." (286). His attendance upon Faustus is only contingently related to the act of conjuration, as Mephostophiles goes on to point out:

> For when we hear one rack the name of God,
> Abjure the scriptures, and his saviour Christ,
> We fly in hope to get his glorious soul;
> Nor will we come unless he use such means
> Whereby he is in danger to be damned.

(287-91)

From this exchange we are told that dabbling in black magic does little in itself: it serves only to reveal the spiritual condition of the dabbler to interested parties. Damnation is a real danger, but devils have no power to ensure it: they only wait in hope, lending what encouragement they can.

Blind to the truth of limitation, both in the devil and himself, Faustus proceeds with his pact. He desperately wants it to be valid. But is it? In answer to this vital question, the A- and B-versions of *Doctor Faustus* part company. In the B-version the pact is binding, for at the end of the allotted time the devils not only claim their due but have no difficulty in exacting it — if we are to judge by the mess which the scholars find the next morning, the dismembered remains of Faustus scattered about his room. In B, the scholars report their gory find in a short added scene. The A-version ends with a terrifying vision of damnation, but without physical concomitants. He apparently dies on his last words, and the departure of the devils with his body is merely dramatic confirmation of his damnation. Their physical presence is always in doubt: twice in the last hundred lines of the play, Faustus is seen to be the victim of hallucinations or private visions. The first of these two occasions is in his last scene with the scholars:

> FAUSTUS
> Look: comes he not? comes he not?
> SECOND SCHOLAR
> What means Faustus?
> THIRD SCHOLAR
> Belike he is grown into some sickness by being
> over-solitary.
>
> (1410–13)

And again:

> FAUSTUS
> I would lift up my hands, but
> see — they hold them, they hold them!
> ALL
> Who, Faustus?
> FAUSTUS
> Lucifer and Mephostophiles.
>
> (1440–43)

The second occasion is in the last soliloquy, where Faustus sees both God and devils:

> O, I'll leap up to my God! Who pulls me down?
> See, see where Christ's blood streams in the firmament;
> One drop would save my soul, half a drop. Ah, my Christ!
> Ah, rend not my heart for naming of my Christ —
> Yet will I call on Him — oh, spare me Lucifer!
> Where is it now? 'Tis gone.
> And see where God stretcheth out his arm
> And bends his ireful brows.
>
> (1483–90)

On both occasions Marlowe emphasises the inwardness of demonic reality. The manifestation of the devils in the last few lines of the A-version is an invitation for us to share in Faustus' inward vision, but no more. The spurious final scene of the B-version, though founded in *EFB*, shows the injudicious addition of material derived from folklore but not in accord with the received intellectual tradition concerning witchcraft. Perhaps, it may be objected, Marlowe himself preferred folklore to the intellectual tradition, but such a view does not accord with the play as a whole, the play as preserved in the A-version. For the moment, however, let us return to the pact itself.

Mephostophiles prepares Faustus for the ceremonial signing of the pact by using formal legal terminology. Renaissance men believed more surely than we do today that the laws of men are made in the image of the laws of God, but their horror at Mephostophiles' blasphemous recourse to legal terms would have been tempered with amusement: that litigious age had a better work-a-day familiarity with legal forms and terms than we do, and those who felt a shudder of dread would also have been struck by the quaint incongruities in what Mephostophiles demands. For Mephostophiles' use of legal language is both bogus and confused. Let us consider some examples.

Mephostophiles stipulates that Faustus must "buy my service with his soul" (473). However, "buy" more properly signifies a money contract of sale than the barter arrangement which Faustus is proffered. Mephostophiles then asks Faustus to "bequeath" (475) his soul, but bequest is a legal act which has nothing to do either with sale or barter. In the next line Mephostophiles requires "a deed or gift", but alienation of property by gift is unrelated to sale, barter, and bequest, and is not consistent with them. What bequest and gift have in common is that both are free acts of will and can only be valid when unforced and without consideration. Again, the "security" (477) that Lucifer craves is not proper to the legal relationships already mentioned. This helter-skelter misapplication of legal terms points to the larger truth that the pact into which Faustus is about to enter is illegal and void. In English law and even more so in the Roman law which Renaissance humanists so much admired—we recall the first scene in which Faustus turned to the Roman law of Justinian—immoral contracts are not binding. For at this point law and theology interpenetrate.

It is axiomatic in the law of property that one can only dispose of what one owns. Faustus proposes to dispose of what is not his to give: in terms of the Christian theology prevailing in Marlowe's day, man is God's creature and as such only God can make the disposition of a soul, to his own company in heaven or to the devil in hell. Parables in the synoptic gospels frequently speak of life as a stewardship, as in the parable of the talents, or in terms of day-labour in service of a king or rich land-owner. A steward or labourer is not an owner but at most a temporary custodian who must account to his master. Again law and theology come together: the principle of Roman law which Faustus earlier rejected in "a petty case of paltry legacies" (60) should have served to remind him that one cannot bequeath what one does not own. Faustus has not the power to "give both body and soul to Lucifer" (550) as he purports to do in the document of the pact.

Another ground for voiding a contract such as the document purports to be is that it depends on conditions that cannot be fulfilled. Where an impossible condition is only of minor or incidental significance, that condition can simply be ignored and the contract remains valid in other respects, but the first condition which Faustus imposes—namely that he shall be "a spirit in form and substance" (538-39)—is both central to his demands and quite impossible of performance. A spirit, in this context, is an incorporeal rational being that is supernatural or at least extranatural, i.e. a good or evil angel like those who visit Faustus. In Renaissance writings on witchcraft and magic, "spirit" usually refers to evil angels, i.e. devils. What Faustus fails to allow for is the difference in essence fixed by God between angels, and men. Both can enjoy heaven or suffer hell, but not in the same way: man is essentially a combination of body and spirit and remains so for eternity; he cannot call upon another created being to change his essential nature. Only God can do that. Man remains man as angel remains angel, whether on earth, in heaven, or in hell. Lucifer cannot change Faustus into a spirit.

Witchcraft was enough of a Renaissance obsession for ordinary members of Marlowe's audience to have spotted a characteristic ploy by the powers of darkness in the first condition: they knew that the devil could achieve nothing without the permissive will of God and that in setting himself up as pseudo-God he was acting as *simia Dei*, or the ape of God. Diabolical power was but shallow mimicry; any of the many manuals on witchcraft could have told them that. They would not have been surprised by the first condition, but they would have known it was impossible.

The fact that Faustus gains something from the pact — if what passes between him, the Emperor, the Vanholts, and the Horse-courser can be accounted gains — is no bar to his repudiating it, even at the last. A contract that is *contra bonos mores* is unenforcible and Faustus is in a stronger position than Lucifer, for in law what has been performed by one party under an immoral contract cannot be reclaimed by him, nor can he demand specific performance from the other party.

If the pact has no standing in law, it also has none in the broader, less formal intuitions of folklore. It is a commonplace in European folklore and literature that a pact with the devil can be repudiated without harmful effects, as examples from *The Golden Legend* testify.[51] Probably the best known of these is the story first dramatised by Hrostwitha and again in Marlowe's time as the Low German *Theophilus drama*. Such stories of a pact with the devil may be seen as inversions of those legends wherein a saint is given special protection by an angel. In the patristic and Augustinian thought from which such legends derive, the devil is still subject to the permissive will of God, so "The tempter, even when he springs his trap on man, is still an agent of a higher power. Accordingly, the devil in his dealings with men has reason to expect foul play and in most cases he says so; neither deed nor signature can protect his claims."[52]

Most of what has been suggested so far concerning the pact with the devil in law, theology, and folklore is adumbrated in the most topical of Renaissance sources for Marlowe and his audience — the writings on witchcraft itself. We have already mentioned that from the mid-sixteenth to the early seventeenth century there was a spate of tracts on witchcraft as an accompaniment to the great increase in the number of witchcraft trials. There is remarkable conformity among the writers on witchcraft, partly, it seems, because later writers tended to echo their predecessors and partly because there was a common body of received doctrine in what they wrote. From Sprenger and Kramer, co-authors of the foundation text, *Malleus Maleficarum*, through Remy, Boguet, Bodin, Guazzo, and Godelmann (to name but a few) down to King James I in his *Daemonologie*, there is firm belief in the reality of evil and with it a reality of human practitioners in league with diabolical powers.

Some of the witchcraft writings bear very closely upon what happens in *Doctor Faustus*. Let us return to the impossible first condition of the pact, "that Faustus may be a spirit in form and substance." Transformation was closely associated with magic among the ignorant masses, it seems, for many writers specifically refute alleged transformations into other categories of being. Godelmann adopts the standard theological view that God alone has the power to change the essence of being. The authors of *Malleus Maleficarum* declare: "Whoever believes that it is possible for any creature to be transformed into another shape or likeness, except by the Creator himself, who made all things, and by whom all things are created, is without doubt an infidel and worse than a pagan" (I, Q.x, p. 61). And Remy affirms that "Metamorphoses were true in appearance only but not in fact; for the eyes are deceived by the glamorous art of the demons which can cause such appearances" (II. v., p. 108). In *Doctor Faustus* there seems to be a direct thematic link between the purported transformation of Faustus into spirit and the transformation of the Vintner, Robin and Ralph in the goblet-stealing scene. Put out of humour with these three (even devils find human beings irritating), Mephostophiles says: "Vanish villains, th'one like an ape, another like a bear, the third an ass . . ." (1026-27). There is no suggestion in the text that he can actually transform them, for he says *like* an ape and *like* a bear. The three disappear from the play at this point and we hear no more of them. This is in the A-version; the B-version of the scene characteristically places no limitation on the actual power of Mephostophiles to transform the pranksters. It is a general tendency of the B-version to extend and aggrandise the magical business, as in the following scene, with the transformation of the injurious knight.

In the A-version, Faustus himself admits limitations to his diabolically-derived powers and in his scene with the Emperor specifically disclaims ability to transform the essence of beings. He says: "But if it like your Grace, it is not in my ability to present before your eyes, the true substantial bodies of those two deceased princes . . ." (1092-94) when bidden to conjure up Alexander the Great and his paramour. In the B-version this disclaimer, again characteristically, is omitted; instead the B-version of the scene affirms that magic really works. In the A-version the hold of devils over men is illusory — though a man of Faustus' psychological appetencies may choose to enslave himself — and if there is little that devils can really do to men in life, there is nothing at all they can do in determining the moment of death, which is God's prerogative. By pretence and trickery, however, they may achieve indirectly what they cannot do by direct action.

One concomitant of the pact with the devil, according to the writers on witchcraft, is that human witches have sexual intercourse with demonic *incubi* and *succubi*. A good deal of critical ink has been unnecessarily and laboriously spilt in earnest argument over whether such an act is forgivable. It is, in any case, too easily assumed that Faustus has committed it. The point made again and again in the witchcraft writings is that the repentant witch will always be forgiven even though, as the *Malleus Maleficarum* puts it, the witch's sins be "more grievous than those of the bad angels and our first parents" (I, Q. xiii, p. 73). The *Malleus Maleficarum* insists that a witch's guilt cannot be greater than Adam's, for "Adam, and others who have sinned when in a state of perfection or even of grace, could more easily because of the help of grace have avoided their sins— especially Adam who was created in grace —than many witches, who have not shared such gifts. Therefore the sins of such are greater than all the crimes of witches" (I, Q. xiv, p. 74). Just before the end of our play, one of the scholars urges Faustus to remember that "God's mercies are infinite" (1418-19). When Faustus replies:

> But Faustus' offence can ne'er be pardoned.
> The serpent that tempted Eve may be saved,
> but not Faustus . . .

discerning members of an Elizabethan audience would have recognised not only a case of inverted pride but also an inversion of standard opinion.

What happens to Faustus at the end of the play is far more subtle and disturbing in the A-version than in B, with its reportage of portents and the gathering of mangled limbs. The A-version conforms with the insistence of writers on witchcraft that devils do not and cannot work through direct action but through devious and indirect means, through "second and natural causes."[53] When Faustus shows dangerous signs of repentance in response to the Old Man's exhortations, Mephostophiles threatens poor Faustus: "Revolt or I'll in piecemeal tear thy flesh" (1355). But this is one of Mephostophiles' grosser lies and the fact that Faustus cannot see it has no more truth in it than the vaunt of a professional wrestler who declares that he will break his antagonist in half is a mark of Faustus' decline in intellect and discrimination.

On the evidence of the A-text, Marlowe himself used *EFB* with discernment and restraint. It seems probable that Mephostophiles' empty threat, reinforced by the luridly sensational account of Faustus' *sparagmos* in the crude source of *EFB*, inspired Rowley—or whoever it was who wrote the last scene in the B-version. We are assured by the Epilogue to the A-version that Faustus does die, but the manner of his death is never explicitly stated. The false clue which the author of the added scene at the end of the B-version picked up from the Old Man episode and *EFB* is counter-balanced by a significant dramatic moment that occurs just before Mephostophiles threatens to tear Faustus apart. At the very moment when Faustus over-reacts to the Old Man's strictures on his sinful life by despairing of forgiveness, Mephostophiles hands Faustus a dagger (1334–38). Handing a dagger was a conventional emblem of temptation to despair in sixteenth-century drama.[54] It occurs in many plays—Macbeth's dagger of the mind is probably the most refined application of it—and is also to be found in the Despair episode of *The Faerie Queene* (Book I, canto ix). The ultimate act of despair is suicide, which the emblem of the proffered dagger dramatises so eloquently. In traditional thought the killing of oneself is a mortal sin from which there is no time to repent and so it is the most sure way to damnation.

Writers on witchcraft agree that the devil tries to make sure of witches for the enlargement of his kingdom by urging them to commit suicide. Remy states that "as an end to a life of crime and impiety, the demon insistently urges and impels his subjects to kill themselves with their own hand" (III, vi, p. 161). Guazzo affirms that Satan "is permitted to tempt men, but not to coerce them. For this reason it is that he does not himself cast despairing souls against their wills into the waters, or hang them by a rope from a beam, or stab them with knives; he only lures them to commit such madness" (II, xiii, p. 130). Given the general principle that devils can work only through natural causes, and indirectly at that, the specific application that they cannot enforce the death of a human being at any moment they choose follows clearly enough.

Nevertheless, in Marlowe's play the devils do come at the appointed hour and Faustus does die on the stroke of midnight. It would require an ingeniously forced reading even of the A-version to assert otherwise. How then does Faustus die? Let us, however, exclude the rowdy devils' picnic of the B-version as being spurious on every possible ground. Suicide is a possibility: as we have seen, there are enough pointers in that direction both within the play and in the received doctrines on witchcraft which lie behind the play. One could countenance a director's right to have Faustus fondling and turning over in his hand the dagger given by Mephostophiles only a few minutes earlier in stage time as he begins his last speech:

> Ah Faustus,
> Now hast thou but one bare hour to live . . .

(1471-72)

However, one could not countenance a dénouement in which Faustus deliberately plunges the dagger into his heaving breast as the devils materialise. Such a dénouement would be in accord with an Elizabethan audience's expectations as to how a witch might end his life, but this would again be forcing the text of the A-version of *Doctor Faustus*. We never learn precisely how Faustus dies but we have established how he does *not* die. It is more profitable to ask why he dies.

Why, then, does Faustus die at the precise moment he has expected to? The answer lies, in part at least, in his expectation. The sight of the devils materialising could be enough in itself; that is another partial explanation. There is a more compelling reason: expectation and manifestation are conjoined in his perverted faith. In Reformation Protestantism the traditional Catholic emphasis on faith is reaffirmed and intensified. Faith, in the first generation of theologians after Luther, was commonly analysed into three constituents — knowledge (*notitia*), assent (*consensus*), and trust (*fiducia*). Through the play we have seen Faustus apply all these elements of faith to his worship of Lucifer. Faith, Renaissance theologians tirelessly reminded themselves, could achieve anything. The fact that Faustus' faith is inverted or perverted does not make it less efficacious. His death, then, is not a vindication of Lucifer's power but of his own spiritual capacity for faith, however perverted. Herein lies the final tragic irony of the play.

Although the last scene in the B-version is dramatically and aesthetically weak as well as being thematically quite confusing, it is not without purpose. One must not too lightly assume that the scene merely reflects the incompetence of the hack-writer — we may assume it was Rowley. In his "adicyones" to the A-version, Rowley also doctored existing material systematically. In order to present a more sensational play and a longer play — audiences to the A-version in the later 1590s may well have felt that they were not getting their money's worth in terms of sheer quantity — it was necessary to add more magic, and more effective magic at that. Rowley's immediate task was to set forth for the wonder of beholders not the folly of magic but the power of magic. To avoid accusations of blasphemy, and perhaps to salve his own conscience, he had to treat magic so that it would lead to disaster for the persevering magician; and the disaster would have to be presented in terms commensurate with the previous successes of magic. Also, if the devils were to drag Faustus off to hell in final fulfilment of the pact's validity, there would have to be appropriate sentiments of Christian revulsion to counter the enhanced role of Lucifer and his ministers. Accordingly, to satisfy both these needs there had to be a scene following Faustus' demise and so Rowley wrote one, going back, as he had done in other additional material for the play, to the vulgar *EFB*. This last scene proclaims with enough moral satisfaction to make the audience feel vindicated in their witnessing of sensational magic: "Faustus' end be such/As every Christian heart laments to think on" (B2106-07). The last scene in B would certainly have fulfilled popular demand, but it would have been at variance with informed, intellectual opinion.

Only when we approach Marlowe's tragedy in its original, or more original, version of the A-text do we become properly aware that the mode and manner and instant of Faustus' death are not the necessary conclusion to the pact he made with the devil. Only then do we encounter a tragic figure whose final suffering is also his final insistence on his vision of himself, one who is destroyed, paradoxically, in his very demand for identity. In a play of many ironies, it is the final irony which is the most profound: Faustus is necessarily destroyed by the faith he freely chose, having found no other choice possible.

8. Enter Faustus in his Study

'Enter Desdemona in her bed' is a telegraphic stage direction which has entertained generations of readers whose editions of *Othello* have followed the rubric of the First Folio. Whilst theatrical historians dispute as to the method by which intimate, small-scale scenes might have been presented in the Elizabethan or Jacobean theatre, the drollness of such stage directions may indicate that the ensuing action takes place within an "inner stage", and that the action is revealed to our gaze by the sudden drawing back of a curtain. 'Here Prospero discovers Ferdinand and Miranda playing at chess' seems to tell us this almost literally, and reminds us of yet another revelation of Truth the Daughter of Time, the point where Paulina draws back the curtain before the living statue in the anagnorisis of *The Winter's Tale*. Such *coups de théâtre* present us, in a commingling of the art of dramatist and producer, with a living tableau, a framed graphic effigy which, for an audience accustomed to decoding the iconography of costume, paraphernalia and blocking, invites a spontaneous but detailed analysis of the iconic elements present on stage.[55] The daring of Marlowe's use of this sort of stage tableau is hence considerable; the main action of *Doctor Faustus* commences, not with an imbroglio where courtiers agitatedly discuss an offstage battle or a political conspiracy or a miraculous birth, but with a static speaking picture whose elements are a solitary man reading at random a number of books. For the purposes of dramatic immediacy, we may imagine these books on stage as a collection of massy tomes. If any of Marlowe's original audience had been acquainted with Dürer's engraving of St Jerome in his study, they might well have been reminded of it, or of an illumination in a manuscript produced in some medieval scriptorium, for it suggests overwhelmingly, through its image of the retired scholar, the life of contemplation.

In the opening lines of the play, the Chorus has prepared us for the paradox of the initial tableau, for he has stressed those elements which, uncharacteristically for the drama of this age, will be absent from the play. Military campaigns, chivalry and amorous intrigue, the political wheel of Fortune, and heroic derring-do—all these dramatically alluring aspects of the life of action will *not* characterise the story we are to witness.

The antithesis between the life of contemplation and the life of action is at least as old as the conclusion to Plato's *Symposium*, where, in a final tableau that was to haunt the imagination of Europe for two thousand years, Socrates the embodiment of philosophy and Alkibiades the embodiment of the public life confront one another and dispute as to which is the better choice (212d–223d). The idea that one's life might be for ever determined by a hugely significant dilemma encountered at its outset was a commonplace to the Renaissance, and such mythological set-pieces as the Judgment of

In occafionem.

To my Kinſman M. GEFFREY WHITNEY.

Figure 6

Figure 7

In Aſtrologos.

Figure 8

Three emblems
from Geoffrey
Whitney's
*A Choice
of Emblemes*
(1586)

Paris or the Choice of Hercules were incessantly glossed as embodiments of this situational dilemma. The contrast between the *vita activa* and the *vita contemplativa* was a stark one, and amounted really to the decision to embrace the fallen world of society and post-lapsarian Time, or to embrace the religious ideal of withdrawal summed up in the concept of pastoral *otium*. The idea that certain spots in time were dedicated to moral choices of particular importance and intensity is summed up in the concept of *occasio*, and there can be little doubt that for Marlowe's audience in the 1590's the spectacle of Faustus' initial psychomachia would have provided an especially pungent instance of *occasio*.[56]

We might for the moment defer our discussion of the elements which compound Faustus' dilemma, and notice the method which, all unwittingly, he has adopted. 'A practise there is among us to determine doubtful matters, by the opening of a book, and letting fall a staff; which notwithstanding are ancient fragments of Pagan divinations. The first an imitation of *Sortes Homericae*, or *Virgilianae*, drawing determinations from verses casually occurring . . . Nor was this only performed in heathen Authors, but upon the sacred text of Scripture . . .'[57] So wrote Sir Thomas Browne in 1646, and even today the practice of consulting the Bible by opening it at random, eyes shut, and trusting that the thrust of a pin will impale a text of particular significance, is not altogether extinct. Marlowe's irony here is elegant and profound, for Faustus deems himself to be languidly consulting his personal library at random. So he is, but there is an order behind his bored page-hopping which is not apparent to him. Commentators on this scene are accustomed, quite correctly, to indicating in their notes that Faustus misunderstands or misapplies the texts he consults. It should be noticed that Faustus' misapplication is in a particular mode, viz., he isolates a line or verse or phrase from its context, and neglects to read the ensuing amplification or qualification. The notes to the text will indicate the particularities, but his overall error would have been as apparent to a Reformation Protestant audience as it would have been to a medieval Catholic one — Faustus is reading the mere letter of the text, and not the spirit. Or, more specifically, he is neglecting to read his books typologically.[58]

The distinction between reading the letter and reading the spirit is essential for an understanding of much sixteenth century religious thought, as it is for an understanding of the English mystery-play cycles of the fifteenth and early sixteenth centuries. Basic Pauline texts are Romans 7.6 — 'But now we are delivered from the Law, being dead unto it, wherein we were holden, that we shulde serve in newnes of Spirit, and not in the oldenes of the letter' and 2 Corinthians 3.5-6 — 'Not that we are sufficient of our selves, to thinke anie thing, as of our selves: but our sufficiencie is of God. Who also hathe made us able ministers of the New testament, not of the letter but of the Spirit: for the letter killeth, but the Spirit giveth life.' The gloss which the Geneva Bible gives to the latter text explains that Moses was the minister of the letter, but Christ provides the spirit, 'meaning, the spiritual doctrine, which is in our hearts,' The practical result of this is that God's revealed word is viewed as functioning in three modes: it is revealed through the literal meaning of the Old Testament, it is revealed through the spiritual or allegorical meaning of the Old Testament, where individual incidents are believed to provide point-by-point prophetic parallels with incidents in the New Testament, and thus to vindicate them as the fulfilment of God's plan, and, for those of a millenarian bent of mind, it is provided in the individual events of the day-to-day life of the warfaring and wayfaring Christian, who finds the ultimate Biblical fulfilment in the meaningful revelation of his own experience. So, the Old Testament image, or type, predicts the New Testament fulfilment, or antitype, as the sacrifice of Isaac predicts, detail by detail, the sacrifice of Christ; Protestantism develops the distinctive personal antitype in the here-and-now of the individual's experience. This application of Scripture to the individual is akin to what medieval exegetes called the tropological or moral sense.[59] Faustus is unable to read his library, therefore, in any truly critical or exegetical or spiritual way; imprisoned in the letter of the printed word, he is, metaphorically, a Jew or Israelite of the old persuasion, unable to grasp the real meaning of the words he reads because he does not accept the historical mission of Christ. Here is a paradox, for Faustus, a scholar, is bound to the literal meanings of untutored ignorance.

The initial scene of Marlowe's play contains another teasing possibility. We have alluded earlier to the *sortes virgilianae*, whereby apparently random texts are searched for their putative inner or arcane meaning and its possible relevance to the spiritual condition of the searcher. For a medieval or Renaissance Christian, there is one overwhelming archetype for such a situation, and it is one of the most powerful and evocative incidents in western literature. It is nothing less than St Augustine's description of the circumstances of his own conversion, and, while the point is not conclusively demonstrable, the parallels present us with the spectacle of Faustus' wicked choice as a parodic inversion of Augustine's rejection of sin. It is plain from the saint's description of his state of mind immediately prior to the incident that he was experiencing what, in modern jargon, would be described as a protracted and intense emotional and moral breakdown.

> I probed the hidden depths of my soul and wrung its pitiful secrets from it, and when I mustered them all before the eyes of my heart, a great storm broke within me, bringing with it a great deluge of tears . . . Somehow I flung myself down beneath a fig tree and gave way to the tears which now streamed from my eyes . . . For I felt that I was still the captive of my sins, and in my misery I kept crying "How long shall I go on saying 'tomorrow, tomorrow'? Why not now? Why not make an end of my ugly sins at this moment?"
>
> I was asking myself these questions, weeping all the while with the most bitter sorrow in my heart, when all at once I heard the sing-song voice of a child in a nearby house. Whether it was the voice of a boy or a girl I cannot say, but again and again it repeated the refrain "Take it and read, take it and read." At this I looked up, thinking hard whether there was any kind of game in which children used to chant words like these, but I could not remember ever hearing them before. I stemmed my flood of tears and stood up, telling myself that this could only be a divine command to open my book of Scripture and read the first passage on which my eyes should fall.[60]

In a state of great agitation, Augustine rushes indoors and seizes the copy of Paul's epistles which he had previously cast down. The passage he reads is Romans 13.13-14, and, unlike Faustus, he has no difficulty in applying it, ecstatically, to his own moral quandary. 'For in an instant, as I came to the end of the sentence, it was as though the light of confidence flooded into my heart and all the darkness of doubt was dispelled.'

The *tolle lege* which Augustine hears the child (or angel) chant in the neighbouring garden should be aligned with two other elements encountered earlier in *The Confes-*

sions. Whilst the immediate derivation of Doctor Faustus from Johannes Fust or Johann Faust seems perfectly plausible, it is at least possible that the name — or both names — derives from the most famous bearer of the sobriquet, the Faustus the Manichaean whom St Augustine encounters earlier in his career (see *Confessions*, Book V).

> In the sight of my God I will describe the twenty-ninth year of my age.

> A Manichean bishop named Faustus had recently arrived at Carthage. He was a great decoy of the devil and many people were trapped by his charming manner of speech. This I certainly admired, but I was beginning to distinguish between mere eloquence and the real truth, which I was so eager to learn. The Manichees talked so much about this man Faustus that I wanted to see what scholarly fare he would lay before me, and I did not care what words he used to garnish the dish. I had already learned that he was very well versed in all the higher forms of learning and particularly in the liberal sciences.
>
> (Pine-Coffin, p. 92).

Augustine waits long and avidly for the coming of Faustus, and is especially anxious to dispute with him because of his own emotional turbulence when confronted with the conflict between divinity and the sciences. Augustine's disillusionement with Faustus is devastatingly summarised in V, 6 of *The Confessions.* 'Other members of the sect whom I happened to meet were unable to answer the questions I raised upon these subjects, but they assured me that once Faustus had arrived I had only to discuss them with him and he would have no difficulty in giving me a clear explanation of my queries and any other difficult problems which I might put forward' (pp. 96-97). Faustus produces a splendid impression when he eventually arrives. He is handsome, charming and eloquent, with all the social graces in abundance, and Augustine is anxious to attain private audience with him in order to analyse at length the issues which trouble him. The audience is eventually arranged.

> I . . . soon discovered that except for a rudimentary knowledge of literature he had no claims to scholarship. He had read some of Cicero's speeches, one or two books of Seneca, some poetry, and such books as had been written in good Latin by members of his sect. Besides his daily practice as a speaker, this reading was the basis of his eloquence, which derived extra charm and plausibility from his attractive personality . . . (p. 98).

After the rejection of Faustus, Augustine moves to Rome and then to Milan, searching for the resolution of his doubts. He finds this resolution in the figure of another public speaker, who conclusively supplants Faustus in his imagination — St Ambrose. The relief provided by Ambrose is quite specific — he frees Augustine from the letter of the Scripture, and teaches him to interpret it.

> . . . in his sermons to the people Ambrose often repeated the text: *The written law inflicts death, whereas the spiritual law brings life* [*sc.*, 2 Corinthians 3.6], as though this were a rule upon which he wished to insist most carefully. And when he lifted the veil of mystery and disclosed the spiritual meaning of texts which, taken literally, appeared to contain the most unlikely doctrines, I was not aggrieved by what he said, although I did not yet know whether it was true . . . it is often the case that a man who has had experience of a bad doctor is afraid to trust himself even to a good one, and in the same way my sick soul, which could not be healed except through faith, refused this cure for fear of believing a doctrine that was false.

The encounter with Ambrose provides the redemptive antithesis to the dismaying encounter with the unlearned scholar Faustus, and its description terminates with a
direct address to the Deity. 'My soul resisted your healing hand, for it was you who prepared and dispensed the medicine of faith and made it so potent a remedy for the
diseases of the world' (pp. 115–116).

Augustine's *Contra Faustum Manichaeum* (*Reply to Faustus the Manichaean*,
AD 400) is largely concerned with the antitheses which we have been discussing so far,
and provides, over the gap of twelve hundred years, the intellectual scaffolding which
enables a man to distinguish between true and false learning, the genuine philosopher
who comprehends and teaches God's true wisdom, and the bogus sophist whose knowledge can never rise above a literal-minded grasp of the mutable fallen world. The
Contra Faustum is devoted chiefly to a discussion of the predictive nature of the Old
Testament, and is hence a defence of the practice of typology, of the reading of the
spirit through the veil of the letter. Book IV, for instance, establishes Faustus' reasons
for rejecting the Old Testament; Book VI contains Augustine's exposition of the relationship between the Old and New Testaments; Book XII contains Faustus' denial
that the prophets of the Old Testament predicted Christ, and Augustine's refutation
of this through typological principles, and Book XVI contains Augustine's elaboration
of this.[61]

If Marlowe's *Doctor Faustus* contains one overwhelming visual icon, this must be, in
any visually sophisticated production, that of the book, the concrete embodiment of
the major motifs of the dramatic action. The book is present in the opening soliloquy,
it marks the graduation of Faustus from neophyte to *illuminatus* at lines 614–628 ('. . .
fain would I have a book wherein . . . Now would I have a book where . . . Let me have
one book more'), and Faustus' last words in the terminal *ars moriendi* are a promise to
burn his books. We might conclude this section of the introduction by attempting to
define in slightly greater detail the identity of these books.

> Thus there are two books from whence I collect my divinity: besides that written one of
> God, another of his servant Nature—that universal and public manuscript that lies
> expansed unto the eyes of all. Those that never saw him in the one have discovered him in
> the other: this was the scripture and theology of the heathens . . . Surely the heathens knew
> better how to join and read these mystical letters than we Christians, who cast a more care-
> less eye on these common hieroglyphics, and disdain to suck divinity from the flowers of
> nature.[62]

So Sir Thomas Browne was to write in 1643, and so, too, thought Browne's contemporary Andrew Marvell, who, strolling through the woods on the estate of his patron
Lord Fairfax, an 'easie Philosopher/Among the Birds and Trees,' could languidly set
himself the exegetical task of decoding the flora and fauna around him.

> Out of these scatter'd Sibyls Leaves
> Strange Prophecies my Phancy weaves:
> And in one History consumes,
> Like Mexique Paintings, all the Plumes.
> What Rome, Greece, Palestine, ere said
> I in this light Mosaick read.
> Thrice happy he who, not mistook,
> Hath read in Natures mystick Book.[63]

Both Browne and Marvell base themselves here on an intellectual tradition which dates from the discovery, in 1419, of the *Hieroglyphica* of Horapollo Niliacus, a work which mistakenly purported to be able to decipher the true meaning of the classical Egyptian hieroglyphs, and which led, through Alciati's *Emblematum Liber* of 1531, to the vogue for emblem literature and iconological dictionaries, and a re-invigorated post-classical tradition by which Ovid and the Greek mythographers could be reinterpreted and moralised in a Christian fashion.[64] This tradition was effectively a metamorphosed view of Biblical typology, and believed that God had revealed himself in various modes to various peoples at various times. Although the manner of his self-revelation might be apparently dissimilar, the core or nucleus was essentially uniform. He had revealed himself to the Jews via the Old Testament, to the Christians via its consummation, the New Testament, and to the 'Gentiles' — the pagans of Greece and Rome — by means of classical mythology. In addition, he had also revealed his hand in history through his handiwork in creation, so that, for minds like Marvell or Browne, God's word could be decoded through the book of nature, perceived as a fourth Testament. It is precisely such a task which Browne sets himself in *The Garden of Cyrus*, where he detects a divine numerological plan in the apparently ubiquitous lozenge shape which has served as the divine template for the Creation in order to mimic, through the quinary of its five points and its centre, the image of the Godhead. 'And for the stability of this number he [the investigator] shall not want the sphericity of its nature, which, multiplied in itself, will return into its own denomination, and bring up the rear of the account. Which is also one of the numbers that makes up the mystical name of God, which, consisting of letters denoting all the spherical numbers — ten, five, and six — emphatically sets forth the notion of Trismegistus, and the intelligible sphere which is the nature of God' (Robbins, p. 186).

As against this approach there is an alternative and antithetical tradition which takes a very different view of nature and of man's orientation to it. This view is based upon traditional exegesis of the character of Original Sin as it is depicted in Genesis. It relates that man's Fall was occasioned primarily by a lust for knowledge, symbolised by the fruit of the Tree of the Knowledge of Good and Evil. Man wished for knowledge in order to rival God's omnipotence, and, seduced by the words of the serpent, he ate the fruit in the belief that it would confer upon him a form of knowledge which would enable him to transcend the state of preternatural grace in which he had been created, and which would make him immortal. Ironically, his sin was rewarded with knowledge, but the knowledge, not of divinity and immortality, but of pain, labour, and death. When Adam fell, the world of created nature fell with him, plunged into the realm of time and the seasons. Its corruption was universal, and extended throughout the enclosed sphere of the moon in the Ptolemaic system. The expulsion from Eden, and man's subsequent life in the corrupt and mutable world of fallen matter, perceived through time and the seasons, is therefore an expression of man's quest for forbidden knowledge. Translated into more contemporaneous terms by thinkers of the Middle Ages, this attitude led to a systematised distinction between the two forms of knowledge, and had important implications for educational theory. The proper study of mankind was, therefore, God, and the goal of education was the acquisition of that form of knowledge which facilitated the salvation of one's own soul. Such knowledge consisted not in the accumulation of facts and hypotheses about the corrupt and fallen world, which was synonymous with transgression and death, but rather, the gradual acquisition, through prayer and penance, of moral wisdom. To study theology, queen of the sciences, was to acquire *sapientia*, and it was incumbent on man, therefore, to read the book of the word of God's direct revelation. To investigate the world of fallen matter, to know the workings of the creature rather than the divine plan of the creator, was to acquire merely the dead and unrelated trivia which constituted *scientia*. To study nature, or to acquire, in the modern meaning of the word, science, was to ally oneself, by implication, with the regent and ruler of this world, the Devil. It is to this book, the book of nature, that Marlowe's Faustus turns, and the opening scene of the play presents him, in terms of powerful iconic stage imagery, as closing the books of divine revelation, rejecting *sapientia*, and wilfully replicating and reliving Adam's primal sin by opting for the book of nature, the acquisition of mere *scientia*.[65]

This view of what is permissible and what is forbidden knowledge is obviously in stark contrast to the view which we have seen expressed by Browne and Marvell. Both views co-existed throughout the sixteenth and seventeenth centuries, and it is evident that their opposition impinges upon the comparable Renaissance nexus of the Art versus Nature controversy. Eventually, both views are transcended by the pragmatic view of modern investigative science, but the process was a gradual one, and was punctuated by such documents as Bacon's *Advancement of Learning*, which pleaded for a more empirical approach to knowledge than the passive acceptance of earlier authorities, Sprat's *History of the Royal Society*, which adopts the Enlightenment attitude that fine scholastic distinctions and ambiguities in language are the enemies of political order and scholarly research, and Addison's *Dialogues on the Usefulness of Ancient Medals*, which ridicules the associative or hieroglyphic way of interpreting the world which is an essential aspect of the magical cast of mind as we have been observing it.

The attitude which Marlowe expounds in *Doctor Faustus* is, for its day, a highly respectable one. The pact which Faustus concludes with the Devil is merely the exoteric, folkloristic exemplification of the pact he has already concluded when he opts for the corrupt reward-system of the acquisition of *scientia* and relives the Fall of Adam. It is an attitude which is summed up in George Herbert's poem *Vanitie I*, where 'the fleet Astronomer,' 'the nimble Diver,' and 'the subtil Chymick,' respectively thread the spheres of the universe with mechanically assisted vision, peer into the depths of the ocean, and examine the minute principles of matter, in order to comprehend the outer macrocosm, but neglect to look inward, through the corporeal walls of the microcosm of their own being to read the word of God in its final decalogue, carved on the stony surface of their own hearts. 'Poore man, thou searchest round/To finde out death, but missest life at hand.'[66] Faustus spends twenty-four years reading the book of his own wilfulness, which is the book of corrupt and fallen nature. All this time, he must struggle in anguish to reject the words written on his own heart and expounded by the Good Angel. Or, as we might put it in a more secular age, he refuses to listen to his own conscience.[67] More than half a century later, Faustus' scholarly conference with Mephostophiles will have its reverse counterpart when Milton's Adam quizzes Raphael and the angel sternly bids him to refrain from the study of astronomy.

> . . . heaven is for thee too high
> To know what passes there; be lowly wise:
> Think only what concerns thee and thy being;
> Dream not of other worlds, what creatures there

Live, in what state, condition or degree,
Contented that thus far hath been revealed
Not of earth only but of highest heaven.[68]

That nature is a book which God has compiled for the edification and instruction of man is an idea at least as old as the twelfth century Latin writer Alanus de Insulis, whom Chaucer cites with approval in *The Parliament of Fowls*. 'Omnis mundi creatura,' wrote Alanus, 'quasi liber, et pictura/Nobis est, et speculum'. 'Everything in the world is, for us, like a book, or a picture, or a mirror.' And, only a year after Marlowe's death, a fashionable English astrologer called George Hartgill published a book of astronomical tables whose frontispiece carries a fanciful depiction of the author. 'He stands in a setting like the Garden of Eden with a city in the background and holds the *verbum dei* in one hand and an armillary sphere in the other. Beneath his feet a plaque identifies him as a "Christian philosopher," while a balloon from his mouth announces, "I shall contemplate the word and the works of Jehovah." Above this scene, in a starry sky, shine the sun and the moon, adding their customary suggestion of both time and eternity.'[69] Perhaps Hartgill was a sincere and pious man. Or perhaps, like the other magus whose story commences in a few pages time, he was really pursuing *scientia* for the world of profit and delight which he hoped it would bring.

---

1 For further biographical reading on Marlowe, see John Bakeless, *The Tragical History of Christopher Marlowe*, 2 vols (Cambridge, Mass.: Harvard University Press, 1942); Frederick Boas, *Christopher Marlowe: A Biographical and Critical Study* (Oxford: Clarendon Press, 1940); J. L. Hotson, *The Death of Christopher Marlowe* (London: Nonesuch Press, 1925); M. Kelsall, *Christopher Marlowe* (Leiden: E. J. Brill, 1981); Paul H. Kocher, *Christopher Marlowe* (Chapel Hill: University of North Carolina Press, 1946); and A. L. Rowse, *Christopher Marlowe: A Biography* (rev. ed., London: Macmillan, 1981).

2 On the subject of school and university curricula, see J.-J. Denonain, "Un nommé Christopher Marlowe, gentleman", *Caliban* 1 (1964), 51-74.

3 MS. *Acts of the Privy Council*, vol. VI, June 29, 1587; quoted by Bakeless, I, 77.

4 *An advertisement written to a Secretarie of my L. Treasurers of Ingland, by an Inglishe Intelligencer* (1592), p. 18; as quoted by Bakeless, I, 129-30.

5 Harleian MS. 6853, fols. 185-86, formerly numbered 170-71; quoted by Bakeless, I, 110-11.

6 Kyd's second letter to Sir John Puckering, Lord Keeper of the Privy Seal, Harleian MS. 6848, fol. 154; quoted by Bakeless, I, 114.

7 Recorded in a government spy's report, known as "Remembraunces of wordes and matters against Richard Cholmeley", Harleian MS. 6848, fol. 190; quoted by Bakeless, I, 125.

8 As quoted by Bakeless, I, 156.

9 H. A. Shield, in "The Death of Marlowe", *NQ* NS4 (1957), 101-103, suggests that even the owner of the Deptford Tavern, Mrs Eleanor Bull, was associated through her marriage with the Walsingham spy-circle.

10 Paul H. Kocher, "The English *Faust Book* and the Date of Marlowe's *Faustus*", *MLN* 55 (1940), 95-101, at p. 100.

11 Curt A. Zimansky, "Marlowe's *Faustus*: The Date Again", *PQ* 41 (1962), 181-87.

12 See Constance B. Kuriyama, "Dr Greg and *Doctor Faustus*: The Supposed Originality of the 1616 Text", *ELR* 5 (1975), 171-97, at 181ff; and the Introduction to Roma Gill's *Doctor Faustus* (London: Ernest Benn, 1965), xvii.

13 Robert A. H. Smith, "A Note on *Doctor Faustus* and *The Taming of a Shrew*", *NQ* NS26 (1979), 116; Smith follows R. A. Houk, "*Doctor Faustus* and *A Shrew*", *PMLA* 62(1947), 950-57. See also Kuriyama, 181-85. The fact that some passages from *Faustus B* are closer to *A Shrew* has been much debated, but if, as seems likely, Rowley had a hand in both plays, the later echoes in *Faustus B* are unsurprising. The

differences between *Faustus A* (1604) and *Faustus B* (1616) are discussed in Section 4 of this Introduction.

14 Further, but not decisive, support for the early date is given by MacD. P. Jackson in "Three Old Ballads
and the Date of *Doctor Faustus*", *AUMLA* 36 (1971), 187-200. See also Paul H. Kocher's "The Early
Date for Marlowe's *Faustus*", *MLN* 58 (1943), 539-42; and Bakeless, I, 275-77. Against the early date,
the main contender is W. W. Greg, in *Marlowe's Doctor Faustus: 1604-1616* (Oxford: Clarendon Press,
1950), 1-10.

15 See Bakeless, I, 297.

16 Greg, at p. 9, following Chambers, rejects this evidence; his dismissal of Bakeless' argument (I, 298) is
based on less convincing counter-possibilities.

17 P. M. Palmer & R. P. More, *The Sources of the Faust Tradition* (New York: Oxford University Press,
1936), p. 87.

18 J. W. Smeed, *Faust in Literature* (London: Oxford University Press, 1975), p. 2.

19 C. E. Mish, "Black Letter as a Social Discriminant in the Seventeenth Century", *PMLA* 68 (1953), cited
by Arieh Sachs, "The Religious Despair of Doctor Faustus", *JEGP* 63 (1964), 633-634.

20 "*Doctor Faustus*: from Chapbook to Tragedy", *Essays in Literature* (West Illinois University) 3 (1976),
3-16. See notes 1-5, pp. 14-15, for a bibliographical resumé of the major discussions.

21 Medieval and Renaissance theories on the nature of Hell are of immense interest for the student of
Doctor Faustus. There is an excellent discussion of the subject in C. A. Patrides, *Premises and Motifs in
Renaissance Thought and Literature* (Princeton: Princeton Univ. Press, 1982), pp. 182-199.

22 Published in 1663.

23 *The Library*, Series IV, 26 (1946), 272-94.

24 Greg, p. 66. The lost-manuscript argument occupies pp. 63-97.

25 *Henslowe's Diary*, edited by Foakes and Rickert (Cambridge: Cambridge University Press, 1968), p. 206.

26 *Doctor Faustus*, edited by Roma Gill (London: Ernest Benn, 1965); *Doctor Faustus*, edited by John
Jump (London: Methuen, 1962); and *Christopher Marlowe: The Complete Plays*, edited by J. B. Steane
(Harmondsworth: Penguin, 1969).

27 Bowers reviewed Greg's *Parallel Texts* in his article, "The Text of Marlowe's *Faustus*", *MP* 49 (1952),
195-204; he recanted in "Marlowe's *Dr Faustus*: The 1602 Additions", *SB* 26 (1973), 1-18.

28 2 vols (Cambridge: Cambridge University Press, 1973).

29 Michael H. Keefer, "Verbal Magic and the Problem of the A and B Texts of *Doctor Faustus*", *JEGP* 82
(1983), 324-46, at p. 324.

30 *ELR* 5 (1975), 171-97.

31 *ELR* 11 (1981), 111-47, at p. 115.

32 *NQ* NS 30 (1983), 133-43.

33 Cited above, note 29.

34 David M. Bevington, *From* Mankind *to Marlowe: Growth of Structure in the Drama of Tudor England*
(Cambridge, Mass.: Harvard University Press, 1962).

35 Paul H. Kocher argues that Marlowe's friend, Thomas Nashe, wrote the comic sub-plot in his article,
"Nashe's Authorship of the Prose Scenes in *Faustus*", *MLQ* 3 (1942), 17-40. Kocher unnecessarily
assumes that Marlowe did not write the prose scenes, but his argument makes it seem likely that if there
was a collaborator in these scenes it was indeed Nashe.

36 See also p. xl of this Introduction.

37 Wayne Shumaker, *The Occult Sciences in the Renaissance: a Study in Intellectual Patterns* (Berkeley,
Los Angeles and London: University of California Press, 1972), p. 156.

38 A modern mathematician might merely remark at this point, of course, that the sum of the digits in all
such products is always nine or a multiple of nine, and that we can quickly determine by this method
whether any number is divisible by nine. What for a medieval or Renaissance thinker would be the occult aspect of the problem would be relegated by a nineteenth or twentieth century mathematician to the
field of 'recreational mathematics' or 'mathematical entertainments'.

39 A description of the major characteristics of numerology, or number symbolism, is outside the scope of
this edition. The interested reader should consult Edward Foster Hopper's *Medieval Number Symbolism*
(1938; New York: Norwood Editions, 1977), which is the best single introduction to the subject.

40 See Chapter 1, 'The Greek Origins of Number Symbolism', in Christopher Butler's *Number Symbolism*
(London: Routledge and Kegan Paul, 1970), pp. 1-21.

41 Discussions of Renaissance magic are legion, but the subject is highly controversial, and the tyro should
proceed with caution, as many studies are written by latter-day occultist enthusiasts whose views can be

wayward and misleading. The work of Shumaker, cited above, can be recommended without reservation; see especially chapters two and three, 'Witchcraft' and 'White Magic', pp. 60–159. An excellent and highly influential study is that of D. P. Walker, *Spiritual and Demonic Magic from Ficino to Campanella* (1958; Notre Dame: University of Notre Dame Press, 1975). The standard work on the 'cunning . . . Agrippa, Whose shadows made all Europe honour him', is Charles G. Nauert Jr.'s *Agrippa and the Crisis of Renaissance Thought* (Urbana: University of Illinois Press, 1965). See especially chapters nine and ten, 'Agrippan Magic and Renaissance Culture' and 'The Magical World', pp. 222–291. Two books by Frances A. Yates are of great interest — *Giordano Bruno and the Hermetic Tradition* (London: Routledge and Kegan Paul, 1964), and *The Occult Philosophy in the Elizabethan Age* (London: Routledge and Kegan Paul, 1979) — although many reviewers have objected to Dame Frances' passionate contention that there was an extensive occultist underground movement throughout sixteenth century Europe.

[42] See the diagrams reproduced for chapter 5, 'Man, the Microcosm', of Joscelyn Godwin's *Robert Fludd* (London: Thames and Hudson, 1979), pp. 68–75.

[43] See Joseph Leon Blau, *The Christian Interpretation of the Cabala* (1944; Port Washington: Kennikat Press, 1965).

[44] There is no satisfactory modern edition of Agrippa's *De Occulta Philosophia* (1533) which is also readily accessible to the average student, nor is there a trustworthy English translation. The reader with sufficient Latin to tackle the original may consult the facsimile edition edited by Karl Anton Nowotny (Graz, Austria: Akademische Druck und Verlagsanstalt, 1967). See also Nowotny's 'The Construction of Certain Seals and Characters in the Work of Agrippa of Nettesheim', *JWCI* 12 (1949), 46–57. The same issue, pp. 196–199, contains I. R. F. Calder's 'A Note on the Magic Squares in the Philosophy of Agrippa of Nettesheim'.

[45] Lynn Thorndike, *A History of Magic and Experimental Science*, vol. 2 (New York: Columbia University Press, 1923), p. 912. Book V of this volume, 'The Thirteenth Century' (pp. 305–984), provides an expert and highly readable account of the major seminal figures, including chapters devoted to Roger Bacon (V, 61), the notorious *Picatrix* (V, 66), Arnold of Villanova (V, 68), and Peter of Abano (V, 70).

[46] A magic square is a diagram, somewhat similar to a modern crossword puzzle in appearance by virtue of the subordinate squares (cells) with which it is divided. The most basic magic square contains nine cells, but vastly larger and more complex versions are possible. Numbers are placed in these cells in such a fashion that they produce the same sum whether added vertically, horizontally, or diagonally. This sum is known as the magic constant, and can be expressed mathematically as $\frac{1}{2}n(1 + n^2)$ for any square of n units along one side. The total of all the numbers in the square is $\frac{1}{2}n^2(1 + n^2)$. The famous SATOR/AREPO . . . conundrum, which has been responsible for an entire exegetical industry, is a 25-cell magic square where letters are substituted for numbers. Magic squares, which had no apparent counterparts in nature, were thought by some Renaissance authorities to stand in some sort of intimate relationship to permanent truths existing in a higher realm than that of the world of the senses. Magic squares originated in China in the ninth century AD, and reached Europe, enormously subtilised and allegorised by Arab scholars, in the fourteenth century, where they had a considerable intellectual impact. See S. V. R. Camman, 'The Evolution of Magic Squares in China', *Journal of the American Oriental Society* 80 (1960), 116–124; and 'Old Chinese Magic Squares', *Sinologica* 7 (1962), 14–53.

[47] See David Pingree, 'A New Look at *Melencolia I*', *JWCI* 43 (1980), 257–258, and Terence Lynch, 'The Geometric Body in Dürer's Engraving *Melencolia I*', *JWCI* 45 (1982), 226–232.

[48] Turner published not only his version of the *Heptameron*, but also, between the same covers, the alleged fourth book of the *De Occulta*, the *Isagoge* of Georg Pictorius Villinganus, and '*Arbatel of Magick*'. The privately produced facsimile reprint by Askin Publishers (London, 1978) is useful, but the modern introduction (pp. vii–xvi) is not objective in tone or attitude.

[49] *Religio Medici*, edited by Robin Robbins, revised ed. (Oxford, 1982), p. 33.

[50] Some of these works are accessible in modern editions and translations; *Malleus Maleficarum*, trans. and ed. by Montague Summers (London: John Rodker, 1928); Remy, *Demonolatry*, trans. E. A. Ashwin and ed. Montague Summers (London: John Rodker, 1930); Guazzo, *Compendium Maleficarum*, trans. E. A. Ashwin and ed. Montague Summers (London: John Rodker, 1929); Scot, *The Discoverie of Witchcraft*, ed. by Hugh Ross Williamson (Arundel: Centaur Press, 1964); where the above works are referred to again, page references are to the modern editions. The views of the various writers are well summarised by Shumaker, Chapter 2 "Witchcraft", pp. 60–107. For a very full treatment of the subject of witchcraft in the Renaissance, see Keith Thomas, *Religion and the Decline of Magic* (London: Weidenfeld and Nicolson, 1971).

51 Howard Seiferth, "The Concept of the Devil and the Myth of the Pact in Literature Prior to Goethe", *Monatschafte* 44(1952), 271–89, at pp. 283–85.

52 Seiferth, pp. 284–85. In England, successive legislation made pacts with the devil a criminal offence; see Keith Thomas, pp. 442–44 and 456.

53 Henri Boguet (c. 1590), *An Examen of Witches*, trans. E. A. Ashwin and ed. Montague Summers (London: John Rodker, 1929), p. xlii.

54 T. W. Craik, *The Tudor Interlude* (Leicester: Leicester University Press, 1958), pp. 51–52.

55 For an analysis of such effects, see John Doebler, *Shakespeare's Speaking Pictures* (Albuquerque: University of New Mexico Press, 1974), pp. 1–20 and passim.

56 See Figure 6, where Whitney's emblem provides a characteristic depiction. For a highly influential discussion of the modes of time relevant to the first and last scenes of *Doctor Faustus* — viz., *kairos* and *aion* — see Erwin Panofsky, 'Father Time', in *Studies in Iconology* (1939; New York: Harper and Row, Icon Editions, 1972), pp. 69–93.

57 Sir Thomas Browne, *Pseudodoxia Epidemica* V, chapter 23, 7.

58 There are good introductions to the study of typology for literary students in Beryl Smalley, *The Study of the Bible in the Middle Ages* (1952; Oxford: Blackwell, rev. ed., 1983) and Earl Miner (ed.), *Literary Uses of Typology* (Princeton: Princeton Univ. Press, 1977).

59 Barbara K. Lewalski, 'Typology and Poetry: a Consideration of Herbert, Vaughan and Marvell', in Earl Miner (ed.), *Illustrious Evidence: Approaches to English Literature of the Early Seventeenth Century* (Berkeley: University of California Press, 1975), p. 43.

60 From R. S. Pine-Coffin (trans.), *Saint Augustine: Confessions* (Harmondsworth: Penguin, 1961), p. 177. The incident is the culmination of Book VIII, 12. The overall significance of Augustinian theology for *Doctor Faustus* has been examined by Douglas Cole in *Suffering and Evil in the Plays of Christopher Marlowe* (Princeton: Princeton Univ. Press, 1962), pp. 194–231. The possible presence of the conversion scene, and the problematical presence of Faustus the Manichean, have already been discussed by Claude J. Summers and Ted-Larry Pebworth, 'The Conversion of St Augustine and the B-Text of *Doctor Faustus*', *Renaissance and Renascences in Western Literature* 1, ii (1979), 1–8, and J. P. Brockbank, *Marlowe: Doctor Faustus* (London: Edward Arnold, 1962), pp. 1–15. The reader is warned, though, that these writers' methods and conclusions differ considerably from those of the present study.

61 Philip Schaff (ed.), *A Select Library of the Nicene and Post-Nicene Fathers of the Christian Church*, vol. IV, 'St Augustin: the Writings against the Manichaeans and Against the Donatists', trans. Richard Stothert (repr. Grand Rapids: Eerdmans Publishing Co., 1956), pp. 155ff. See esp. pp. 161–264.

62 *Religio Medici* I, 16 (Robbins, pp. 16–17).

63 *Upon Appleton House*, st. 73, in H. M. Margoliouth (ed.), *The Poems and Letters of Andrew Marvell*, I (Oxford: Clarendon Press, rev. ed., 1971), p. 80.

64 See Don Cameron Allen, *Mysteriously Meant* (Baltimore: Johns Hopkins Press, 1970), and Noel Purdon, *The Words of Mercury* (Salzburg, Austria: Institut für Englische Sprache und Literatur, 1974).

65 The conventional distinction between the two processes of cognition is made very lucidly by St Augustine in *Confessions* X, 35 (Pine-Coffin, pp. 241–244).

66 F. E. Hutchinson (ed.), *The Works of George Herbert* (Oxford: Clarendon Press, 1945), pp. 85–86.

67 For a classic discussion of the subject, see E. R. Curtius, *European Literature and the Latin Middle Ages* (New York: Bollingen Foundation, 1953), chapter 16: 'The Book as Symbol', especially section 7, 'The Book of Nature', pp. 319–326.

68 *Paradise Lost* VIII, lines 172–178. The notes to the first 200 lines of Book VIII provided by John Carey and Alastair Fowler in their edition of *The Poems of John Milton* (London: Longman, 1968) will be of considerable assistance to the student of this aspect of *Doctor Faustus*. Adam seems to have mastered the distinction between the two forms of knowledge in a way that Faustus has not. '. . . not to know at large of things remote/From use, obscure and subtle, but to know/That which before us lies in daily life,/Is the prime wisdom' (lines 191–194). But his expertise is short-lived. See also J. M. Evans, *Paradise Lost and the Genesis Tradition* (Oxford: OUP, 1968).

69 S. K. Heninger Jr., *The Cosmographical Glass: Renaissance Diagrams of the Universe* (San Marino: Huntington Library, 1977), p. 11.

Select Bibliography

1. Bibliographies

Chan, Lois Mai, assisted by S. A. Pedersen. *Marlowe Criticism: A Bibliography*. Boston: G. K. Hall, 1978.

Danson, Lawrence. 'Recent Studies in Elizabethan and Jacobean Drama'. *Studies in English Literature* 23: 2 (1983), 329-60.

Friedenreich, Kenneth, ed. *Christopher Marlowe: An Annotated Bibliography since 1950*. Metuchen, NJ: Scarecrow Press, 1979.

Huffman, Clifford Chalmers, comp. 'Tudor and Stuart Drama: A Bibliography, 1966-1971'. *Educational Theater Journal* 24 (1972), 169-78.

―――. comp. *Tudor and Stuart Drama* (Goldentree Bibliographies). O. B. Hardison, Jr., ed. Evanston, Illinois: AHM Publishers, 1978.

Kimbrough, Robert. 'Christopher Marlowe'. In *The Predecessors of Shakespeare: A Survey and Bibliography of Recent Studies in English Renaissance Drama*. Terence P. Logan and Denzell S. Smith, eds. Lincoln: Univ. of Nebraska Press, 1973, 3-55.

Palmer, D. J. 'Marlowe'. In *English Drama excluding Shakespeare: A Select Bibliographical Guide*. Stanley Wells, ed. London: Oxford Univ. Press, 1975, 42-53.

Penninger, Frieda Elaine. *English Drama to 1660 (excluding Shakespeare): A Guide to Information Sources*. Detroit: Gale Research Company, 1976. Section 20, 'Christopher Marlowe', 285-99.

Post, Jonathan F. S. 'Recent Studies of Marlowe (1968-1976)'. *English Literary Renaissance* 7 (1977), 382-99.

Ribner, Irving, comp. *Tudor and Stuart Drama* (Goldentree Bibliographies). New York: Appleton-Century Crofts, 1966.

2. Concordances

Crawford, Charles. *The Marlowe Concordance*, 2 vols, 1911-1932. New York: Burt Franklin, 1964 (reprint).

Fehrenbach, Robert J. *et al.*, eds. *A Concordance to the Plays, Poems, and Translations of Christopher Marlowe*. Ithaca and London: Cornell Univ. Press, 1983.

Ule, Louis, ed. *A Concordance to the Works of Christopher Marlowe*. The Elizabethan Concordance Series. Hildesheim: Georg Olms Verlag, 1979.

3. Editions of Doctor Faustus since 1900

a. *In Collected Works*

Boas, Frederick S., ed. In *Collected Works*, ed. R. H. Case. London: Methuen, 1930-33. Vol. 5, 1932.

Bowers, Fredson, ed. *The Complete Works of Christopher Marlowe*, 2 vols. New York and London: Cambridge Univ. Press, 1973, Vol. 1.

Gill, Roma, ed. *The Plays of Christopher Marlowe*. London: Oxford Univ. Press, 1971.

Kirschbaum, Leo., ed. *The Plays of Christopher Marlowe*. Cleveland and New York: World Publishing Company (Meridian Books), 1962.

Pendry, E. D. and Maxwell, J. C., eds. *Christopher Marlowe: Complete Plays and Poems*. London: Dent, and Totowa, New Jersey: Rowman & Littlefield, 1976.

Ribner, Irving, ed. *The Complete Plays of Christopher Marlowe*. New York: Odyssey Press, 1963.

Ridley, M. R., ed. *Christopher Marlowe: Plays and Poems* (Everyman's Library, No. 383). London: Dent, 1955.

Steane, J. B., ed. *The Complete Plays of Christopher Marlowe*. Harmondsworth and Baltimore: Penguin, 1969.

Tucker Brooke, C. F., ed. *The Works of Christopher Marlowe*. Oxford: Clarendon Press, 1910.

b. *Single Text Editions*

Barnet, Sylvan, ed. *Doctor Faustus*. New York: New American Library, 1969.

Doctor Faustus 1604 and 1616: A Scolar Press Facsimile. Menston: Scolar Press, 1970.

Gill, Roma, ed. *Doctor Faustus* (New Mermaids). London: Ernest Benn, 1965.

Greg, W. W. ed. *Marlowe's Doctor Faustus 1604-1616: Parallel Texts*. Oxford: Clarendon Press, 1950.

Jump, John D., ed. *The Tragical History of the Life and Death of Doctor Faustus*. London: Methuen; Cambridge, Massachusetts: Harvard Univ. Press, 1962. (Revels Edition of the Works of Christopher Marlowe.) Clifford Leech, ed.

Kocher, Paul H., ed. *The Tragical History of Doctor Faustus*. The Crofts Classics. New York: Harlan Davidson, 1950.

Ribner, Irving, ed. *Doctor Faustus: Text & Major Criticism*. New York: Odyssey Press, 1966.

Walker, Keith, ed. *Doctor Faustus* (Fountainwell Drama Texts). Edinburgh: Oliver & Boyd, 1973.

Wright, Louis B. and LaMar, Virginia A., eds. *The Tragedy of Doctor Faustus*. New York: Washington Square Press, 1959.

4. Critical and Textual Studies: Doctor Faustus

Baker, Donald C. 'Ovid and Faustus: The *Noctis Equi*'. *Classical Journal* 55 (1959), 126-8.

Barber, C. L. 'The Form of Faustus' Fortunes Good or Bad'. *Tulane Drama Review* 8: 4 (1964), 92-119.

Barnes, Celia. 'Matthew Parker's Pastoral Training and Marlowe's *Doctor Faustus*'. *Comparative Drama* 15: 3 (1981), 258-67.

Beckerman, Bernard. 'Scene Patterns in *Doctor Faustus* and *Richard III*'. In E. A. J. Honigmann, ed. *Shakespeare and His Contemporaries: Essays in Comparison*. Manchester: Manchester U.P., 1986, 33-41.

Birringer, Johannes H. *Marlowe's 'Doctor Faustus' and 'Tamburlaine': Theological and Theatrical Perspectives*. Berne, Frankfurt, New York: Peter Lang, 1983.

———. 'The Daemonic Flight of Dr. Faustus: Hope and/or Escape?' *Massachusetts Studies in English* 8(3) 1982, 17-26.

Bland, Thomas Albert, Jr. 'Staging and Theology in the A- and B-Texts of *Doctor Faustus*'. DAI 47 (1987): 3045A.

Blackburn, William. '"Heavenly Words": Marlowe's Faustus as a Renaissance Magician'. *English Studies in Canada* 4: 1 (1978), 1-14.

Bluestone, Max. '*Libido Speculandi*: Doctrine and Dramaturgy in Contemporary Interpretations of *Doctor Faustus*'. In *Reinterpretations of Elizabethan Drama: Selected Papers of the English Institute, 1968*, Norman Rabkin, ed. New York: Columbia Univ. Press, 1969, 33-88

Boccia, Michael. 'Faustus Unbound: a Reconsideration of the Fate of Faustus in Christopher Marlowe's *Doctor Faustus*'. *The USF Language Quarterly* [Florida] 25(1-2) (1986), 8-12.

Bowe, Elaine C. 'Doctrines and Images of Despair in Christopher Marlowe's *Doctor Faustus*, and Edmund Spenser's *The Faerie Queene*'. DAI 29 (1969), 2206A.

Bowers, Fredson, 'Marlowe's *Dr Faustus*: The 1602 Additions'. *Studies in Bibliography* 26 (1973), 1–18.

————. 'The Text of Marlowe's *Faustus*'. *Modern Philology* 49 (1952), 195–204.

Brandt, Bruce E. 'Marlowe's Helen and the Soul-in-the Kiss Conceit'. *Philological Quarterly* 64(1) (1985), 118–21.

Brockbank, Philip. 'Marlowe: *Doctor Faustus*'. *Studies in English Literature* 6, David Daiches, ed. London: Edward Arnold, and Great Neck, N. Y.: Barron's Educational Series, 1962.

Brooke, Nicholas. 'The Moral Tragedy of Doctor Faustus'. *Cambridge Journal* 7 (1952), 662–87.

Burnett, Mark Thornton. 'Two Notes on Metre and Rhyme in *Doctor Faustus*'. *Notes and Queries* 33 (1986), 337–8.

Burwick, Frederick. 'Marlowe's *Doctor Faustus*: Two Manners, the Argumentative and the Passionate'. *Neuphilologische Mitteilungen* 70 (1969), 121–45.

Campbell, Lily Bess. '*Doctor Faustus*: A Case of Conscience'. *Publications of the Modern Language Association* 67 (1952), 219–39.

Carpenter, Nan C. '"Miles" versus "Clericus" in Marlowe's *Faustus*'. *Notes and Queries* 197 (1952), 91–93.

————. 'Music in *Doctor Faustus*: Two Notes'. *Notes and Queries* 195 (1950), 180–81.

Cheney, Patrick. 'Love and Magic in *Doctor Faustus*: Marlowe's Indictment of Spenserian Idealism'. *Mosaic* 17 (1984), 93–109.

Covella, Francis Delores. 'The Choral Nexus in *Doctor Faustus*'. *Studies in English Literature* 26 (1986), 201–15.

Cox, Gerald H., III. 'Marlowe's Doctor Faustus and "Sin against the Holy Ghost"'. *Huntington Library Quarterly* 36 (1973), 119–37.

Craik, T. W. 'Faustus' Damnation Reconsidered'. *Renaissance Drama* NS 2 (1969), 189–96.

Creswell, Rosemary. '*Doctor Faustus* and the Renaissance World'. *Sydney Studies in English* (1975–76), 13–31.

Davidson, Clifford. 'Doctor Faustus of Wittenberg'. *Studies in Philology* 59 (1962), 514–23.

————. 'Renaissance Dramatic Forms, Cosmic Perspective, and Alienation'. *Cahiers élisabethains* 27 (1985), 1–16.

Deats, Sara M. '*Doctor Faustus*: From Chapbook to Tragedy'. *Essays in Literature*, 3: 1 (1976), 3–16.

————. 'Ironic Biblical Allusion in Marlowe's *Doctor Faustus*'. *Medievalia et Humanistica* 10 (1981), 203–16.

————. 'The Dialectic of Gender in Four of Marlowe's Plays'. *University of Hartford Studies in Literature* 20(1) (1988), 13–36.

Defaye, Claudine. 'Mephistophilis est-il un démon authentique?' *Etudes Anglaises* 32 (1979), 1–10.

Dent, R. W. 'Ramist Faustus or Ramist Marlowe?' In *Studies Presented to Tanno F. Mustanoja on the Occasion of His Sixtieth Birthday. Neuphilologische Mitteilungen* 73 (1972), 63–74.

Dollerup, Cay. 'The Earliest Space Voyagers in the Renaissance, Heliocentric Solar System'. In Luk de Vos, ed. *Just the Other Day: Essays on the Suture of the Future*. Antwerp: EXA (1985), 103–14.

Doyle, Charles Clay. 'One Drop of Christ's Streaming Blood: A Gloss on *Doctor Faustus*'. *Cahiers Elisabethains* 17 (1980), 85–7.

Dreher, Diane Elizabeth. '"Si Pecasse Negamus": Marlowe's Faustus and the *Book of Common Prayer*'. *Notes and Queries* 30: 2 (April 1983), 143–44.

Empson, William. *Faustus and the Censor: The English Faust Book and Marlowe's 'Doctor Faustus'*. Ed. John Henry Jones. Oxford: Blackwell, 1987.

Eriksen, Roy T. *The Forme of Faustus' Fortunes: A Study of 'The Tragedie of Doctor Faustus (1616)'*. Oslo: Solum Forlag; Atlantic Highlands, N.J.: Humanities Press, 1987.

Fabian, Bernhard. 'A Note on Marlowe's *Faustus*'. *English Studies* 41 (1960), 365–68.

Farnham, Willard, ed. *Twentieth Century Interpretations of Doctor Faustus*. Englewood Cliffs, N. J.: Prentice Hall, 1969.

Fisch, Harold. 'The Pact with the Devil'. *Yale Review* 69 (1980), 520–32.

Fitz, L. T. '"More than Thou Hast Wit to Ask": Marlowe's Faustus as Numskull'. *Folklore* 88 (1977), 215–19.

Fleissner, Robert F. *The Prince and the Professor*. Heidelberg: Carl Winter, 1986.

Fontane, Marilyn Stall. 'When and What is Damnation?' *Publications of the Arkansas Philological Association* 11 (1985), 27–32.

Forsyth, Neil. 'Heavenly Helen'. *Etudes de lettres* 4 (1987), 11–21.

French, A. L. 'The Philosophy of *Dr Faustus*'. *Essays in Criticism* 20 (1970), 123–42.

Frey, Leonard H. 'Antithetical Balance in the Opening and Close of *Doctor Faustus*'. *Modern Language Quarterly* 24 (1963), 350–53.

Galloway, Andrew. '*Doctor Faustus* and the Charter of Christ'. *Notes and Queries* 35 (1988), 36–8.

Gatti, Hilary. *The Renaissance Drama of Knowledge*. London and New York: Routledge, 1989.

Goebel, Julius. 'The Etymology of Mephistopheles'. *Transactions and Proceedings of the American Philological Association* 35 (1904), 148–56.

Gilbert, Allan H. 'A Thousand Ships', *Modern Language Notes* 67 (1951), 477–78.

Gill, Roma. '"Such Conceits as Clownage Keeps in Pay": Comedy and *Dr Faustus*'. In *The Fool and the Trickster: Essays in Honour of Enid Welsford*, Paul V. A. Williams, ed. Cambridge: Brewer; Totowa, NJ: Rowman & Littlefield, 1979, 55–63.

———. '*Doctor Faustus*: the Texual Problem'. *University of Hartford Studies in Literature* 20(1) (1988), 52–60.

Golden, Kenneth L. 'Myth, Psychology, and Marlowe's *Doctor Faustus*'. *College Literature* 12 (1985), 202–10.

Goldfarb, Russell and Clare. 'The Seven Deadly Sins in *Doctor Faustus*'. *College Language Association Journal* 13 (1970), 350–63.

Goodman, Ailene S. 'Alchemistic Diabolism in the *Faust* of Marlowe and Goethe'. *Journal of Evolutionary Psychology* 5 (1984), 166–70.

Greg, W. W. 'The Damnation of Faustus'. *Modern Language Review* 41 (1946), 97–107.

Haile, H. G. *The History of Dr Johann Faustus: Recorded from the German*. Urbana: Univ. of Illinois Press, 1965.

Hart, Jeffrey. 'Prospero and Faustus'. *Boston University Studies in English* 2: 4 (1956–57), 197–206.

Hattaway, Michael. 'The Theology of Marlowe's *Doctor Faustus*'. *Renaissance Drama* NS 3 (1970), 51–78.

Hawkins, Sherman. 'The Education of Faustus'. *Studies in English Literature* 6 (1966), 193–209.

Heller, Erich. 'Faust's Damnation: The Morality of Knowledge'. *Listener*, 11 January 1962, 60–62.

Honderich, Pauline. 'John Calvin and Doctor Faustus'. *Modern Language Review* 68 (1973), 1–13.

Henke, James T. 'The Devil Within: A *Doctor Faustus* for the Contemporary Audience'. *Elizabethan Miscellany* 2. Salzburg: Institut für Englische Sprache & Literatur, 1978, 31–46.

Ingram, R. W. '"Pride in Learning goeth before a fall": Doctor Faustus' Opening Soliloquy'. *Mosaic* 13: 1 (1978), 73–80.

Jackson, M. P. 'Three Old Ballads and the Date of *Doctor Faustus*'. *AUMLA* 36 (1971), 187–200.

Jantz, Harold. 'An Elizabethan Statement on the Origin of the German Faust Book, with a Note on Marlowe's Sources'. *Journal of English and Germanic Philology* 51 (1952), 137–53.

Jensen, Enjer J. 'Heroic Convention and *Doctor Faustus*'. *Essays in Criticism* 21 (1971), 101-106.

Jobe, Don. 'Marlowe's *Doctor Faustus*'. *Explicator* 44(3) (1986), 12-14.

Jump, John D., ed. *Marlowe: Doctor Faustus: A Casebook*. London: Macmillan, 1969.

Kaula, David. 'Time and Timelessness in *Everyman* and *Doctor Faustus*'. *College English* 22 (1960), 9-14.

Keefer, Michael H. 'Verbal Magic and the Problem of the A and B Texts of *Doctor Faustus*'. *Journal of English and Germanic Philology* 82: 3 (1983), 324-46.

———. 'Misreading Faustus Misreadings: the Question of Context'. *Dalhousie Review* 65 (1985), 511-33.

———. 'History and the Canon: the Case of *Doctor Faustus*'. *University of Toronto Quarterly* 56 (1987), 498-522.

Kiessling, Nicolas. 'Doctor Faustus and the Sin of Demonality'. *Studies in English Literature* 15 (1975), 205-11.

Knowlton, Edgar C. '"Indian Moors" and *Doctor Faustus*'. *Cahiers Elisabethains* 23 (1983), 93-98.

Kocher, Paul H. 'The Early Date for Marlowe's *Faustus*'. *Modern Language Notes* 58 (1943), 539-42.

Kuriyama, Constance Brown. 'Dr Greg and *Doctor Faustus*: The Supposed Originality of the 1616 Text'. *English Literary Renaissance* 5 (1975), 171-97.

Lake, David J. 'Three Seventeenth-Century Revisions: *Thomas of Woodstock*, *The Jew of Malta*, and *Faustus B*'. *Notes and Queries* 30: 2 (April 1983), 133-43.

Langston, Beach. 'Marlowe's *Faustus* and the *Ars Moriendi* Tradition'. In *A Tribute to George Coffin Taylor: Studies and Essays, Chiefly Elizabethan, by His Students and Friends*, Arnold Williams. ed. Chapel Hill: Univ. of North Carolina Press, 1952, 148-67.

Longo, Joseph. 'Marlowe's *Doctor Faustus*: Allegorical Parody in Act V'. *Greyfriar* 15 (1974), 38-49.

McAlindon, T. 'Classical Mythology and Christian Tradition in Marlowe's *Doctor Faustus*'. *Publications of the Modern Language Association* 81 (1966), 214-23.

———. 'The Ironic Diction and Theme in Marlowe's *Doctor Faustus*'. *Review of English Studies* 32 (1981), 129-41.

McCullen, Joseph T. 'Dr Faustus and Renaissance Learning'. *Modern Language Review* 51 (1956), 6-16.

Mangan, Michael. *Christopher Marlowe: Doctor Faustus*. Harmondsworth: Penguin, 1987 [Penguin Masterstudies].

Manley, Frank. 'The Nature of Faustus'. *Modern Philology* 66 (1969), 218-31.

Marienstrass, Richard. 'Les Termes du contrat dans *Everyman* et *Doctor Faustus*'. In *De Shakespeare à T. S. Eliot: Mélanges offerts à Henri Fluchère*, M.J. Durry, R. Ellrodt, and M.-T. Jones-Davies, eds. Paris: Didier, 1976, 19-29.

Martin, Betty C. '*Shore's Wife* as a Source of the Epilogue of *Doctor Faustus*'. *Notes and Queries* 195 (1950), 182.

Matalene, H. W., III. 'Marlowe's *Faustus* and the Comforts of Academicism'. *English Literary History* 39 (1972), 495-519.

Maxwell, J. C. 'Notes on Dr Faustus'. *Notes and Queries* NS 11 (1964), 262.

Mebane, John S. *Renaissance Magic and the Return of the Golden Age: the Occult Tradition and Marlowe, Jonson, and Shakespeare*. Lincoln: University of Nebraska Press, 1989.

Muir, Kenneth. 'Marlowe's *Doctor Faustus*'. *Philologica Praegensia* 9 (1966), 395-408.

Nagarajan, S. 'The Philosophy of Doctor Faustus'. *Essays in Criticism* 20 (1970), 485-87.

Nicoll, Allardyce. 'Passing Over the Stage'. *Shakespeare Survey* 12 (1959), 47-55.

Norton Smith, John. 'Marlowe's *Faustus* (I. iii. 1-4)'. *Notes and Queries* 25 (1978), 436-37.

O'Brien, Margaret P. 'Christian Belief in *Doctor Faustus*'. *English Literary History* 37 (1970), 1-11.

Okerlund, A. N. 'The Intellectual Folly of Doctor Faustus.' *Studies in Philology* 74 (1977), 258-78.

Ornstein, Robert. 'The Comic Synthesis in *Doctor Faustus*'. *English Literary History* 22 (1955), 165-72.

———. 'Marlowe and God: The Tragic Theology of *Doctor Faustus*'. *Publications of the Modern Language Association* 83 (1968), 1378-85.

Ostrowski, Witold. 'The Interplay of the Subjective and Objective in Marlowe's *Dr Faustus*'. In *Studies in Language and Literature in Honor of Margaret Schlauch*, M. Bahmer, S. Helsztynski, and J. Krzyzanowski, eds, 1966, 293-305.

Palmer, D. J. 'Magic and Poetry in *Doctor Faustus*'. *Critical Quarterly* 6 (1964), 56-67.

Pearce, T. M. 'Jasper Heywood and Marlowe's *Doctor Faustus*'. *Notes and Queries* 197 (1952), 200-201.

Pettitt, Thomas. 'The Folk-Play in Marlowe's *Doctor Faustus*'. *Folklore* 9: 1 (1980), 72-77.

Pittock, Malcolm. 'God's Mercy is Infinite: Faustus' Last Soliloquy'. *English Studies* 65 (1984), 302-11.

Podis, JoAnne. 'The Concept of Divinity in *Doctor Faustus*'. *Theatre Annual* 27 (1971-1972), 89-102.

Ransom, Marian, Roderick Cooke, and T. M. Pearce. '"German Valdes and Cornelius" in Marlowe's *Doctor Faustus*'. *Notes and Queries* NS 9 (1962), 329-31.

Rayburn, Stephen E. 'Marlowe's *Doctor Faustus* and Medieval Judgement Day Drama'. *Publications of the Mississippi Philological Association* 1985, 33-9.

Reynolds, J. A. 'Faustus's Flawed Learning'. *English Studies* 57: 4 (1976), 329-36.

———. 'Marlowe's *Dr Faustus*: "Be a Divine in a Show" and "When All Is Done Divinity Is Best"'. *American Notes and Queries* 13 (1975), 131-3.

Ricks, Christopher. '*Doctor Faustus* and Hell on Earth'. *Essays in Criticism* 35 (1985), 101-20.

Riehle, Wolfgang. 'Marlowe's *Doctor Faustus* and Renaissance Italy: Some Observations and Suggestions'. In Wolf-Dietrich Bald and Horst Weinstock, eds. *Medieval Studies Conference, Aachen 1983: Language and Literature*. Frankfort: Peter Lang, 1984, 185-95.

Rosador, Kurt Tetzel von. '*Doctor Faustus*: 1604 and 1616'. *Anglia* 90 (1972) 470-93.

———. 'Supernatural Soliciting: Temptation and Imagination in *Doctor Faustus* and *Macbeth*'. In E. A. J. Honigmann, ed. *Shakespeare and His Contemporaries: Essays in Comparison*. Manchester: Manchester U.P., 1986, 42-59.

Rozett, Martha Tuck. *The Doctrine of Election and the Emergence of Elizabethan Tragedy*. Princeton: Princeton U.P., 1984.

Ryan, Lawrence V. 'Panurge and the Faustian Dilemma'. *Stanford Literature Review* 2 (1985), 147-63.

Sachs, Arieh. 'The Religious Despair of Doctor Faustus'. *Journal of English and Germanic Philology* 63 (1964), 625-47.

Sanders, Wilbur. 'Marlowe's *Doctor Faustus*'. *Melbourne Critical Review*, 7 (1964), 78-91.

Seiferth, Howard. 'The Concept of the Devil and the Myth of the Pact in Literature Prior to Goethe'. *Monatschafte* 44 (1952), 271-89.

Sewall, Richard B. *The Vision of Tragedy*. New Haven and London: Yale Univ. Press, 1959.

Shapiro, I. A. 'The Significance of a Date'. *Shakespeare Survey* 8 (1955), 100-105.

Smith, Warren D. 'The Nature of Evil in *Doctor Faustus*'. *Modern Language Review* 60 (1965), 171-75.

Smith, Robert A. H. 'A Note on *Doctor Faustus* and *The Taming of a Shrew*'. *Notes and Queries* NS26 (1979), 116.

———. '"Faustus End" and *The Wounds of Civil War*'. *Notes and Queries* 32 (1985), 16-17.

Snow, Edward A. 'Marlowe's *Doctor Faustus* and the Ends of Desire'. In *Two Renaissance Mythmakers: Marlowe and Jonson*, Alvin Kernan, ed. Baltimore: Johns Hopkins Press, 1977, 70-110.

Snyder, Susan. 'Marlowe's Doctor Faustus as an Inverted Saint's Life'. *Studies in Philology* 63 (1966), 565-77.
———. 'The Left Hand of God: Despair in Medieval and Renaissance Tradition'. *Studies in the Renaissance* 12 (1965), 18-59.
Steadman, John M. 'Averroes and Dr Faustus: Some Additional Parallels'. *Notes and Queries* NS 9 (1962), 327-29.
———. 'Faustus and Averroes'. *Notes and Queries* NS 3 (1956), 416.
Storm, McIvin. 'Faustus First Soliloquy: The End of Every Act'. *Massachusetts Studies in English* 8(4) (1982), 40-9.
Stroup, Thomas B. '*Doctor Faustus* and *Hamlet*: Contrasting Kinds of Christian Tragedy'. *Comparative Drama* 5 (1971), 243-53.
Summers, Claude J. and Ted-Larry Pebworth. 'Marlowe's *Faustus* and the Earl of Bedford's Motto'. *English Language Notes* 9 (1972), 165-67.
———. 'The Conversion of St. Augustine and the B-Text of *Doctor Faustus*', *Renaissance and Renascences in Western Literature* 1: 2 (1979), 1-8.
Tanner, James T. F. '*Doctor Faustus* as Orthodox Christian Sermon'. *Dickinson Review* 2 (1969), 23-31.
Teague, Francis. 'Spectacle in *Faustus*'. *Cahiers Elisabethains* 17 (1980), 83-84.
Traci, Philip. 'Marlowe's Faustus as Artist: A Suggestion about the Theme of the Play'. *Renaissance Papers* (1966), 3-9.
Versfeld, Martin. 'Some Remarks on Marlowe's *Faustus*'. *English Studies in Africa* 1 (1958), 134-43.
Warren, Michael J. '*Doctor Faustus*: The Old Man and the Text'. *English Literary Renaissance* 11: 2 (1981), 111-47.
Waswo, Richard, 'Damnation, Protestant Style: Faustus, Macbeth, and Christian Tragedy'. *Journal of Medieval and Renaissance Studies* 4 (1974), 63-99.
Waugh, Butler. 'Deep and Surface Structure in Traditional and Sophisticated Literature: Faust'. *South Atlantic Bulletin* 33: 3 (1968), 14-17.
West, Robert H. 'The Impatient Magic of Dr Faustus'. *English Literary Renaissance* 4 (1974), 218-40.
Westlund, Joseph. 'The Orthodox Christian Framework of Marlowe's *Faustus*'. *Studies in English Literature* 3 (1963), 191-205.
Wion, Philip K. 'Marlowe's *Doctor Faustus*, the Oedipus Complex, and the Denial of Death'. *Colby Literary Quarterly* 16 (1980), 190-204.
Wymer, Roland. 'When I Behold the Heavens': A Reading of *Doctor Faustus*'. *English Studies* 67 (1986), 505-10.
Young, David. '"Where the Bee Sucks": A Triangular Study of *Doctor Faustus*, *The Alchemist*, and *The Tempest*'. In *Shakespeare's Romances Reconsidered*, J. M. Kay and H. E. Jacobs, eds. Lincoln: Univ. of Nebraska Press, 1978, 149-66.
Zimansky, Curt A. 'Marlowe's *Faustus*: The Date Again'. *Philogical Quarterly* 41 (1962), 181-87.

5. Critical, Textual, and Biographical Studies: Marlowe (general)

Alexander, Peter. 'Shakespeare, Marlowe's Tutor'. *Times Literary Supplement*, 2 April 1964, 280.
Ando, Sadao. *A Descriptive Syntax of Christopher Marlowe's Language*. Tokyo: Univ. of Tokyo Press, 1976.
Ardolino, Frank. 'Come and Go: Marlowe's Imperative Mode'. *Journal of Evolutionary Psychology* 8 (1987), 115-27.
Bakeless, John. *The Tragical History of Christopher Marlowe*, 2 vols., Cambridge, Mass.: Harvard Univ. Press, 1942.

Barber, C. L., ed. *Creating Elizabethan Tragedy: the Theater of Marlowe and Kyd.* Chicago: University of Chicago Press, 1988.

Battenhouse, Roy W. 'Marlowe Reconsidered: Some Reflections on Levin's *Overreacher*'. *Journal of English and Germanic Philology* 52 (1953), 531-42.

Bevington, David M. *From Mankind to Marlowe: Growth of Structure in the Popular Drama of Tudor England.* Cambridge, Massachusetts: Harvard Univ. Press, 1962.

Bloom, Harold, ed. *Christopher Marlowe.* New York: Chelsea, 1986.

Boas, Frederick S. *Christopher Marlowe: A Biographical and Critical Study,* 1940. Oxford: Clarendon Press, 1953 (revised).

Bobin, Donna. 'Marlowe's Humor'. *Massachusetts Studies in English* 2 (1969), 29-40.

Bradbrook, Muriel C. *English Dramatic Form: A Study of Its Development.* London: Chatto & Windus, 1965, 41-61.

———. 'Shakespeare's Recollection of Marlowe'. In *Shakespeare's Styles: Essays in Honour of Kenneth Muir,* Philip Edwards, I.-S. Ewbank, and G. K. Hunter, eds. Cambridge: Cambridge Univ. Press, 1980, 191-204.

———. *Themes and Conventions of Elizabethan Tragedy,* 1935. Cambridge: Cambridge Univ. Press, 1966.

Brandt, Bruce Edwin. *Christopher Marlowe and the Metaphysical Problem Play.* Salzburg: Institut für Anglistik & Amerikanistik, 1985.

Brooke, C. F. Tucker. 'The Reputation of Christopher Marlowe'. *Transactions of the Connecticut Academy of Arts and Sciences* 25 (1922), 347-408.

Brooke, Nicholas. 'Marlowe the Dramatist'. In *Elizabethan Theatre* (Stratford-upon-Avon Studies, 9), John Russell Brown and Bernard Harris, eds. London: Edward Arnold and New York: St Martin's Press, 1966, 86-105.

Brooks, Harold. 'Marlowe and Early Shakespeare'. In *Christopher Marlowe* (Mermaid Critical Commentaries). Edited by Brian Morris, 67-94. See entry for Morris in this section.

Brown, John Russell. 'Marlowe and the Actors'. *Tulane Drama Review* 8: 4 (1964), 155-73.

Bynum, James J., Jr. 'Isolation, Metamorphosis, and Self-Destruction in the Plays of Christopher Marlowe'. *DAI* 34 (1973), 719A-20A (Emory University).

Clay, Charlotte N. *The Role of Anxiety in English Tragedy: 1580-1642.* (Salzburg Studies in English Literature under the Direction of Professor Erwin A. Stürzl. Jacobean Drama Studies, No. 23.) Editor: James Hogg, Salzburg: Institut für Englische Sprache und Literatur, 1974, 87-114.

Clemen, Wolfgang. *English Tragedy before Shakespeare,* translated by T. S. Dorsch. London: Methuen, 1961.

Cole, Douglas. 'Christopher Marlowe, 1564-1964: A Survey'. *Shakespeare Newsletter* 14 (1964), 44.

———. *Suffering and Evil in the Plays of Christopher Marlowe.* Princeton: Princeton Univ. Press, 1962. New York: Gordian Press, 1974.

Cornelius, Richard M. *Christopher Marlowe's Use of the Bible.* New York: Lang, 1984.

Cutts, John P. *The Left Hand of God: A Critical Interpretation of the Plays of Christopher Marlowe.* Haddonfield, N. J.: Haddonfield House, 1973.

———. 'The Marlowe Canon'. *Notes and Queries* NS 6 (1959), 71-74.

Dameron, J. Lasley. 'Marlowe's "Ships of War"'. *American Notes and Queries* 2 (1963), 19-20.

Danson, Laurence. 'Christopher Marlowe: The Questioner'. *English Literary Renaissance* 12 (1982), 3-29.

Das, Sisr Kamar. 'Christopher Marlowe and the Modern Reader'. *Bulletin of the Department of English: Calcutta* 6: 3 (1970-71), 7-14.

Denonain, Jean-Jacques. 'Christopher Marlowe, dramaturge "en mage"?' *Caliban* 10 (1974), 57-76.

———. 'Un nommé Christopher Marlowe, Gentleman'. *Caliban* 1 (1964), 51-74.

Doran, Madeleine. *Endeavours of Art: A Study of Form in Elizabethan Drama*. Madison: Univ. of Wisconsin Press, 1954.

Eagle, Roderick. 'The Mystery of Marlowe's Death'. *Notes and Queries* 197 (1952), 399–402.

Ellis-Fermor, Una M. *Christopher Marlowe*. 1927; Hamden, Conn.: Archon Books, 1967.

Fraser, Russell. 'On Christopher Marlowe'. *Michigan Quarterly Review* 12 (1973), 136–59.

Freeman, Arthur. 'Marlowe, Kyd, and the Dutch Church Libel'. *English Literary Renaissance* 3 (1973), 44–52.

Friedenreich, Kenneth *et al.*, (eds). *'A Poet and a Filthy Play-Maker': New Essays on Christopher Marlowe*. New York: AMS Press, 1988.

Frye, Roland Mushat. 'Theological and Non-Theological Structures in Tragedy'. *Shakespeare Studies* 4 (1968), 132–48.

Garber, Marjorie. '"Infinite Riches in a Little Room": Closure and Enclosure in Marlowe'. In *Two Renaissance Mythmakers: Christopher Marlowe and Ben Jonson* (Selected Papers from the English Institute, 1975–76, New Series, No. 1), edited, with a Foreword, by Alvin Kernan. Baltimore and London: Johns Hopkins Press, 1977, 3–21.

————. 'Marlovian Vision, Shakespearean Revision'. *Research Opportunities in Renaissance Drama* 22 (1979), 3–9.

Giamatti, A. Bartlett. 'The Arts of Illusion'. *Yale Review* 61 (1972), 530–43.

Godshalk, William L. *The Marlovian World Picture*. The Hague: Mouton, 1974.

Goldman, Michael. 'Marlowe and the Histrionics of Ravishment'. In *Two Renaissance Mythmakers: Christopher Marlowe and Ben Jonson* (Selected Papers from the English Institute. New Series, No. 1), edited, with a Foreword, by Alvin Kernan. Baltimore & London: Johns Hopkins Press, 1977, 22–40.

Greenblatt, Stephen G. 'Marlowe and Renaissance Self-Fashioning'. In *Two Renaissance Mythmakers: Christopher Marlowe and Ben Jonson* (Selected Papers from the English Institute, 1975–1976), edited, with a Foreword, by Alvin Kernan. Baltimore and London: Johns Hopkins Press, 1977, 41–69.

Hardin, Richard F. 'Marlowe and the Fruits of Scholarism'. *Philological Quarterly* 63 (1984), 387–400.

Hawkins, Harriet. *Poetic Freedom and Poetic Truth*. Oxford: Oxford Univ. Press, 1976.

Henderson, Philip. *Christopher Marlowe*. London: Longmans, Green & Co., 1952. (2nd ed. New York and Brighton: Barnes & Noble, Harvester Press, 1974.)

Hoelzel, Alfred. *The Paradoxical Quest: a Study of Faustian Vicissitudes*. New York: Lang, 1988.

Hoffman, Calvin. *The Murder of the Man Who Was 'Shakespeare'*. New York: Messner, 1955. (Reprinted New York: Grossett & Dunlap, 1960.)

Homan, Sidney R. 'Chapman and Marlowe: The Paradoxical Hero and the Divided Response'. *Journal of English and Germanic Philology* 68 (1969), 391–406.

Honey, William. *The Shakespeare Epitaph Deciphered*. London: Mitre Press, 1969.

Hotson, J. L. *The Death of Christopher Marlowe*. London: Nonesuch Press, 1925.

Hoy, Cyrus. 'Shakespeare, Sidney, and Marlowe: The Metamorphoses of Love'. *Virginia Quarterly Review* 51 (1975), 448–58.

Huebert, Ronald. 'Tobacco and Boys and Marlowe'. *Southern Review* 92 (1984), 206–24.

Hughes, Pennethorne. 'The Vogue for Marlowe'. *Month* 8 (1952), 141–51.

Kelsall, M. *Christopher Marlowe*. Leiden: E. J. Brill, 1981.

Kiefer, Frederick. *Fortune and Elizabethan Tragedy*. San Marino: Huntington Library Pubs, 1983.

Knights, L. C. 'The Strange Case of Christopher Marlowe'. In *Further Explorations*. Stanford: Stanford Univ. Press, 1965, 75–98.

Knoll, Robert E. *Christopher Marlowe* (Twayne's English Authors Series, No. 74). New York: Twayne, 1969.

Kocher, Paul H. *Christopher Marlowe: A Study in His Thought, Learning, and Character.* Chapel Hill: Univ. of North Carolina Press, 1946.

Kott, Jan. *The Bottom Translation: Marlowe and Shakespeare and the Carnival Tradition.* Trans. Daniela Miedzyrzecka and Lillian Vallee. Evanston: Northwestern University Press, 1987.

Kuriyama, Constance B. *Hammer or Anvil: Psychological Patterns in Christopher Marlowe's Plays.* New Brunswick: Rutgers Univ. Press, 1980.

––––––. 'Marlowe, Shakespeare, and the Nature of Biographical Evidence'. *University of Hartford Studies in Literature* 20(1) (1988), 1–12.

Leech, Clifford. 'The Acting of Marlowe and Shakespeare' (The Second George Fullmer Reynolds Lecture for 1963), reprinted in *Colorado Quarterly* 13: 1 (1964), 25–42.

––––––. 'Marlowe's Humor'. In *Essays on Shakespeare and Elizabethan Drama in Honor of Hardin Craig.* Richard Hosley, ed. Columbia: Univ. of Missouri Press, 1962, 69–81.

––––––. 'When Writing Becomes Absurd' (First of two George Fullmer Reynolds Lectures for 1962), reprinted in *Colorado Quarterly* 13: 1 (1964), 3–24; and in *The Dramatist's Experience with other Essays in Literary Theory.* London: Chatto & Windus; and New York: Barnes & Noble, 1970, 64–86.

––––––. ed. *Marlowe: A Collection of Critical Essays* (Twentieth Century Views Series), Maynard Mack, ed. Englewood Cliffs, New Jersey: Prentice Hall, 1964.

Leech, Clifford and Anne Lancashire, eds. *Christopher Marlowe: Poet for the Stage.* New York: AMS Press, 1986.

Leggatt, Alexander. 'The Critical Fortunes of Christopher Marlowe'. *Queen's Quarterly* 88: 1 (1981), 93–99.

Levin, Harry. 'Marlowe Today'. *Tulane Drama Review* 8: 4 (1964), 22–31.

––––––. *The Overreacher: A Study of Christopher Marlowe.* Cambridge, Massachusetts: Harvard Univ. Press, 1952. (Reprinted, Boston: Beacon Press, 1964.)

Lewis, W. 'In the Shade of the Tree of Knowledge: Marlowe and Calderon'. *Inti: Revista de Literatura Hispánica* 5–6 (1977), 125–33.

Logan, Robert A. 'The Sexual Attitudes of Marlowe and Shakespeare'. *University of Hartford Studies in Literature* 19(2–3) (1987), 1–23.

McAleer, John J. 'Marlowe's Solar Symbolism'. *Drama Critique* 3: 3 (1960), 111–31.

MacIntyre, James Malcolm. 'Marlowe's Use of Rhetorical Figures'. *DAI* 23 (1963), 2518–19 (University of Illinois).

Maclure, Millar, ed. *Marlowe: The Critical Heritage 1588–1896.* London: Routledge & Kegan Paul, 1979.

Mahood, M. M. *Poetry and Humanism,* 1950. New York: W. W. Norton, 1970 (reprinted with corrections).

Margeson, J. M. R. *The Origins of English Tragedy.* Oxford: Clarendon Press, 1967.

Masinton, Charles G. *Christopher Marlowe's Tragic Vision: A Study in Damnation.* Athens, Ohio: Ohio Univ. Press, 1972.

––––––. 'Marlowe's Artists: The Failure of Imagination'. *Ohio University Review* 11 (1969), 22–35.

Maxwell, J. C. 'The Plays of Christopher Marlowe'. In *The Age of Shakespeare.* Pelican Guide to English Literature, Vol. 2, Boris Ford, ed. Harmondsworth: Penguin Books, 1956 (revised 1963), 162–78.

Meehan, Virginia M. *Christopher Marlowe: Poet and Playwright Studies in Poetical Method* (De Proprietatibus Litterarum. Series Practica, 81). The Hague: Mouton, 1974.

Misra, K. S. 'The Archetypal Symbol in Marlowe'. *Journal of English* 5 (1978), 10–40.

Morris, Brian, ed. *Christopher Marlowe* (Mermaid Critical Commentaries). London: Ernest Benn, 1968.

Mundy, P. D. 'The Ancestry of Christopher Marlowe'. *Notes and Queries* NS 2 (1954), 328–31.

Nozaki, Mutsumi. 'The Comic Sense in Marlowe Reconsidered'. *Shakespeare Studies* 9 (1970-71), 1-27.

O'Neill, Judith, ed. *Critics on Marlowe*. Coral Gables, Florida: Univ. of Miami Press, 1970.

Oras, Ants. 'Lyrical Instrumentation in Marlowe: A Step Towards Shakespeare'. *Studies in Shakespeare*, 74-87 (University of Miami Publications in English and American Literature, No. 1). Coral Gables: Univ. of Miami Press, 1953.

Page, R. I. 'Christopher Marlowe and Matthew Parker's Library'. *Notes and Queries*, NS 24 (1977), 510-14.

Palmer, D. J. 'Elizabethan Tragic Heroes'. In *Elizabethan Theatre* (Stratford-upon-Avon Studies, No. 9), John Russell Brown and Bernard Harris, eds. London: Edward Arnold; and New York: St Martin's Press, 1966, 11-35.

———. 'Marlowe's Naturalism'. In *Christopher Marlowe* (Mermaid Critical Commentaries), Brian Morris, ed., 151-175. [See entry this section.]

Parkes, H. B. 'Nature's Diverse Laws: The Double Vision of the Elizabethans'. *Sewanee Review* 58 (1950), 402-18.

Peery, William. 'Marlowe's Irreverent Humor — Some Open Questions'. *Tulane Studies in English* 6 (1957), 15-29.

Pinciss, Gerald. *Christopher Marlowe* (World Dramatists Series). New York: Frederick Ungar Publishing Co., 1975.

Poirier, Michel. *Christopher Marlowe*. 1951. London: Chatto & Windus, 1968.

Potter, Robert. *The English Morality Play*. London and Boston: Routledge & Kegan Paul, 1975.

Powell, Jocelyn. 'Marlowe's Spectacle'. *Tulane Drama Review* 8: 4 (1964), 195-210.

Price, Hereward T. 'Shakespeare and His Young Contemporaries'. *Philological Quarterly* 41 (1962), 37-57.

Rabkin, Norman and Bluestone, Max, eds. *Shakespeare's Contemporaries*. Englewood Cliffs, New Jersey: Prentice-Hall, 1961 (reprinted and expanded, 1971).

Ribner, Irving. *The English History Play in the Age of Shakespeare*, 1957. London: Methuen, 1965 (revised edition).

———. 'Greene's Attack on Marlowe: Some Light on *Alphonsus and Selimus*'. *Studies in Philology* 52 (1955), 162-71.

———. 'Marlowe and Shakespeare'. *Shakespeare Quarterly* 15: 2 (1964), 41-53. Also issued as commemorative volume, *Shakespeare 400*, James G. McManaway, ed. New York: Holt, Rinehart, & Winston, 1964 (same pagination).

———. 'Marlowe and the Critics'. *Tulane Drama Review* 8: 4 (1964), 211-24.

———. 'Marlowe's "Tragicke Glass"'. In *Essays on Shakespeare and Elizabethan Drama in Honor of Hardin Craig*, Richard Hosley, ed. Columbia: Univ. of Missouri Press, 1962, 91-114.

Röhrman, Hendrick. *Marlowe and Shakespeare: A Thematic Exposition of Some of Their Plays*. Arnhem: Van Loghum Slaterus, 1953.

Rowse, A. L. *Christopher Marlowe: A Biography*. 1964. London: Macmillan, 1981 (revised edition).

Sanders, Wilbur. *The Dramatist and the Received Idea: Studies in the Plays of Marlowe and Shakespeare*. Cambridge: Cambridge Univ. Press, 1968.

Sellin, Paul R. 'The Hidden God: Reformation Awe in Renaissance Literature'. In *The Darker Vision of the Renaissance: Beyond the Fields of Reason* (U.C.L.A. Center for Medieval and Renaissance Contributions, No. 6), Robert S. Kinsman, ed. Berkeley and Los Angeles: Univ. of California Press, 1974, 147-96.

Shepherd, Simon. *Marlowe and the Politics of Elizabethan Theatre*. Brighton, Sussex: Harvester Press, 1986.

Shield, H. A. 'Charles Sledd, Spymaster'. *Notes and Queries* NS 7 (1960), 47-48.

———. 'The Death of Marlowe'. *Notes and Queries* NS 4 (1957), 101-103.

Sims, James H. *Dramatic Uses of Biblical Allusion in Marlowe and Shakespeare* (University of Florida Monographs in the Humanities, No. 24). Gainesville: Univ. of Florida Press, 1966.

Speaight, Robert. 'Marlowe: The Forerunner'. *Review of English Literature* 7: 4 (1966), 26-41.

Sprott, S. E. 'Drury and Marlowe'. *Times Literary Supplement*, 2 August 1974, 840.

Steane, J. B. *Marlowe: A Critical Study*. Cambridge: Cambridge Univ. Press, 1964.

Stroup, Thomas B. *Microcosmos: The Shape of the Elizabethan Play*. Lexington: Univ. of Kentucky Press, 1965.

———. 'Ritual in Marlowe's Plays'. *Comparative Drama* 7 (1973), 198-221.

Summers, Claude J. *Christopher Marlowe and the Politics of Power* (Elizabethan and Renaissance Studies, No. 22), James Hogg, ed. Salzburg: Institut für Englische Sprache und Literatur, 1974, vi + 203 pp.

Talbert, Ernest W. *Elizabethan Drama and Shakespeare's Early Plays: An Essay in Historical Criticism*. Chapel Hill: Univ. of North Carolina Press, 1963.

Thurston, Gavin. 'Christopher Marlowe's Death'. *Contemporary Review* 205 (1964), 156-59, 193-200.

Tomilson, T. B. *A Study of Elizabethan and Jacobean Tragedy*. Cambridge: Cambridge Univ. Press, 1964.

Urry, William. 'Marlowe and Canterbury'. *Times Literary Supplement*, 13 February 1964 136.

———. *Christopher Marlowe and Canterbury*. Ed. Andrew Butcher. London: Faber and Faber, 1988.

Waith, Eugene M. *The Herculean Hero in Marlowe, Chapman, Shakespeare, and Dryden*. New York: Columbia Univ. Press; London: Chatto & Windus, 1962.

———. *Ideas of Greatness: Heroic Drama in England*. London: Routledge & Kegan Paul, 1971.

———. *Patterns and Perspectives in English Renaissance Drama*. Newark: University of Delaware Press, 1988.

Weil, Judith E. R. *Christopher Marlowe: Merlin's Prophet*. Cambridge: Cambridge Univ. Press, 1977.

Welsh, Robert Ford. 'The Printing of Early Editions of Marlowe's Plays: *Tamburlaine* (1590); *The Massacre at Paris* (1592?); *Edward II* (1594); *Dido* (1594); *Doctor Faustus* (1604, 1616); *The Jew of Malta* (1633)'. *DAI* 25 (1964), 2968-69 (Duke University).

Wernham, R. B. 'Christopher Marlowe at Flushing in 1592'. *English Historical Review* 91 (1976), 344-45.

Wham, Benjamin. 'Marlowe's Mighty Line: Was Marlowe Murdered at Twenty-Nine?'. *American Bar Association Journal* 46 (1960), 509-13.

Wickham, Glynne. '*Exeunt to the Cave*: Notes on the Staging of Marlowe's Plays'. *Tulane Drama Review* 8: 4 (1964), 184-94.

Williams, David Rhys. *Shakespeare, Thy Name Is Marlowe*. New York: Philosopher's Library, 1966.

Williamson, Hugh Ross. *Kind Kit: An Informal Biography of Christopher Marlowe*. London: Michael Joseph, 1972.

Wilson, Frank Percy. *Marlowe and the Early Shakespeare*. Being the Clark Lectures presented at Trinity College, Cambridge, 1951. Oxford: Clarendon Press, 1953.

Wraight, A. D. *In Search of Christopher Marlowe: A Pictorial Biography*, photography by Virginia F. Stern. London: MacDonald, 1964.

Zimansky, Curt A. 'Comment on Marlowe'. *Times Literary Supplement*, 6 April 1956, 207.

Zucker, David H. *Stage and Image in the Plays of Christopher Marlowe* (Elizabethan and Renaissance Studies, No. 7), James Hogg, ed. Salzburg: Institut für Englische Sprache und Literatur, 1972.

6. Related Material

Agrippa von Nettesheim, Heinrich Cornelius. *De Occulta Philosophia, sive de magia libri tres*, 1533, Karl Anton Nowotny, ed. Graz, Austria: Akademische Druck u. Verlagsanstalt, 1967.

———. *Of Geomancy*. Robert Turner, trans. London, 1655. London: Askin Publishers, 1978 (reprint).

Allen, Don Cameron. *The Star-Crossed Renaissance: the Quarrel about Astronomy and its Influence in England*. Durham, North Carolina: Duke Univ. Press, 1941.

———. *Doubt's Boundless Sea: Skepticism and Faith in the Renaissance*. Baltimore: Johns Hopkins Press, 1964.

———. *Image and Meaning*. Baltimore: Johns Hopkins Press, rev. ed., 1968.

———. *Mysteriously Meant*. Baltimore: Johns Hopkins Press, 1970.

Altman, Joel B. *The Tudor Play of Mind: Rhetorical Inquiry and the Development of Elizabethan Drama*. Berkeley: Univ. of California Press, 1978.

Anon. *Mary of Nemegen* (Antwerpen, 1518). H. Morgan and A. J. Barnouw, eds. Cambridge, Mass.: Harvard Univ. Press, 1934 (facsimile reprint).

Ashe, Dora Jean. 'The Non-Shakespearean Bad Quartos as Provincial Acting Versions', *Renaissance Papers*, 1 (1954), 57–62.

Saint Augustine. *The City of God*. Marcus Dods, trans. New York: Random House, 1950.

———. *Confessions*. R. S. Pine-Coffin, trans. Harmondsworth: Penguin, 1961.

Ayers, P. K. 'The Protestant Morality Play and Problems of Dramatic Structure'. *Essays in Theatre* 2(2) (1984), 94–110.

Barroll, J. Leeds, Alexander Leggatt, Richard Hosley and Alvin Kernan, *The Revels History of Drama in English*, Vol. 3, 1576–1613. London: Methuen, 1975.

Barkan, Leonard. *Nature's Work of Art: The Human Body as Image of the World*. New Haven and London: Yale Univ. Press, 1975.

Barker, Walter L. 'The English Pantalones: A Study in Relations between the Commedia Dell'arte and Elizabethan Drama.' *DAI* 27 (1967), 3419A (University of Connecticut).

Berry, Lloyd E., ed. *The Geneva Bible: A Facsimile of the 1560 Edition*. Madison: Univ. of Wisconsin Press, 1969.

Blau, Joseph Leon. *The Christian Interpretation of the Cabala in the Renaissance*. New York: Columbia Univ. Press, 1944. Port Washington: Kennikat Press, 1965 (reprint).

Bloomfield, Morton W. *The Seven Deadly Sins: An Introduction to the History of a Religious Concept with Special Reference to Medieval English Literature*. East Lansing: Michigan State College Press, 1952.

Boase, T. S. R. *Death in the Middle Ages*. London: Thames & Hudson, 1972.

The Book of Common Prayer, 1559: the Elizabethan Prayer Book, ed. John E. Booty. Washington, D.C.: Folger Shakespeare Library, 1976.

Brody, Alan. *The English Mummers and Their Plays: Traces of Ancient Mystery*. London: Routledge & Kegan Paul, 1971.

Browne, Sir Thomas. *Pseudodoxia Epidemica. The Works of Sir Thomas Browne*, Vol. II. Geoffrey Keynes, ed. London: Faber, 1928. Oxford Univ. Press, 1964 (revised edition).

———. *Religio Medici, Hydriotaphia*, and *The Garden of Cyrus*. Robin Robbins, ed. Oxford: Clarendon Press, 1982.

Butler, Christopher. *Number Symbolism*. London: Routledge & Kegan Paul, 1970.

Butler, E. M. *The Fortunes of Faust*. Cambridge: Cambridge Univ. Press, 1952.

———. *The Myth of the Magus*. Cambridge: Cambridge Univ. Press, 1949.

———. *Ritual Magic*. Cambridge: Cambridge Univ. Press, 1948.

Calder, I. R. F. 'A Note on Magic Squares in the Philosophy of Agrippa of Nettesheim'. *Journal of the Warburg and Courtauld Institutes* 12 (1949), 196–99.

Calvin, John. *Institutes of the Christian Religion*. John T. McNeill, ed., Ford L. Battles, trans., 2 vols. Philadelphia: Westminster Press, 1960.

Cassirer, Ernst. *The Individual and the Cosmos in Renaissance Philosophy*. Mario Domandi, trans. 1927. Philadelphia: Univ. of Pennsylvania Press, 1963 (reprint).

Chambers, E. K. *The Elizabethan Stage*, 4 vols. Oxford: Oxford Univ. Press, 1923.

Chew, Samuel C. *The Pilgrimage of Life*. New Haven: Yale Univ. Press, 1962. New York: Kennikat Press, 1973 (reprint).

Clemen, Wolfgang. *English Tragedy before Shakespeare*. T. S. Dorsch, trans. London: Methuen, 1961.

Cohen, Walter. 'The Reformation and Elizabethan Drama'. *Shakespeare Jahrbuch* [Weimar] 120 (1984), 45-52.

Comper, Frances M. M., ed. *The Book of the Craft of Dying*. London: Longmans Green, 1917.

Conley, John. 'The Doctrine of Friendship in *Everyman*'. *Speculum* 44 (1969), 374-82.

Cooper, Geoffrey and Wortham, Christopher, eds. *Everyman*. Nedlands: Univ. of Western Australia Press, 1980.

Craig, Hardin. 'Morality Plays and Elizabethan Drama'. *Shakespeare Quarterly* 1 (1950), 64-72.

Craik, T. W. *The Tudor Interlude*. Leicester: Leicester Univ. Press, 1962.

Cruden, Alexander. *Cruden's Complete Concordance to the Old and New Testaments*. Guildford and London: Lutterworth Press, 1954 (revised edition).

Curtius, E. R. *European Literature and the Latin Middle Ages*. Willard R. Trask, trans. Bollingen Series no. 36, New York: Bollingen Foundation, 1953.

Davidson, Clifford, C. J. Gianakaris and John H. Stroupe, eds. *Drama in the Renaissance: Comparative and Critical Essays*. New York: AMS Press, 1986.

Dessen, Alan C. *Elizabethan Drama and the Viewer's Eye*. Chapel Hill: Univ. of North Carolina Press, 1977.

Diehl, Huston. "'To Put Us in Remembrance': The Protestant Transformation of Images of Judgement." In David Bevington, ed., *Homo, Memento Finis: The Iconography of Just Judgment in Medieval Art and Drama*. Kalamazoo: Western Michigan University, Medieval Institute Publications, 1985, 179-208.

Doebler, John. *Shakespeare's Speaking Pictures*. Albuquerque: Univ. of New Mexico Press, 1974.

Doran, Madelaine. *Endeavors of Art: A Study of Form in Elizabethan Drama*. Madison: Univ. of Wisconsin Press, 1954.

Eden, H. K. F. and Lloyd, Eleanor, eds. *The Book of Sundials*. London: Bell, 1890 (3rd edition).

Ettin, Andrew V. 'Magic into Art: the Magician's Renunciation of Magic in English Renaissance Drama'. *Texas Studies in Literature and Language* 19 (1977), 268-93.

Evans, J. M. *Paradise Lost and the Genesis Tradition*. Oxford: Oxford Univ. Press, 1968.

Evans-Pritchard, Edward Evan. *Witchcraft, Oracles and Magic among the Azande*. Oxford: Clarendon Press, 1937.

Farnham, Willard. *The Medieval Heritage of Elizabethan Tragedy*. Berkeley: Univ. of California Press, 1936.

Fischer, Sandra K. *Econolingua: A Glossary of Coins and Economic Language in Renaissance Drama*. Newark: University of Delaware Press, 1985.

Foakes, R. A. and Rickert, R. T., eds. *Henslowe's Diary*. 1961. Cambridge: Cambridge Univ. Press, 1968 (reprint).

French, Peter J. *John Dee: the World of an Elizabethan Magus*. London: Routledge & Kegan Paul, 1972.

Frye, Northrop. 'Vision and Cosmos'. In David H. Hirsch and Nehama Ashkenazy, eds. *Biblical Patterns in Modern Literature*. Brown Judaic Studies 77, 1984.

Garin, Eugenio. *Astrology in the Renaissance: the Zodiac of Life*. Carolyn Jackson and June Allen, trans. London: Routledge & Kegan Paul, 1983.

Gibson, H. N. *The Shakespeare Claimants: A Critical Survey of the Four Principal Theories Concerning the Authorship of Shakespearean Plays*. New York: Barnes & Noble, 1962. London: Methuen, 1971 (reprinted edition).

Godwin, Joscelyn. *Robert Fludd: Hermetic Philosopher and Surveyor of Two Worlds*. London: Thames & Hudson, 1979.

Goltra, Robert J., Jr. 'Five Ceremonial Magicians of Tudor-Stuart Drama'. *Emporia State Research Studies* 33(2) (1984), 5-36.

Greenblatt, Stephen. *Renaissance Self-Fashioning: From More to Shakespeare*. Chicago: Univ. of Chicago Press, 1980.

Guazzo, Francesco. *Compendium Maleficarum*. E. A. Ashwin, trans., Montague Summers, ed. London: John Rodker, 1929.

Hammond, Gerald. 'The Bible and Literary Criticism I'. *Critical Quarterly* 25: 2 (1983) 5-20.

Happé, Peter, ed. *English Mystery Plays: a Selection*. Harmondsworth: Penguin, 1975.

———. *Four Morality Plays*. Harmondsworth: Penguin, 1979.

Hardison, O. B., Jr. 'Blank verse before Milton'. *Studies in Philology* 81 (1984), 253-74.

Harris, Anthony. *Night's Black Agents: Witchcraft and Magic in Seventeenth Century English Drama*. London: Manchester Univ. Press, 1980.

Heninger, S. K., Jr. *The Cosmographical Glass: Renaissance Diagrams of the Universe*. San Marino: Huntington Library, 1977.

———. *Touches of Sweet Harmony: Pythagorean Cosmology and Renaissance Poetics*. San Marino: Huntington Library, 1974.

Henkel, Arthur and Schöne, Albrecht. *Emblemata: Handbuch zur sinnbildkunst des XVI. und XVII. jahrhunderts*. Stuttgart: J. B. Metzlersche Verlagsbuchhandlung, 1967.

Herbert, George. *Works*. F. E. Hutchinson, ed. Oxford: Clarendon Press, 1945.

Historia von D. Johann Fausten (Frankfurt, 1587). Hans Henning, ed. and introd. Halle: Verlag Sprache und Literatur, 1963.

The History of the Damnable Life and Deserved Death of Doctor John Faustus . . . according to the True Copie Printed at Franckfort, and Translated into English by P. F. Gent, 1592. The English Experience Series, no. 173. Amsterdam and New York: Da Capo Press, Theatrum Orbis Terrarum, 1969 (facsimile reprint).

The History of the Damnable Life and Deserved Death of Doctor John Faustus . . . William Rose, ed. London: Routledge, n.d. [1925].

The History of the Damnable life and the Deserved Death of Doctor Faustus. Hildesheim: Georg Olms, 1985. [Facsimile reprint of the 1592 edition].

Holmyard, E. J. *Alchemy*. Harmondsworth: Penguin, 1957.

Hopper, Vincent Foster. *Medieval Number Symbolism: Its Sources, Meaning and Influence on Thought and Expression*. New York: Columbia Univ. Press, 1938. Columbia University Studies in English and Comparative Literature no. 132. New York: Norwood Editions, 1977 (facsimile reprint).

Horstmann, Carl, ed. *The Boke of the Craft of Dying*. In *Yorkshire Writers: Richard Rolle . . . and His Followers*, 2 vols. London: Swan Sonnenschein, 1895-96.

Hughes, Robert. *Heaven and Hell in Western Art*. London: Weidenfeld & Nicolson, 1968.

Hulse, Clark. 'Recent Studies of Literature and Painting in the English Renaissance'. *English Literary Renaissance* 15 (1985), 122-40.

James I of England. *Demonology*. G. B. Harrison, ed. Edinburgh: Edinburgh Univ. Press, 1966.

Johnson, Francis R. *Astronomical Thought in Renaissance England*. Baltimore: Johns Hopkins Press, 1937.

———. 'Marlowe's "Imperial Heaven"'. *ELH* 12 (1945), 35-44.

———. 'Marlowe's Astronomy and Renaissance Skepticism'. *ELH* 13 (1946), 241-54.

Kaiser, Walter. 'The Wisdom of the Fool'. In *Dictionary of the History of Ideas*, Philip P. Wiener, ed. New York: Scribner's, 1973, Vol. 4, pp. 515-20.

Kocher, Paul H. *Science and Religion in Elizabethan England*. San Marino: Huntington Library, 1953. New York: Octagon Books, 1969 (reprint).

Koestler, Arthur. *The Sleepwalkers*. London: Hutchinson, 1959.

Kuhn, Thomas P. *The Copernican Revolution: Planetary Astronomy in the Development of Western Thought.* Cambridge, Massachusetts: Harvard Univ. Press, 1957.

Lanham, Richard A. *The Motives of Eloquence: Literary Rhetoric in the Renaissance.* New Haven: Yale Univ. Press, 1976.

Levin, Harry. *The Myth of the Golden Age in the Renaissance.* New York: Oxford Univ. Press, 1969 (2nd edition).

Levin, Richard. *The Multiple Plot in English Renaissance Drama.* Chicago: Univ. of Chicago Press, 1971.

Lievsay, John L. *The Elizabethan Image of Italy.* Ithaca, New York: Cornell Univ. Press and Folger Shakespeare Library, 1964.

Lynch, Terence. 'The Geometric Body in Durer's Engraving *Melencolia I*'. *Journal of the Warburg and Courtauld Institutes* 45 (1982), 226-32.

Luther, Martin. *A Compend of Luther's Theology*, Hugh Thomson Kerr, ed. Philadelphia: Westminister Press, 1943.

———. *On the Bondage of Will.* J. I. Packer and O. R. Johnston, eds. 1957. Cambridge: James Clarke & Co., 1973 (reprint).

———. *The Precious and Sacred Writings of Martin Luther.* John N. Lenker, ed. 15 vols. Minneapolis: The Luther Press, 1903-10.

Mair, Lucy. *Witchcraft.* London: Weidenfeld & Nicholson, 1973 (2nd edition). World University Library.

Marvell, Andrew. *Poems and Letters.* H. M. Margoliouth, ed., 2 vols. Oxford: Clarendon Press, 1971 (3rd edition).

McKerrow, Ronald B. *Printers' and Publishers' Devices in England and Scotland, 1485–1640.* London: The Bibliographical Society, 1949.

McPherson, David. 'Three Charges against Sixteenth- and Seventeenth-Century Playwrights: Libel, Bawdy and Blasphemy'. *Medieval and Renaissance Drama in England* 2 (1985), 269-82.

Meagher, Robert E. *An Introduction to Augustine.* New York: New York Univ. Press, 1978.

Milton, John. *Poems.* John Carey and Alastair Fowler, eds. London: Longman, 1968.

Miner, Earl, ed. *Illustrious Evidence: Approaches to English Literature of the Early Seventeenth Century.* Berkeley: Univ. of California Press, 1975.

———. *Literary Uses of Typology from the Late Middle Ages to the Present.* Princeton: Princeton Univ. Press, 1977.

Munitz, Milton K., ed. *Theories of the Universe.* New York: Free Press of Glencoe, 1957.

Nauert, Charles G., Jr. *Agrippa and the Crisis of Renaissance Thought.* Urbana: Univ. of Illinois Press, 1965.

Nicolson, Marjorie Hope. *The Breaking of the Circle: Studies in the Effect of the 'New Science' on Seventeenth-Century Poetry.* New York: Columbia Univ. Press, 1960 (revised edition).

Nowotny, Karl Anton. 'The Construction of Certain Seals and Characters in the Work of Agrippa of Nettesheim'. *Journal of the Warburg and Courtauld Institutes* 12 (1949), 46-57.

O'Brien, Gordon W. 'Recent Studies of Elizabethan Stage Magic'. *Cauda Pavonis* 5(1) (1986), 4-8.

Ong, Walter J. *Ramus, Method, and the Decay of Dialogue.* 1958. New York: Octagon Books, 1974 (reprint).

Owst, G. R. *Literature and Pulpit in Medieval England.* 1933; Oxford: Blackwell, 1961.

The Oxford Dictionary of the Christian Church. F. L. Cross and E. A. Livingstone, eds. 2nd edition, 1974; Oxford: Oxford Univ. Press, 1978.

Palmer, P. M. and More, R. P., eds. *The Source of the Faust Tradition from Simon Magus to Lessing.* New York: Oxford Univ. Press, 1926.

Panofsky, Erwin. *Studies in Iconology.* New York: Icon Editions, 1972 (3rd edition).

Patrides, C. A. *Premises and Motifs in Renaissance Thought and Literature.* Princeton: Princeton Univ. Press, 1982.

––––––. 'Renaissance and Modern Views of Hell'. *Harvard Theological Review* 57 (1964), 217–36.

Pingree, David. 'A New Look at *Melencolia I*'. *Journal of the Warburg and Courtauld Institutes* 43 (1980), 257–8.

Plato. *Timaeus and Critias*. H. D. P. Lee, trans. Harmondsworth: Penguin, 1971.

Porter, Harry C. *Reformation and Reaction in Tudor Cambridge*. 1958. Hamden, Conn.: The Shoe String Press, 1972 (reprint).

Purdon, Noel. *The Words of Mercury: Shakespeare and English Mythography of the Renaissance*. Elizabethan and Renaissance Studies no. 39. Salzburg: Institut für Englische Sprache und Literatur, 1974.

Quint, David. *Origin and Originality in Renaissance Literature*. New Haven and London: Yale Univ. Press, 1983.

Remy, Nicolas. *Demonolatry*. E. A. Ashwin, trans., Montague Summers, ed. London: John Rodker, 1930.

Richardson, Alexander. *The Logician's Schoolmaster, or a Comment upon Ramus' Logicke*. London, 1629.

Ricoeur, Paul. *The Symbolism of Evil*. 1967. Boston: Beacon Press, 1969 (reprint).

Rose, Elliot. *A Razor for a Goat*. Toronto: Univ. of Toronto Press, 1962.

Rosen, Barbara, ed. *Witchcraft*. Stratford-upon-Avon Library no. 6. London: Edward Arnold, 1969.

Russell, Jeffrey Burton. *Witchcraft in the Middle Ages*. Ithaca and London: Cornell Univ. Press, 1972.

Sandys, George. *Ovids Metamorphosis Englished, Mythologiz'd, and Represented in Figures*. 1632. New York: Garland Press, 1976 (facsimile reprint).

Scot, Reginald. *The Discoverie of Witchcraft*. Hugh Ross Williamson, ed. Arundel: Centaur Press, 1964.

Schaff, Philip, ed. *A Select Library of the Nicene and Post-Nicene Fathers of the Christian Church*, Vol. 4. Grand Rapids: Eerdmans Publishing Co., 1956.

Seznec, Jean. *The Survival of the Pagan Gods*. Princeton: Princeton Univ. Press, 1953.

Shumaker, Wayne. *The Occult Sciences in the Renaissance: A Study in Intellectual Patterns*. Berkeley and Los Angeles: Univ. of California Press, 1972.

Smalley, Beryl. *The Study of the Bible in the Middle Ages*. Oxford: Blackwell, 1982 (3rd edition).

Smeed, J. W. *Faust in Literature*. London: Oxford Univ. Press, 1975.

Spenser, Edmund. *The Faerie Queene*. J. C. Smith, ed., 2 vols. Oxford: Clarendon Press, 1909.

Spivack, Charlotte. *The Comedy of Evil on Shakespeare's Stage*. Rutherford: Fairleigh Dickinson Univ. Press, 1978.

Sprenger, Jakob and Heinrich Kramer. *Malleus Maleficarum*. Montague Summers, trans. and ed. London: John Rodker, 1928.

Stevens, David, ed. *English Renaissance Theatre History: A Reference Guide*. Boston: G. V. Hall, 1982.

Strauss, Walter L. *The Complete Engravings, Etchings and Drypoints of Albrecht Dürer*. New York: Dover Publications, 1972.

St. Thomas Aquinas. *Summa Theologiae*. London: Blackfriar, and Eyre & Spottiswoode, 1964–81. Kenelm Foster, O.P., ed., 1968.

Thomas, Keith. *Religion and the Decline of Magic*. Harmondsworth: Penguin, 1973.

Thompson, Stith. *Motif-index of Folk Literature: a Classification of Narrative Elements in Folk-tales, Ballads, Myths, Fables, Medieval Romances, Exempla, Fabliaux, Jestbooks and Local Legends*, 6 vols. Bloomington: Indiana Univ. Press, 1955 (reprinted 1966).

Thorndike, Lynn. *A History of Magic and Experimental Science During the First Thirteen Centuries of Our Era*, 8 vols. New York: Columbia Univ. Press, 1922–1958.

Tilley, Morris Palmer. *A Dictionary of the Proverbs in England in the Sixteenth and Seventeenth Centuries*. Ann Arbor: Univ. of Michigan Press, 1950.

Tomlinson, Charles. *Poetry and Metamorphosis*. Cambridge: Cambridge Univ. Press, 1983.

Trevor-Roper, H. R. *The European Witch-Craze of the 16th and 17th Centuries*. Harmondsworth: Penguin, 1969.

Trousdale, Marion. *Shakespeare and the Rhetoricians*. Chapel Hill: Univ. of North Carolina Press, 1982.

Tuchman, Barbara. *A Distant Mirror*. New York: Knopf, 1978.

Walker, D. P. *The Decline of Hell: Seventeenth-Century Discussions of Eternal Torment*. London: Routledge & Kegan Paul, 1964.

———. *Spiritual and Demonic Magic from Ficino to Campanella*, 2nd ed., 1969. Notre Dame: Univ. of Notre Dame Press, 1975 (reprint).

Whitney, Geoffrey. *A Choice of Emblemes*, 1586. English Emblem Books no. 3. Menston: Scolar Press, 1969 (facsimile reprint).

Woodes, Nathaniel. *The Conflict of Conscience*, 1581. Oxford: Malone Society, 1952 (facsimile reprint).

Yates, Frances A. *Giordano Bruno and the Hermetic Tradition*. London: Routledge & Kegan Paul, 1964.

———. *The Occult Philosophy in the Elizabethan Age*. London: Routledge & Kegan Paul, 1979.

NOTES AND TEXT

0.1   Chorus: Elizabethan dramatists introduced the term in respectful emulation of Greek tragedy, but applied it to the single commentator of the morality play tradition. The first Chorus is, in effect, a prologue. Prologues became less common towards the end of the Queen Elizabeth's reign: "Th'epilogue is in fashion; prologues no more", *The Birth of Hercules* c. 1597 (Dr David Lake).

1-6   It is uncertain whether Marlowe is alluding to his own plays; see J. P. Cutts, "The Marlowe Canon", *NQ* NS6 (1959), 71 74. Marlowe may be drawing attention to his daring in writing a tragedy which has nothing to do with love or war.

2   mate: allied himself with. (*OED* Mate. v^2, *trans.*) incorrectly gives the opposite meaning for this instance.

6   Muse: the Muses, nine sister goddesses in Greek mythology, were invoked severally for different kinds of inspiration. Renaissance poets often invoked an undifferentiated Muse; Marlowe may even be referring to himself (cf. Milton's *Lycidas*, 19 21).
        vaunt [B; A, daunt].
        heavenly verse: periphrasis for the high style, customarily used for tragedy.

8   Faustus: the name would have been pronounced as spelt by Henslowe, the Elizabethan theatre manager, in his *Diary*: "Fostes".

12   Rhodes: Roda, now known as Stadtroda.

13   Wittenberg [B; A Wertenberg]. Its university was made famous by Martin Luther and Philipp Melanchthon, who taught there.

15   divinity: theology, as a university discipline (*OED* Divinity. 4)

16   A round-about way of saying that Faustus was an adornment.

17   graced: Cambridge confers degrees by "grace of the Senate"; Marlowe takes the terminology of his own university.

18 26   sweet . . . glutted . . . surfeits . . . sweet: It was a medieval commonplace that the first sin of Adam and Eve was gluttony, in taking the forbidden fruit from the tree of knowledge. In his necromancy (25), Faustus may be seen to replicate original sin. On the imagery of gluttony in the play, see C. L. Barber, "The form of Faustus' fortunes good or bad", *TDR* 8 (1964), 92 119; see also W. D. Smith, "The nature of evil in *Dr Faustus*", *MLR* 60 (1965), 171 75.

18   . . . whose sweet delight disputes: who takes delight in debating.

20   cunning: knowledge, in the sense of special skill; also, skill in the occult arts (*OED* Cunning. *sb.* 3 and 4).
        self-conceit: conceit meant concept or idea in common Elizabethan usage, but the more modern sense of self-opiniatedness seems intended (*OED* Conceit. *sb*. I. 1 and II. 6).

21   waxen wings: the myth of Daedalus and Icarus, commonly known through Ovid's *Metamorphoses* (III. 180-230), was popular among moralists and emblem writers. In Geoffrey Whitney's *Choice of Emblemes* (Leyden, 1586) Icarus is a warning to those seeking forbidden knowledge, expecially astrology. See p. xlix of the present edition, figure 8, and Sandys' *Ovids Metamorphosis*, p. 291.

23   falling to: becoming involved in (*OED* Fall. *v.* X. 66.a), with secondary suggestion of falling from grace into sin (*OED* Fall. *v.* III. 25.b). Mounting too high (21) and then falling is the Renaissance paradigm of tragedy. See W. Farnham, *The Medieval Heritage of Elizabethan Tragedy* (Oxford, 1937) and H. Levin, *The Overreacher* (Cambridge, Mass., 1952).

25   necromancy [B; A negromancy]: an etymological confusion, whereby medieval Latin transformed necromancy (from Greek: nekros = corpse) into nigromancy (niger = black), was intensified through the Spanish-derived variant of negromancy.

The Tragical History of Doctor Faustus

Enter CHORUS

CHORUS

Not marching now in fields of Thracimene,
Where Mars did mate the Carthaginians,
Nor sporting in the dalliance of love
In courts of kings, where state is overturned,
Nor in the pomp of proud audacious deeds,   5
Intends our Muse to vaunt his heavenly verse:
Only this — Gentlemen — we must perform
The form of Faustus' fortunes, good or bad.
To patient judgements we appeal our plaud,
And speak for Faustus in his infancy: 10
Now is he born, his parents base of stock,
In Germany, within a town called Rhodes;
Of riper years to Wittenberg he went,
Whereas his kinsmen chiefly brought him up.
So soon he profits in divinity,   15
The fruitful plot of scholarism graced,
That shortly he was graced with doctor's name,
Excelling all, whose sweet delight disputes
In heavenly matters of theology;
Till, swollen with cunning of a self-conceit,   20
His waxen wings did mount above his reach,
And melting heavens conspired his overthrow.
For, falling to a devilish exercise,
And glutted more with learning's golden gifts,
He surfeits upon cursed necromancy;   25
Nothing so sweet as magic is to him,
Which he prefers before his chiefest bliss;
And this the man that in his study sits.

Exit.

29f.   The sequence in Faustus' soliloquy may owe something to Lyly's *Euphues*: "Philosophie,
          Physicke, Divinitie, shal be my studie." (ed. Bond, i. 241). However, Lyly and Marlowe were
          probably drawing independently on commonplace formulations.

30   profess: teach, make one's profession (*OED* Profess. *v.* I. i.c and II. 6)

31   commenced: graduated as Master of Arts or Doctor (*OED* Commence. *v.* 4); another Cambridge
          usage (see note to 17).
          be a divine in show: this seems inconsistent with Faustus' assertion that "When all is done, divinity
          is best" (65). One explanation is that 31 contains a fossil-form of reference to *EFB*, which makes
          Faustus a necromancer from the beginning of his career: see J. A. Reynolds, "Be a divine . . .",
          ANQ 13 (1975), 131–33.

32   level: aim (*OED* Level. *v.* II. 6.d), with connotations of taking aim with a weapon (II. 7.b).

33–35   Faustus proclaims Aristotle, yet quotes from Aristotle's Renaissance adversary, Peter Ramus, in
          35. Explanations are offered by F. Burwick in "Marlowe's *Dr Faustus*: Two manners . . ." *NM* 70
          (1969), 121–45, at 125; and R. W. Dent in "Ramist Faustus or Ramist Marlowe?", *NM* 73 (1972),
          63–74.

35   *Bene disserere est finis logices*: to dispute well is the goal of logic. [A and B: *logicis*.]

37   miracle: in Christian tradition, an action or occurrence produced by the special intervention of
          God for a religious end.

40   *Oncaymaeon*: becomes *Oeconomy* in later editions. Bullen recognized the strange word as a
          phonetic transliteration of the Greek *on kai me on*, i.e. being and not being, a phrase from a
          Cambridge Ramist, Alexander Richardson. Dent, p. 70 (see note to 33–35).

41   *ubi desinit philosophus, ibi incipit medicus*: where the philosopher leaves off, the physician
          begins. Though adapted from Aristotle's *De Sensu* 436a, this saying seems to have been prover-
          bial; in a Paul's Cross sermon of 1578, Thomas White says: "Where the Philosopher ends, the
          Physition begyns, and after the Phisition, comes the Divine when senses and all are gone."

43   eternized: immortalized (see note to 52).

44–45   *Summum bonum medicinae sanitas*: the greatest good of medicine is health. In translating this
          axiom of Aristotle (*Nichomachean Ethics*, 1094.a.8), Faustus interpolates "our body's" and
          thereby interprets *sanitas* in a purely physical sense.

47   aphorisms: probably alluding to the *Aphorisms* of Hippocrates, the father of western medicine.

48   bills: prescriptions (*OED* Bill. *sb.* 3.5.b)
          plague: a general name for infections of epidemic proportions and with great mortality (*OED*
          Plague. *sb.* 3.a and b). Outbreaks caused the London theatres to be closed for extended periods,
          most notably in 1582 and 1592–94.

52–53   Faustus aspires to work miracles, apparently alluding to Christ's raising of Lazarus from the dead
          (John 11. 1–44).

55   Justinian: the emperor Justinian (483–565 A.D.) codified the entire system of Roman Law; the
          Institutes form a major part. Roman Law became highly influential again during the Renais-
          sance.

56–57   *Si una . . . valorum rei*: if one thing is bequeathed to two persons, one shall have the thing, the
          other the value of the thing. This passage, from the part of the *Institutes* (ii.20) which deals with
          impossible bequests, is not quoted exactly and seems to come from a sixteenth-century redaction
          of Roman Law.

Enter FAUSTUS *in his Study.*

FAUSTUS

Settle thy studies, Faustus, and begin
To sound the depth of that thou wilt profess.   30
Having commenced, be a divine in show,
Yet level at the end of every art,
And live and die in Aristotle's works.
Sweet *Analytics,* 'tis thou hast ravished me:
Bene disserere est finis logices.   35
Is to dispute well logic's chiefest end?
Affords this art no greater miracle?
Then read no more, thou hast attained the end;
A greater subject fitteth Faustus' wit.
Bid *Oncaymaeon* farewell; Galen, come: 40
Seeing *ubi desinit philosophus, ibi incipit medicus.*
Be a physician, Faustus, heap up gold,
And be eternized for some wondrous cure.
Summum bonum medicinae sanitas:
The end of physic is our bodies' health.   45
Why, Faustus, hast thou not attained that end?
Is not thy common talk sound aphorisms?
Are not thy bills hung up as monuments,
Whereby whole cities have escaped the plague
And thousand desperate maladies been eased?   50
Yet art thou still but Faustus, and a man.
Wouldst thou make man to live eternally?
Or, being dead, raise them to life again?
Then this profession were to be esteemed.
Physic farewell! Where is Justinian?   55
Si una eademque res legatur duobus,
Alter rem, alter valorum rei . . .
A petty case of paltry legacies.
Exhereditare filium non potest pater nisi . . .

59-64   *Exhereditare filium non potest pater nisi* . . .: a father cannot disinherit his son unless . . . (*Institutes* ii.13). In Roman Law there was a very strong presumption in favour of the natural heir. Renaissance jurists admired Roman Law as being compatible with Christian ethics. A reads *exhaereditari*.

61   Law [B; A Church]: though emended to "law" by later editors, "Church" is defensible: Faustus would have been grounded in Canon Law at Wittenberg, and Justinian's *Institutes* were a basic Canon Law text.

62   This [B; A, His].

64   Too servile [B; The Diuell A]: the A-text is clearly wrong here; the B-text editor substituted the most likely assonant word. In Elizabethan English, "servile" would have been pronounced as though spelt "servill".

66   Jerome's Bible: attaining approximately final form in the sixth century, it was the only widely available version of Holy Scripture before the vernacular translations of the Reformation and Renaissance.

67-70   Faustus is quoting, first from Romans 6.23 and then from 1 John 1.8, but neither quotation is exact. See J. C. Maxwell, "Notes on *Dr Faustus*", *NQ*, NS11 (1964) 262. Both quotations are out of context: each passage is half of an antithetically-balanced statement; the quoted portions emphasize man's sinfulness, but the omitted portions affirm God's mercy and forgiveness.

68   death: spiritual death, i.e. damnation, though the fact of physical death was attributed to the original sin of Adam and Eve.

75   Ay [A and B, I]: The A-text conventionally prints "I" for the affirmative interjection. We have silently emended in all subsequent occurrences.

77   Divinity, adieu: Faustus returns the study of divinity to God, i.e. *à Dieu*.

79   Metaphorically, these "heavenly" books represent the fallen world: see Curtius, "The Book as Symbol", *European Literature and the Latin Middle Ages* (New York, 1953), 302-47. See 607-28 and note,
[A, Negromantike].

80   lines: as used in geomancy, the art of divination by means of signs derived from the earth: "Geomancie is a Science and Art which consisteth of points, prickes, and lines, made in steade of the foure elements." See Francis Sparry, trans. *Cattan's Geomancie* (1591), 1.
circles: a standard term in astrology and astronomy (*OED* Circle. *sb*. 2.a) and therefore complementary to the "lines" of geomancy, but also commonly applied to rites of magic and necromancy (*OED* Circle. *sb*. 3).
scenes: a problematical word, omitted from B. Greg and Gill reasonably suggest "signs", but until late seventeenth century "sayings" would have been a closer homophone, in that "scenes" was rhymed with "trains" (See Dryden, *The Works of Virgil*, "*Georgics*" III. 38). A meaning of "sayings" contemporary with Marlowe was "spells" or "incantations" (*OED* saying. *vbl. sb.* 2.d).
letters: magicians used combinations of the letters forming the name of God in conjuring devils.
characters: cabbalistic or magical signs; also the astrological symbols of planets (*OED* Character. *sb*. 1.5)

84   artisan: one who practises or cultivates an art.

82-84   Possibly an allusion to Mark 8.36: "For what shal it profite a man, thogh he shoulde winne the whole worlde, if he lose his soule?". See note to 1426-34.

86   command: a general distinction between religion and magic is that the religious person prays in supplication, whereas the magician believes he has the power to command supernatural forces. The magician's aspirations are burlesqued in the comic scenes.

88   Raising the wind and rending the clouds are traditional images for the power of God: see Psalm 147, Genesis 8.1, Isaiah 27.8, Proverbs 30.4, Ecclesiastes 5.16, Micah 2.11, and Matthew 8.26; magicians commonly claim such powers, as does Prospero in Shakespeare's *The Tempest*.

90   Man's aspiring nature is a recurrent motif in Marlowe's plays, as in *1 Tamburlaine* II. vii. 18-20.

92   The play's *exordium*, or introductory prelude, ends at this point. For discussion see R. W. Ingram, "Pride in Learning Goeth Before a Fall': Dr Faustus' Opening Soliloquy," *Mosaic* 13 (1979-80), 73-80; C. L. Summers and T.-L. Pebworth "The Conversion of St Augustine and the B-Text of *Doctor Faustus*," *RRWL* 1, ii (1979), 1-8; and J. A. Reynolds "Faustus' flawed Learning," *ES* (1976), 329-36.

Such is the subject of the *Institute*   60
And universal body of the Law.
This study fits a mercenary drudge,
Who aims at nothing but external trash,
Too servile and illiberal for me.
When all is done, divinity is best.   65
Jerome's Bible, Faustus, view it well:
Stipendium peccati mors est. Ha! *Stipendium . . .*
The reward of sin is death: that's hard.
Si peccasse negamus, fallimur,
Et nulla est in nobis veritas: 70
If we say that we have no sin,
We deceive ourselves, and there's no truth in us.
Why then, belike we must sin,
And so consequently die.
Ay, we must die an everlasting death.   75
What doctrine call you this — *Che sera, sera?*
What will be, shall be? Divinity, adieu.
These metaphysics of magicians
And necromantic books are heavenly.
Lines, circles, scenes, letters, and characters: 80
Ay, these are those that Faustus most desires.
O what a world of profit and delight,
Of power, of honour, of omnipotence,
Is promised to the studious artisan?
All things that move between the quiet poles   85
Shall be at my command. Emperors and kings
Are but obeyed in their several provinces,
Nor can they raise the wind or rend the clouds;
But his dominion that exceeds in this
Stretcheth as far as doth the mind of man.   90
A sound magician is a mighty god:
Here, Faustus, try thy brains to gain a deity.

93   Wagner: the pronunciation of his name would have been anglicized in Marlowe's day, i.e. first
          syllable as in English "wag". See note to 8.

94   Valdes and Cornelius: no plausible historical attribution for Valdes has been suggested.
          Cornelius cannot be the occultist Cornelius Agrippa (see 146 and note), but by Marlowe's time
          the name would have had a suitable resonance for anyone wishing to establish himself as a magi-
          cian. See Ransom, Cooke and Pearce, *NQ* NS(9) (1962), 329-31.

98.1   Good Angel and Evil Angel: allegorical figures as externalized forces of internal conflict were
          common in the religious morality plays of the fifteenth century, e.g. *The Castle of Perseverance*
          (c. 1410-25) and the convention continued in secularized drama thereafter, e.g. Skelton's *Mag-
          nyfycence* (c. 1515-18). The *Psychomachia* (= spiritual battle) by the early Christian writer,
          Prudentius, is generally regarded as a source for this allegorical motif.

99-104   Damned book . . . scriptures . . . nature's treasury: in popular Christian tradition, Adam's sin
          infected nature as well as himself and nature fell with him, partaking in his corruption. In the
          Ptolemaic astronomic system, which was interpreted in spiritual terms, all created matter
          beneath the sphere of the moon was mutable and corrupted by the fall. This dichotomy led to the
          concept of two sorts of knowledge—*sapientia*, true wisdom, which was obtained by reading the
          book of God's word (The Bible) and listening to God's universal law (one's conscience); and *scien-
          tia*, profane knowledge, which was pursued by reading the devil's book, i.e. the physical corrupt
          world of nature. Renaissance magi and proto-scientists set out to prove that nature was not
          entirely corrupt but an alternative source of divine illumination written in coded signs or "hiero-
          glyphs". Faustus' Good Angel is not so sure.

105   Jove: this pagan name for the chief of the Roman gods was frequently applied to the Christian
          God, not only as an exercise in syncretism but also to avert accusations of blasphemy. Man's
          desire to usurp the role of God was part of the temptation to which Adam succumbed: see Genesis
          3.5. As Roma Gill succinctly points out: "there is special force in this, coming from the Evil
          Angel."

106   commander: the Evil Angel reminds Faustus that the magician is not a dependent suppliant
          before supernatural powers, but rather their controller (see note to 86).

107   glutted: since it involved the eating of forbidden fruit (Genesis 3.6) gluttony was often thought to
          be the original sin; but it was also traditional to see Adam's and Eve's sin as the epitome of all the
          seven deadly sins. See 18-26 and note.

Enter WAGNER.

Wagner, commend me to my dearest friends,
The German Valdes and Cornelius;
Request them earnestly to visit me.   95

WAGNER
I will, sir.

Exit.

FAUSTUS
Their conference will be a greater help to me
Than all my labours, plod I ne'er so fast.

Enter the GOOD ANGEL *and the* EVIL ANGEL.

GOOD ANGEL
O Faustus, lay that damned book aside
And gaze not on it, lest it tempt thy soul   100
And heap God's heavy wrath upon thy head.
Read, read the scriptures; that is blasphemy.

EVIL ANGEL
Go forward, Faustus, in that famous art
Wherein all nature's treasury is contained:
Be thou on earth as Jove is in the sky,   105
Lord and commander of these elements.

Exeunt.

FAUSTUS
How am I glutted with conceit of this!

109   ambiguities: uncertainties. It is a commonplace of Renaissance thought that man's position in the world is ambiguous: unlike other earthly inhabitants, he was seen to be part flesh and part spirit; mortal because of his fallen fleshly nature and immortal in his soul; and, in his fallen state, uncertain of his spiritual salvation or damnation. Ambiguity is also inherent within the occultist and Neoplatonist traditions, where aspects of the fallen world could be moralized *in bono* or *in malo*, i.e. favourably or unfavourably.

110   desperate: in this context, simply "risky" or "reckless" but with connotations of being done in a state of spiritual despair (*OED* Desperate. *a*.4 and 5).

114   delicates: delicacies.

117   Possibly an allusion to Greene's *Friar Bacon and Friar Bungay* (before 1592); Friar Bacon planned to "circle England round with brass" through magic.

119   public schools: university lecture rooms.
          skill: emended by Dyce and later editors to "silk". Nashe's marginalia include the enigmatic jotting: "Faustus: studie in indian silke." However, in *The Rape of Lucrece* Shakespeare speaks of "skill-contending schools" (1018), meaning cleverness, expertness, or special knowledge (*OED* Skill. *sb*. 5, 6, and 7).

120   bravely: splendidly. Students were required to wear plain dress in Marlowe's day.

122   Prince of Parma: Spanish governor-general of the Netherlands from 1579 to 1592. The reference is topical, for Parma was to have participated in the invasion of England with the Armada in 1588.

124   engines: machines.
          brunt: assault, fury.

125   fiery keel: the Netherlanders had used a fireship to destroy a bridge built by their Spanish overlord when he blockaded Antwerp in 1585.

132   fantasy: in scholastic psychology, the faculty by which objects are perceived (*OED* Fantasy. *sb*. 1.*a*).

134   necromantic [Negromantique A]: see note to 25.

Shall I make spirits fetch me what I please,
Resolve me of all ambiguities,
Perform what desperate enterprise I will? 110
I'll have them fly to India for gold,
Ransack the ocean for orient pearl,
And search all corners of the new-found world
For pleasant fruits and princely delicates.
I'll have them read me strange philosophy, 115
And tell the secrets of all foreign kings.
I'll have them wall all Germany with brass,
And make swift Rhine circle fair Wittenberg.
I'll have them fill the public schools with skill,
Wherewith the students shall be bravely clad. 120
I'll levy soldiers with the coin they bring,
And chase the Prince of Parma from our land,
And reign sole king of all our provinces.
Yea, stranger engines for the brunt of war
Than was the fiery keel at Antwerp's bridge 125
I'll make my servile spirits to invent.
Come, German Valdes and Cornelius,
And make me blest with your sage conference.
Valdes, sweet Valdes, and Cornelius,

Enter VALDES *and* CORNELIUS.

Know that your words have won me at the last 130
To practise magic and concealed arts;
Yet not your words only, but mine own fantasy,
That will receive no object for my head,
But ruminates on necromantic skill.
Philosophy is odious and obscure; 135
Both law and physic are for petty wits;
Divinity is basest of the three,
Unpleasant, harsh, contemptible, and vile:

141   concise syllogisms [Consissylogismes A]: succinct logical arguments.

142   gravelled: confounded, nonplussed, perplexed (*OED* Gravel. *v.* 4).

144   problems: in the special, scholastic sense of questions proposed for discussion (*OED* Problem. 2).

145   Musaeus: a legendary pre-Homeric poet, who, in Virgil's *Aeneid* (VI. 666-67) guides Aeneas through the underworld to find his dead father Anchises. Marlowe may be conflating this incident with the story of Orpheus, tutor of Musaeus, who descended into Hades where he charmed the spirits with his song in order to rescue his wife Eurydice (see Ovid, *Metamorphoses* X. 1-68), for, in the Renaissance, Orpheus was thought to be the originator of the occult Neoplatonic tradition and his visit to Hades was allegorized as the initiate's mystic death to his old life and rebirth into a new. Alternatively, Marlowe may be allowing Faustus to blur distinctions between heaven and hell, as he does elsewhere (see 303), for Virgil placed Musaeus among the happy souls. See B. Fabian, "A Note on Marlowe's *Faustus*," *ES*, 41 (1960), 365-68.

146   Agrippa: Henry Cornelius Agrippa von Nettesheim (1486-1535), author of the *De Occulta Philosophia* and the *De Vanitate Scientiarum*, was a central figure for the Renaissance vision of the magus. See Charles G. Nauert Jr., *Agrippa and the Crisis of Renaissance Thought* (Urbana, 1965); D. P. Walker, *Spiritual and Demonic Magic from Ficino to Campanella* (Notre Dame, 1958; and Frances Yates, *The Occult Philosophy in the Elizabethan Age* (London, 1979).

147   shadows: spectral forms or phantoms: probably used by Marlowe as a synonym for "familiars" (*OED* Shadow. *sb.* 7).

150   Indian Moors: Moors were any dark-skinned people; here specifically American Indians.

151   spirits [B; A, subjects].
     every element: matter was still thought to be compounded of the four elements, a concept going back to Empedocles (5th century B.C.) and elaborated by Aristotle. In alchemical theory, each element was presided over by an immanent class of being (Valdes' "spirits") which resided in it. Alchemy consisted of two levels of apprehension: the *exoteric*, which sought to create perfect metal, gold, by restructuring the proportions of the elements within a given base metal; and the *esoteric*, which was concerned with psychic and spiritual transmutations within the practitioner. Shakespeare's Prospero in *The Tempest* may be thought of as an *esoteric* or spiritual alchemist, whereas Faustus and Ben Jonson's Subtle in *The Alchemist* may be thought of as *exoteric* or materialist alchemists. See E. J. Holmyard, *Alchemy* (Harmondsworth: Penguin, 1957), and Jeffrey Hart, "Prospero and Faustus", *BUSE* 2 (1956-57), 197-206. See also note to 755-56.

152, 177   us three . . . we three: Cornelius and Valdes do not reappear in the play, and their function here seems to be primarily numerical, i.e. to suggest a parodic trinity in the Faustian anti-world.

154   Almaine rutters: German cavalrymen.

155   Lapland giants: in an earlier play Marlowe speaks of the Arctic region as being "Inhabited with tall and sturdy men" (*2 Tamburlaine*, I. i.27); giants are common in Norse mythology. Lapland was frequently associated with witchcraft and sorcery.

158   the white breasts [A, their].

159   Venice: in Marlowe's time the wealthiest mercantile city in Europe and as such caught the imagination of Elizabethan dramatists: see Shakespeare's *The Merchant of Venice* and Ben Jonson's *Volpone*.
     argosies: large merchant ships.
     drag [B; A, dregge].

160-161   America's tribute to Philip of Spain is compared with the legendary booty of Jason and his Argonauts. Renaissance yearning for renewal of the heroic age of Greece is evident here. The proximity of argosies (159) to golden fleece (160) does not mean that Marlowe confused argosy with Jason's ship the *Argo*, but rather that in keeping with rhetorical practice he used the sound of a word to anticipate another, thereby linking and mutually enriching two ideas.
     stuffs: an important clue to the relatively early date of the copy from which the A-text was printed. Philip died in 1598 and B-text alters "stuffs" to "stuffed".

'Tis magic, magic that hath ravished me.
Then, gentle friends, aid me in this attempt;   140
And I, that have with concise syllogisms
Gravelled the pastors of the German church
And made the flowering pride of Wittenberg
Swarm to my problems, as the infernal spirits
On sweet Musaeus when he came to hell,   145
Will be as cunning as Agrippa was,
Whose shadows made all Europe honour him.

VALDES

Faustus, these books, thy wit, and our experience
Shall make all nations to canonize us.
As Indian Moors obey their Spanish lords,   150
So shall the spirits of every element
Be always serviceable to us three;
Like lions shall they guard us when we please,
Like Almaine rutters with their horsemen's staves,
Or Lapland giants trotting by our sides;   155
Sometimes like women, or unwedded maids,
Shadowing more beauty in their airy brows
Than in the white breasts of the Queen of Love.
From Venice shall they drag huge argosies,
And from America the golden fleece   160
That yearly stuffs old Philip's treasury,
If learned Faustus will be resolute.

FAUSTUS

Valdes, as resolute am I in this
As thou to live; therefore object it not.

167   The status of astrology was controversial; it was becoming less universally accepted, but Shakespeare and many of his contemporaries seem to have accepted a modified form of it. See D. C. Allen, *The Star-Crossed Renaissance* (Durham, N. Carolina, 1941).

168   Enriched with tongues: the three biblical languages of Latin, Greek, and Hebrew were also used in the arcane diction of magical practices; magicians thought that these languages contained the word of God in its essential form, which could then be manipulated to magical ends. See 246-47, where Faustus anagrammatizes the Hebrew name of Jehovah. He conjures his devil in Latin (254f.). The shamanistic languages of the magus are ridiculed in the comic sub-plot (1015f.) well-seen in minerals: well-informed about the properties of minerals; see note to 151. in [B; not in A].

171   mystery: in the dual sense of (1) that which can only be comprehended through faith and (2) a technical trade secret (*OED* Mystery. *sb*. 1, 2 and 3; *sb*. 2, 2*a* and *b*.)

172   the Delphian oracle: the famous oracle of Apollo at Delphi was revered among occultists. The predictive powers of "sacred Delphos . . . Apollo's temple" were to be invoked by Leontes in *The Winter's Tale* (II. i.184).

180   lusty: "little" in A2 and A3; "bushy" in B1. Evidently the usage puzzled later editors, but lusty may simply mean pleasant (*OED* Lusty. *a*.2).
    grove: in English versions of The Bible from Coverdale (1535) to the Authorized Version (1611), the Hebrew *Asherah*, now understood to be the name of a goddess or a pillar serving as an idol, was mistranslated as "grove" (*OED* Grove. 2). Consequently, there was an implied connection between groves and rites frowned upon by Jewish religion. See, for example, Coverdale's version of 1 Kings 18.10: ". . . the foure hundreth and fiftye prophetes of Baal, and the four hundreth prophetes of ye grove, which eate at Jesabel's table." Perhaps the error was reinforced by the received tradition that druids of pre-Christian religion had worshipped their vegetation gods in groves.

183   Roger Bacon (c. 1212-92) was a scholar whose expertise in several fields earned him the title of *Doctor Mirabilis*. He united an unusual interest in mathematics and the history of science with a thorough-going (for his age) practicality and pragmatism. He is often compared with his later namesake, and Marlowe's contemporary, Francis Bacon, in his empirical approach. Bacon was a controversial figure: he attacked many of his contemporaries and his own works were widely condemned. In his chief work, the *Opus Maius*, Roger Bacon denounces both popular and learned ignorance; champions the intellectual vigour of Aristotle and the medieval Arab philosophers who followed him; appeals for reason in interpreting scripture; defends pagan philosophy; urges modern studies, including optics and the invention of explosives; and insists that speculation should be verified by experiment. Bacon was regarded in the Renaissance as a proto-magus who dabbled in black magic and was protagonist in Robert Greene's play *Friar Bacon and Friar Bungay*, written about the same time as *Dr Faustus*.
    Albanus: probably Pietro d'Abano (c. 1250-1316), humanist and physician; widely known for medical amulets and believed to have been a conjuror.

184   Hebrew Psalter: the Book of Psalms, which would have been of especial significance to the magician because the psalms were attributed to David, whom syncretist magicians identified with Orpheus (see note to 145).
    New Testament: the opening words of St John's gospel were regularly used in conjuration (Ward). Notice the combination of this work (in Greek), with the Hebrew version of the Old Testament and the Latin works of Bacon and Abano; and see note to 168.

189   cunning: see note to 20. In Elizabethan England, a fortune teller, conjuror, wizard, or witch, was often called a "cunning man" or "cunning woman".

CORNELIUS

The miracles that magic will perform   165
Will make thee vow to study nothing else.
He that is grounded in astrology,
Enriched with tongues, well seen [in] minerals,
Hath all the principles magic doth require:
Then doubt not, Faustus, but to be renowned   170
And more frequented for this mystery
Than heretofore the Delphian oracle.
The spirits tell me they can dry the sea
And fetch the treasure of all foreign wrecks,
Ay, all the wealth that our forefathers hid   175
Within the massy entrails of the earth.
Then tell me, Faustus, what shall we three want?

FAUSTUS

Nothing, Cornelius! O, this cheers my soul!
Come, show me some demonstrations magical,
That I may conjure in some lusty grove   180
And have these joys in full possession.

VALDES

Then haste thee to some solitary grove,
And bear wise Bacon's and Albanus' works,
The Hebrew Psalter, and New Testament;
And whatsoever else is requisite   185
We will inform thee ere our conference cease.

CORNELIUS

Valdes, first let him know the words of art,
And then, all other ceremonies learned,
Faustus may try his cunning by himself.

190   rudiments: the first principles of a subject (*OED* Rudiment. 1); also the special meaning in magic
           of "all that which is vulgarly the vertue of worde, herbe, & stone: which is used by unlawful
           charmes, without natural causes . . . such kinde of charmes as commonlie daft wives use" James I,
           Demonology, ed. G. B. Harrison, p. 11.

193   canvass every quiddity: examine every part; quiddity is a scholastic term.

195.2   Just as the Good and Evil Angels provide a morality-play symmetry, so this pair of scholars
           balances the wicked duo of Valdes and Cornelius. There is no need to suppose specific or consis-
           tent identities for these or subsequent scholars (e.g. at 1406f.); they are merely embodiments of
           the academic life.

197   *sic probo*: thus I prove it; a term used in scholastic debate.

200f.   In this scene Wagner apes his master's pretensions and aspirations in the manner of the *zanni* (=
           zany), or servant-clown, from the *Commedia dell'Arte*. Later scenes in the comic sub-plot are
           constructed around the same motif. The *Commedia* was well known in England by Marlowe's
           time and influenced other dramatists, including Shakespeare.

VALDES

First I'll instruct thee in the rudiments, 190
And then wilt thou be perfecter than I.

FAUSTUS

Then come and dine with me, and after meat
We'll canvass every quiddity thereof:
For ere I sleep I'll try what I can do;
This night I'll conjure, though I die therefore. 195

Exeunt.

Enter two SCHOLARS

FIRST SCHOLAR

I wonder what's become of Faustus, that was wont
to make our schools ring with *sic probo.*

SECOND SCHOLAR

That shall we know, for see — here comes his boy.

Enter WAGNER

FIRST SCHOLAR

How now, sirrah, where's thy master?

WAGNER

God in heaven knows. 200

SECOND SCHOLAR

Why, dost not thou know?

206   licentiate: of graduate status; one received a licence from the university to proceed to a higher degree.

215   dunces: originally a nickname for followers of Duns Scotus (c. 1266–1308) and by Marlowe's time applied pejoratively to old-fashioned scholastic cavillers and dull pedants unable to absorb new learning (*OED* Dunce. 3, 4, and 5).

216-17   *corpus naturale . . . mobile*: a scholastic adaptation from Aristotle's definition of physics as the study of things that are natural and capable of movement.

WAGNER

Yes, I know, but that follows not.

FIRST SCHOLAR

Go to, sirrah, leave your jesting, and tell us
where he is.

WAGNER

That follows not necessary by force of argument, that you being licentiate should stand
upon't. Therefore, acknowledge your error and
be attentive.

SECOND SCHOLAR

Why, didst thou not say thou knewst?

WAGNER

Have you any witness on't?

FIRST SCHOLAR

Yes, sirrah, I heard you.

WAGNER

Ask my fellow if I be a thief.

SECOND SCHOLAR

Well, you will not tell us.

WAGNER

Yes, sir, I will tell you. Yet if you were not
dunces you would not ask me such a question:
for is not he *corpus naturale,* and is not that
mobile? Then wherefore should you ask me

218   phlegmatic: phlegm, in medieval physiology, was one of four bodily fluids or "humours". Persons in whom phlegm predominated were inclined to indolence or sloth, one of the Seven Deadly Sins (see 741f.). See also note on cover illustration.

219   wrath . . . lechery: two of the Seven Deadly Sins.

221   place of execution: the inner room where the magicians are gathered. But Wagner's prediction that the two overly-inquisitive scholars are likely to be hanged at the next sessions (court sitting) is a reminder that execution in another sense awaits magicians, conjurors, and other persons seeking forbidden knowledge.

224   precisian: a Puritan; many Puritans were implacably opposed to the performance of drama and it is hardly surprising that they are ridiculed by most of the dramatists, e.g. Shakespeare in *Twelfth Night* and Jonson in *The Alchemist* and *Bartholomew Fair*. See also note to 767-74.

such a question? But that I am by nature phlegmatic, slow to wrath, and prone to lechery — to
love, I would say — it were not for you to come   220
within forty foot of the place of execution,
although I do not doubt to see you both hanged
the next sessions. Thus having triumphed over
you, I will set my countenance like a precisian,
and begin to speak thus: truly, my dear brethren,   225
my master is within at dinner with Valdes and
Cornelius, as this wine — if it could speak — it
would inform your worships; and so the Lord bless
you, preserve you, and keep you, my dear brethren, my dear brethren.   230

Exit

FIRST SCHOLAR

Nay then, I fear he is fallen into that damned art,
for which they two are infamous through the world.

SECOND SCHOLAR

Were he a stranger, and not allied to me, yet
should I grieve for him. But come, let us go and
inform the Rector, and see if he by his grave   235
counsel can reclaim him.

FIRST SCHOLAR

O but I fear me nothing can reclaim him.

SECOND SCHOLAR

Yet let us try what we can do.

Exeunt.

239-42 A difficult passage. In Thomas Bowes' *De La Primaudeye's French Academie* (1589; III. xxxvii) night is also described as "the shadow of the earth." Faustus is evidently conjuring during an eclipse.

240   The constellation of Orion in the ascendant was popularly associated with rain.

242   welkin: sky.

246   Magicians traditionally performed their rites within a circle, an image of infinity and eternity, being without discernible beginning or end (see Plato, *The Symposium*, 189d-193e). In *As You Like It*, Orlando alludes to "a great magician, Obscured in the circle of this forest" (V. iv. 31-34) to account for the enchanted milieu of the Forest of Arden.

246-47 Names in themselves were thought to have especial power (see Genesis 2.19-20). Anagrammatizing the name of God, i.e. pulling it apart and reforming it in different combinations, was a magical way of gaining power and it is to this practice which Mephostophiles later refers as "racking" (287) the name of God. See Introduction, part 5.

247   anagrammatized [B; A, and Agramithist].

248   breviated: abbreviated or abridged; an unusual contraction, probably introduced for word-play, similar to Breviary, the book of readings for each day set for those in Holy Orders.

249   Figures: an astrological term to describe the disposition of the heavens at any given time (*OED* Figure. *sb*. 14).

250   A modern rendition of this line: "And astrological symbols [characters] of the Zodiac [signs] and planets [erring stars]." The planets were though to wander from their proper orbits, hence "erring" from the Latin *errare*, to wander.

251   On the enforced rising of spirits, see K. A. Nowotny, "The Construction of Certain Seals and Characters in the Work of Agrippa of Nettesheim," *JWCI* 12 (1949), 46-57, together with I. R. F. Calder's short note in the same issue, pp 1-4. See also note to 86.

254-262 *Sint mihi . . . Mephostophiles*: May the gods of Acheron be propitious to me. May the triple spirit of Jehovah be gone! Spirits of fire, air, and water, hail! Prince of the East, Beelzebub, monarch of burning hell, and Demogorgon [Demigorgon in A, B], favour us so that Mephostophiles may appear and rise! Why do you delay? By Jehovah, Gehenna, and the holy water which I now sprinkle; and by the sign of the cross which I now make; and by our prayers, may Mephostophiles himself now arise at our command! (Editors' translation).
        Faustus' invocation is modelled loosely on the ninth-century Latin hymn, *Veni creator spiritus*, used at ordinations and consecrations. It was commonly supposed that spirits preferred being addressed in Latin (see note to 168). In Marlowe's England this preference would have reinforced Protestant suspicion about the Roman Catholic Church.

255   *Ignei, aerii, aquatani*: some editors add *terreni* to complete the roll-call of the four elements, but there is no textual authority for the addition.
        appareat [B; apariat in A].

258   Mephostophiles: the name, which occurs in the *Historia* and *EFB* as Mephostophiles, has been spelt in many different ways. See J. Goebel, "The Etymology of Mephistopheles", *TPAPA* 35 (1904), 148-56. All theories must be treated with caution. In the absence of more compelling criteria we have followed Marlowe's source. A's spelling is not consistent.

258 59 *Quid tu moraris?*: from the gibberish of the original A-reading of *quod tumeraris* early editors extracted the probable reconstruction given here, meaning "Why do you delay?" The magician's impatience at the conjured spirit's delay in manifesting itself is a common motif. See P. H. Kocher, *Christopher Marlowe* (Chapel Hill, 1946), pp. 157-58.

256 58 Lucifer is usually designated as Prince of the East (Isaiah 14.12), but in A1 and B1 the title is given to Beelzebub. Demogorgon is first mentioned by the Scholiast on Statius *Theb*. IV. 516 as the Greek infernal deity involved in magic rites. See also notes to 297 and 303.

262   dicatis [B; dicaetis in A].

Enter FAUSTUS *to conjure.*

FAUSTUS

Now that the gloomy shadow of the earth,
Longing to view Orion's drizzling look,   240
Leaps from th'antarctic world unto the sky
And dims the welkin with her pitchy breath,
Faustus, begin thine incantations
And try if devils will obey thy hest,
Seeing thou hast prayed and sacrificed to them.   245
Within this circle is Jehovah's name,
Forward and backward, anagrammatized;
The breviated names of holy saints,
Figures of every adjunct to the heavens,
And characters of signs and erring stars,   250
By which the spirits are enforced to rise.
Then fear not, Faustus, but be resolute
And try the uttermost magic can perform.

Sint mihi dei Acherontis propitii, valeat numen
triplex Jehovae! Ignei, aerii, aquatani spiritus   255
salvete! Orientis princeps Beelzebub, inferni
ardentis monarcha, et Demogorgon, propitiamus
vos ut appareat et surgat Mephostophiles! Quid tu
moraris? Per Jehovam, Gehennam, et consecratam
aquam, quam nunc spargo; signumque crucis   260
quod nunc facio; et per vota nostra, ipse nunc
surgat, nobis dicatus, Mephostophiles!

Enter a DEVIL.

I charge thee to return and change thy shape,
Thou art too ugly to attend on me.
Go, and return an old Franciscan friar: 265

267   virtue: occult efficacy or power (obsolete meaning, but current in Marlowe's day) as well as moral excellence (*OED* Virtue. *sb.* 3 and 9).

272   Now [A2; A1 No].

270-73   obedience . . . force of magic . . . command: another statement of faith in magical powers (see 86 and note).

274   *Quin redis, Mephostophiles, fratris imagine!:* Why do you not return, Mephostophiles, in the shape of a friar? See note to lines 923f. A1 has *regis*; this does not make sense in the context and Boas sensibly emends to *redis*.

275   Mephostophiles' first words echo St Paul's first words to Christ on the road to Damascus, as reported in Acts 9.6. See M. P. O'Brien, "Christian Belief in *Dr Faustus*", *ELH* 37(1970), 1-11.

276-79   The successful magician was believed to have power over the elements. See P. H. Kocher, *Christopher Marlowe* (Chapel Hill, 1946), p. 141. In most cosmogonies, including the Graeco-Roman and the Christian, the universe originates in chaos and is prevented from returning to chaos only by the controlling force of divine harmony. In Renaissance drama, reversion to chaos is a ubiquitous image for the frustration of Divine Providence (see *Othello* III. iii. 92 and *Macbeth* II. iv. 1-20).

280-82   Mephostophiles tells an unpalatable truth that refutes Faustus' ambitions for himself as magician. On the motif of the truthful devil, see H. Seiferth, "The Concept of the Devil . . . Prior to Goethe", *Monatschafte* 44 (1952), 271-89.

That holy shape becomes a devil best.

Exit DEVIL.

I see there's virtue in my heavenly words!
Who would not be proficient in this art?
How pliant is this Mephostophiles,
Full of obedience and humility.   270
Such is the force of magic and my spells.
Now, Faustus, thou art conjuror laureate,
That canst command great Mephostophiles!
Quin redis, Mephostophiles, fratris imagine!

Enter MEPHOSTOPHILES.

MEPHOSTOPHILES

Now, Faustus, what wouldst thou have me do?   275

FAUSTUS

I charge thee wait upon me whilst I live,
To do whatever Faustus shall command,
Be it to make the moon drop from her sphere,
Or the ocean to overwhelm the world.

MEPHOSTOPHILES

I am a servant to great Lucifer   280
And may not follow thee without his leave:
No more than he commands must we perform.

FAUSTUS

Did not he charge thee to appear to me?

284   An instance of what P. H. Kocher calls the "doctrine of voluntary ascent" (*Christopher Marlowe*, Chapel Hill, 1946), p. 160. This doctrine was fairly common.

286   cause . . . *per accidens* [B, A *per accident*]: one of the "vermiculate questions" for which Marlowe's contemporary, Francis Bacon, castigated traditional philosophy was the unnecessary proliferation of intellectual categories. Garbed as a friar, Mephostophiles demonstrates that he is quite at home with medieval scholastic distinctions, of which Francis Bacon said: "Admirable for the fineness of thread and work, but of no substance or profit." Aristotle had laid down the categories of causes (efficient, formal, final, and material) in *Metaphysics* I, 1-10; for his distinction between "proper" and "accidental" causes, see V.2. Compare Faustus' "conjuring speeches" (285) with the semi-literate gibberish of Robin, which seemingly succeeds in raising Mephostophiles against his will (1032-34); the inconsistency suggests that the later passage is considerably contaminated.

287   rack: pull or tear apart, break up (*OED* Rack. *p.* 3.2.b); probably alluding to Faustus' anagrammatizing of Jehovah's name (246-47).

293   abjure the Trinity: the seminal text for the doctrine of the Trinity in the early Church was Matthew 28.19, which also institutes the sacrament of baptism. Thus to reject the Trinity is also to reject one's membership in the Church through baptism. Faustus has already abjured the Holy Trinity implicitly by setting up one of his own with Valdes and Cornelius and also by invoking the three demons, Lucifer, Beelzebub, and Demogorgon (see 256-57). The powers of darkness were commonly supposed to revere an infernal trinity, though there was no agreement on its composition.

295-96   Rendered as one line in A1 and B1.

297   chief . . . Beelzebub: Faustus may seem to be confusing Beelzebub with Lucifer (see 256-58 with note), but in Matt. 12.24-28, Mark 3.22-26, and Luke 11.15-20 the names Satan, Lucifer, and Beelzebub are all used for the chief of devils.

298   dedicate: a word rich in religious associations, as in initiation into an order, the offering of a sacrifice, and the sacramental vows of Baptism and Confirmation.

300   confounds hell in Elysium: identifies hell with Elysium; Faustus asserts a pre-Christian world view and a vision of the after-life based upon such morally neutral descriptions as that of Virgil in *Aeneid* VI. Confound may mean "mix" or "mingle" (*OED* Confound. *v.* 6) but the meaning of "confuse" is also current in Marlowe's time (*OED* Confound. *v.* 7).

301   the old philosophers: may refer to (1) those pagan philosophers who did not believe in eternal punishment (see J. C. Maxwell, "Two Notes on Marlowe's *Faustus*, *NQ* 194 [1949], 334-35 and J. M. Steadman, "Averroes and *Dr Faustus*: Some Additional Parallels", *NQ* NS9[1962]); or (2) more specifically, the magically-minded pagan philosophers (see T. McAlindon, "Classical Mythology and Christian Tradition in Marlowe's *Dr Faustus*", *PMLA* 81[1966], 214-23); or (3) those who, having lived before the coming of Christ, will spend eternity in Limbo, without punishment but not in the vision of God. Line 301 may also be meant to accord with the views of Averroes, the medieval Arab philosopher who did not believe in the survival of individuality after death but who did believe in a corporate, unindividuated survival (see J. M. Steadman, "Faustus and Averroes", *NQ* NS3 [1956], 416).

303   Lucifer thy lord: Lucifer (= light-bearer) is an epithet in Isaiah 14.12 for the King of Babylon, whose fall was often interpreted as symbolizing that of the prince of devils, e.g. by St Jerome and other Fathers of the early Church. Elsewhere Lucifer is associated with Christ as "day star" (see 2 Peter 1.19 and Rev. 22.16). See note to 297.

305   Lucifer is still an angel, though fallen. The essential nature has not been destroyed though its spiritual direction has been perverted. St Thomas Aquinas taught that the angelic will differs from the human will in that one evil act forever fixes the angelic disposition, whereas the human will becomes fixed only at death (*Summa Theologiae* Ia, Q.64, art. 2). Milton describes the essential nature of the fallen angels in *Paradise Lost* I, 589-94 and offers an explanation for their inability to repent or be forgiven in *Paradise Lost* III, 129-32.

MEPHOSTOPHILES

No, I came now hither of mine own accord.

FAUSTUS

Did not my conjuring speeches raise thee? Speak!   285

MEPHOSTOPHILES

That was the cause, but yet *per accidens*,
For when we hear one rack the name of God,
Abjure the scriptures and his saviour Christ,
We fly in hope to get his glorious soul;
Nor will we come unless he use such means   290
Whereby he is in danger to be damned.
Therefore the shortest cut for conjuring
Is stoutly to abjure the Trinity
And pray devoutly to the prince of hell.

FAUSTUS

So Faustus hath already done,   295
And holds this principle:
There is no chief but only Beelzebub,
To whom Faustus doth dedicate himself.
This word 'damnation' terrifies not him,
For he confounds hell in Elysium;   300
His ghost be with the old philosophers.
But leaving these vain trifles of men's souls,
Tell me: what is that Lucifer thy lord?

MEPHOSTOPHILES

Arch-regent and commander of all spirits.

FAUSTUS

Was not that Lucifer an angel once?   305

311-313   Marlowe is using *epistrophe*, the rhetorical device of ending a series of lines with the same word or phrase for emphasis.

314-21   On the ability of damned devils to roam the earth, Aquinas says: ". . . although the demons are not actually bound within the fire of hell while they are in this dark atmosphere, nevertheless their punishment is none the less; because they know that such confinement is in store for them. Hence it is said in the gloss upon James 3.6 'They take the fire of hell with them wherever they go" (*Summa Theologiae* Ia, Q.64, art. 4). See also M. A. O'Brien, "Christian Belief in *Dr Faustus*". *ELH* 37 (1970), 1-11. Another, often complementary, point of view — and one which Marlowe seems to be taking up at 317 — is that hell is both a specific location and a state of being. See *Paradise Lost* IV, 75: "Which way I fly is hell; my self am hell." See also 566-73 and note.

320   ten thousand hells: Marlowe's account is translated from St John Chrysostom (347-407 A.D.), who states that "ten thousand hells are as nothing in comparison with the loss of celestial bliss." *Hom. in St Matt.* xxiii. 9 (Jump).

MEPHOSTOPHILES

Yes, Faustus, and most dearly loved of God.

FAUSTUS

How comes it then that he is prince of devils?

MEPHOSTOPHILES

O, by aspiring pride and insolence,
For which God threw him from the face of heaven.

FAUSTUS

And what are you that live with Lucifer?   310

MEPHOSTOPHILES

Unhappy spirits that fell with Lucifer,
Conspired against our God with Lucifer,
And are forever damned with Lucifer.

FAUSTUS

Where are you damned?

MEPHOSTOPHILES

In hell.   315

FAUSTUS

How comes it then that thou art out of hell?

MEPHOSTOPHILES

Why, this is hell, nor am I out of it.
Thinkst thou that I, who saw the face of God
And tasted the eternal joys of heaven,
Am not tormented with ten thousand hells   320
In being deprived of everlasting bliss?

322 23   Here the lingering angelic quality in Mephostophiles cries out in pain. There is a tradition, going back to Origen and Erigena, that the created spirit, however fallen, will always return to God. Though this doctrine was declared heretical it continued to have a strong underground existence (see W. S. Seiferth, "The Concept of the Devil . . . Prior to Goethe", *Monatschafte* 44 (1952), 271-89, at 281. See also 644 and note.

326   manly fortitude: the Renaissance ideal of the education appropriate to a gentleman included emphasis on the virile arts, e.g. fencing, but Faustus offers to teach manliness to a spirit.

328   these [B; A, those].

329-30   Faustus regards his sin of aspiration as being too great for God to forgive. This inverted form of pride is frequently associated with despair in medieval and Renaissance writing on sin. See also 1420-22 and note.

330   Jove: see 105 and note.

332   four and twenty years [B; A, 24]: twenty-four is traditionally a number of completed time and it is appropriate that Faustus should exchange all eternity for a period which will seem as short as a day. Just so, his final hour on earth, in which he asks for one more day (1478), will be encompassed in a speech of just under sixty lines. See also 383 and note.

335 37   Faustus is using the rhetorical devices of *anaphora* (beginning a series of lines with the same word or phrase) and *parison* (corresponding structure in a sequence of clauses) to formalize his requirements.

343   It was commonly believed that there was more than one soul: the vegetative soul animated plants and guided them in their growth; the sensible soul empowered beasts to act according to their instincts and feelings; and the rational soul, the special property of man, endowed reason. See Trevisa, trans. *Bartholomeus, De Proprietatibus Rerum* (c. 1398). Hence references to a single person having more than one soul and usually three:

> What? will I turn shark upon my friends?
> I scorn it with my three souls.

(Ben Jonson, Poetaster, V. iii. 160-61).

O Faustus, leave these frivolous demands,
Which strike a terror to my fainting soul.

FAUSTUS

What, is great Mephostophiles so passionate
For being deprived of the joys of heaven?   325
Learn thou of Faustus manly fortitude
And scorn those joys thou never shalt possess.
Go bear these tidings to great Lucifer,
Seeing Faustus hath incurred eternal death
By desperate thoughts against Jove's deity: 330
Say he surrenders up to him his soul,
So he will spare him four and twenty years,
Letting him live in all voluptuousness,
Having thee ever to attend on me,
To give me whatsoever I shall ask,   335
To tell me whatsoever I demand,
To slay mine enemies and aid my friends,
And always be obedient to my will.
Go and return to mighty Lucifer,
And meet me in my study at midnight,   340
And then resolve me of thy master's mind.

MEPHOSTOPHILES

I will, Faustus.

Exit.

FAUSTUS

Had I as many souls as there be stars,
I'd give them all for Mephostophiles.
By him I'll be great emperor of the world,   345
And make a bridge through the moving air

348   hills: the land mass on either side of the narrow Straits of Gibraltar.

349   country [B; A land].

354   speculation: contemplation, with connotations of astrological observation of the stars (*OED* Speculation 2.b. and 4).

355.2   *Enter WAGNER and the CLOWN:* Faustus' grandiloquent geo-political fantasy is deflated by the irruption of the comic sub-plot. In this scene Wagner again plays the part of Faustus' *zany* (see 200 and note), his actions reflecting the main plot in that he has become a conjuror without any thought for the consequences. The Clown's hesitation is in contrast; a clown, in Elizabethan usage, is often a jester or fool (*OED* Clown. *sb*. 3), but here clown seems to mean a boorish rustic, crass and rude-mannered (*OED* Clown 1 and 2). The antithesis between the witty fool and the foolish wit, at its most diverting in Shakespeare's comedies and at its most intense in *King Lear*, is already evident in this play. The antithesis often suggests the Christian paradox of the folly of the wise and the wisdom of fools. See W. Kaiser, "The Wisdom of the Fool," in P. P. Wiener (ed.), *Dictionary of the History of Ideas*, (New York: Scribners, 1973), vol. 4, 515-20. The comic scenes recall their origins in morality plays and, at a greater remove, in popular folk drama (see R. Potter, *The English Morality Play: Origins, History and Influence of a Dramatic Tradition* (London: Routledge and Kegan Paul, 1975); and also A. Brody, *The English Mummers and their Plays: Traces of Ancient Mystery* (London: Routledge and Kegan Paul, 1971)).

357-59   Earlier editors have noted that A and B, which differ markedly here, have divergent moments of correspondence with the anonymous *Taming of a Shrew*, upon which Shakespeare drew for *The Taming of the Shrew*. Arguments for the priority of both A and B versions of this scene by comparison with *A Shrew* are possible, but since *A Shrew* is itself derivative and plagiarized from a number of sources it is difficult to come to firm conclusions. For a summary of the debate, see C. B. Kuriyama, "Dr Greg and *Dr Faustus*", *ELR* 5 (1975), 171-97.

357   'swounds [A, swowns]: an abbreviation of the oath "by God's wounds".

358   pickadevants: from the French *pic-à-devant*, a beard cut to a small point.

359   quotha: an archaic interjection meaning "said he" (from "quoth he"), usually contemptuously or sarcastically (*OED* Quotha).

360   comings in: income (*OED* Coming. *vbl. sb¹*. 7.c. cites similar usage in *Henry V*. iv.i. 260).

361   goings out: expenses; but this rueful observation is also the clown's comment on his ragged clothes, as Wagner is not slow to notice (363).

363-64   out of service: unemployed.

364-66   Faustus' greed for knowledge and power, a recurrent motif in the imagery of the play, is echoed in the sub-plot in terms of literal hunger. Wagner's derisive comment reflects upon the scene just past and anticipates the one about to follow, but he seems to be unaware that his own master's bargain will be as unwise as that which he expects of the clown.

To pass the ocean with a band of men;
I'll join the hills that bind the Afric shore
And make that country continent to Spain,
And both contributory to my crown;   350
The emperor shall not live but by my leave,
Nor any potentate of Germany.
Now that I have obtained what I desire,
I'll live in speculation of this art
Till Mephostophiles return again.   355

                                                    Exit.

Enter WAGNER *and the* CLOWN.

WAGNER

Sirrah boy, come hither.

CLOWN

How 'Boy'? 'swounds, boy, I hope you have seen
many boys with such pickadevants as I have.
'Boy', quotha?

WAGNER

Tell me sirrah, hast thou any comings in?   360

CLOWN

Ay, and goings out too, you may see else.

WAGNER

Alas, poor slave! See how poverty jesteth in his
nakedness. The villain is bare, and out of
service, and so hungry that I know he would
give his soul to the devil for a shoulder of   365
mutton, though it were blood raw.

369   B'urlady [A, Burladie]: probably a contraction of "by Our Lady", as used in an oath or expletive. The particular form of contraction suggests that the Clown speaks in a rural accent of the sort best located as "Loamshire".

372   *Qui mihi discipulus*: you who are my pupil; the first line of a school-book Latin poem by William Lily (1466 - 1522), whose work was much used in sixteenth-century grammar schools. The pretentious quotation, designed to impress the yokel, is reminiscent of Faustus' use of the classical languages.

374   Garments of silk were precious, and were rendered yet more expensive by beating precious metals into them for additional decoration.
        stavesacre: *staphisagria*, a plant related to the delphinium family. Its seeds were used as an insecticide against personal parasites.

CLOWN

How? My soul to the devil for a shoulder of mutton,
though 'twere blood raw? Not so, good friend.
B'urlady, I had need have it well roasted, and good
sauce to it, if I pay so dear.   370

WAGNER

Well, wilt thou serve me? and I'll make thee go like
Qui mihi discipulus.

CLOWN

How, in verse?

WAGNER

No, sirrah, in beaten silk and stavesacre.

CLOWN

How? how? knavesacre? Ay, I thought that was all   375
the land his father left him. Do you hear; I would
be sorry to rob you of your living.

WAGNER

Sirrah, I say in stavesacre.

CLOWN

Oho, oho, stavesacre: why then belike, if I were
your man, I should be full of vermin.   380

WAGNER

So thou shalt, whether thou beest with me or no.

383   seven years: seven is another number of completed time, as in the number of days in the week (see also 332 and note). Here Wagner unknowingly anticipates the threat which Mephostophiles will later use to terrify Faustus (see 1355).

384, 387   familiar: literally, belonging to the family; and hence, on an intimate, family footing. Because of Leviticus 20.6 and 20.27, sorcerers were supposed to have attendant spirits in the form of animals. The literature concerning the concept of the familiar in sixteenth- and seventeenth-century witchcraft is immense. See K. Thomas, *Religion and the Decline of Magic* (1971; Harmondsworth: Penguin University Books, 1973); and W. Shumaker, *The Occult Sciences in the Renaissance* (Berkeley: University of California Press, 1972). Belief in the literal presence of witches' familiars was embodied in the witchcraft statute of 1604.

390-96   guilders . . . gridirons . . . French crowns: this exchange occurs only in A. Some editors have suggested that the topical relevance of the exchange rate and the debased value of French crowns dates only from 1595; and from this they argue that the A version of this scene must date from after Marlowe's death in 1593. However, the topicality existed well before 1595, as has been demonstrated by H. E. Cain, in "Marlowe's 'French Crowns'", *MLN*, 49 (1934), 380-84. The disappearance of the joke from the B version is probably an indication that it was no longer topical when the scene was revised, probably after 1602.

            The point of the joke is that a gridiron, a cooking plate that is often circular and has holes in it, looks as many a French crown would have looked: there was an English proclamation in 1587 authorising members of the public to strike holes in any French crowns they came upon because the coinage was debased and many of the crowns were counterfeit. Gill points out that later the money market under James I was less troubled by this kind of counterfeiting.

395   English counters: counters were privately issued coins of no publicly accepted value, but were used for barter purposes in remote rural areas. They were first issued in the late sixteenth century and were still current in the late nineteenth century. The word "counter" was often used to denote forged or debased money (*OED* Counter. sb^3. 2).

397   an hour's warning: a phrase of proverbial force to emphasize the unexpectedness of death and the resultant need for a blameless life. See Rev. 18.10: "For in one houre is thy judgement come" and the warnings given in Matt. 24.36, 42, 44, 50; Mark 13.32; and Luke 12.40, 46. The unexpectedness of death is a constant motif in the morality tradition, e.g. *Everyman*: "O Deth, thou comest whan I had the leest in mynde!" (119).

But sirrah, leave your jesting and bind yourself
presently unto me for seven years, or I'll turn all
the lice about thee into familiars, and they shall
tear thee in pieces.   385

CLOWN

Do you hear, sir? You may save that labour: they
are too familiar with me already. 'Swounds, they
are as bold with my flesh as if they had paid for
my meat and drink.

WAGNER

Well, do you hear, sirrah? Hold: take these   390
guilders.

CLOWN

Gridirons, what be they?

WAGNER

Why, French crowns.

CLOWN

Mass, but for the name of French crowns, a man
were as good have as many English counters.   395
And what should I do with these?

WAGNER

Why now, sirrah, thou art at an hour's warning
whensoever or wheresoever the devil shall fetch
thee.

CLOWN

No, No; here, take your gridirons again.   400

406   Baliol and Belcher: these are not entirely nonsense names. Baliol is an ignorant rendering of Belial, the demon most closely associated with the deadly sin of lechery (see *Paradise Lost* I, 490 505, *Paradise Regained* II. 150, and numerous biblical references); Belcher is probably a corruption of Beelzebub and in this form clearly implies gluttony. In view of the imagery and action of the main plot, Wagner's invocation of two such devils seems wholly appropriate. Since Balliol (sometimes spelt Baliol) is also the name of an Oxford college, there may be a Cantabrigian's joke at the expense of the rival university.

411   tall: handsome, elegant (*OED* Tall. *a.* 2.b).

WAGNER

Truly, I'll none of them.

CLOWN

Truly, but you shall.

WAGNER

Bear witness I gave them him.

CLOWN

Bear witness I give them you again.

WAGNER

Well, I will cause two devils presently to fetch   405
thee away — Baliol and Belcher!

CLOWN

Let your Balio and your Belcher come here, and
I'll knock them! They were never so knocked
since they were devils! Say I should kill one of
them, what would folks say? 'Do ye see yonder   410
tall fellow in the round slop? He has killed the
devil!' So I should be called 'kill-devil' all the
parish over.

Enter two DEVILS *and the* CLOWN *runs up and
down, crying.*

WAGNER

Baliol and Belcher! Spirits away!

Exeunt.

416-17   That evil spirits could adopt human sex and have intercourse with a sorcerer or witch was widely enough believed to have constituted a recurrent motif in witchcraft trials. The clown's he-devil and she-devil would have been more grandiloquently termed *incubus* and *succubus* in superior magical circles.

418-19   The Clown lewdly identifies devils by their sexual characteristics.

423-31   The possibility of downward transformation or metamorphosis by magic anticipates Faustus' own spiritual decline (see 1513-14); the true "Christian fellow" (426) seeks upward metamorphosis through Christ. See M. O'Brien, "Christian Belief in *Dr Faustus*," *ELH* 37 (1970), 1-11, p. 7.

429   frisking flea: a perfectly natural idea for one of the Clown's ilk, of course, but more literary people also had pondered on the liberties a flea might take and there are many witty variants on the motif from Ovid, whom Marlowe had translated (see 745), onwards, and flea poems were practically an independent genre.

431   plackets: an allusion to the female genitals (*OED* Placket. 3.b).

CLOWN

What, are they gone? A vengeance on them — 415
they have vile long nails. There was a he-devil
and a she-devil. I'll tell you how you shall know
them: all he-devils has horns, and all she-devils
has clefts and cloven feet.

WAGNER

Well, sirrah, follow me. 420

CLOWN

But do you hear? If I should serve you, would
you teach me to raise up Banios and Belcheos?

WAGNER

I will teach thee to turn thyself to anything, to a
dog, or a cat, or a mouse, or a rat, or anything. 425

CLOWN

How? A Christian fellow to a dog or a cat, a
mouse or a rat? No, no, sir, if you turn me into
anything, let it be in the likeness of a little,
pretty, frisking flea, that I may be here and
there and everywhere. O, I'll tickle the pretty 430
wenches' plackets! I'll be amongst them, i'faith!

WAGNER

Well, sirrah, come.

CLOWN

But do you hear, Wagner?

438   diametarily: directly, in a straight line (*OED* Diametarily and Diametrally. 2).

439   *quasi vestigias nostras insistere*: as though to walk in our footsteps; but Wagner's syntax is false
           and reveals his own ignorance.

440   fustian: ridiculously lofty, bombastic; also with suggestion of being concocted (*OED* Fustian. B.
           2).

445-47   Faustus inverts Christian ideas and terms; this perversity, together with the mention of
           Beelzebub, may be seen as a trope on Mark 3.22-29, where such behaviour constitutes the sin
           "that shal never have forgiveness", the so-called sin against the Holy Ghost. The Geneva Bible
           gloss to this passage in Mark reads: ". . . when a man fighteth against his own conscience, and
           striveth against the trueth which is reveiled unto him, for such is in a reprobate sense and cannot
           come to repentance." See also Gerald H. Cox, "Marlowe's Doctor Faustus and 'Sin against the
           Holy Ghost'", *HLQ* 36 (1973), 119-37.

WAGNER

How? Baliol and Belcher!

CLOWN

O Lord, I pray sir, let Banio and Belcher go   435
sleep.

WAGNER

Villain, call me Master Wagner, and let thy left
eye be diametarily fixed upon my right heel,
with *quasi vestigias nostras insistere.*

Exit.

CLOWN

God forgive me! he speaks Dutch fustian. Well,   440
I'll follow him, I'll serve him; that's flat.

Exit.

Enter FAUSTUS *in his Study.*

FAUSTUS

Now, Faustus, must thou needst be damned,
And canst thou not be saved?
What boots it then to think of God or heaven?
Away with such vain fancies, and despair;   445
Despair in God, and trust in Beelzebub.
Now go not backward; no Faustus, be resolute.
Why waverest thou? O, something soundeth in mine ears:
'Abjure this magic, turn to God again.'
Ay, and Faustus will turn to God again.   450

452   appetite: desire or inclination, as well as hunger to fulfil natural functions (*OED* Appetite. *sb*. 1, 3, and 4). There may be an allusion to St Paul's rejection of worldly appetites (Romans 16.18) and those "whose God is their belie" (Phil. 3.19). See also J. H. Sims, *Dramatic Uses of the Bible in Marlowe and Shakespeare* (Florida, 1966).

453   fixed: Faustus again asserts despair, and with an obstinate mind; these were supposedly signs of the unforgivable sin against the Holy Ghost (see note to 445-47).

455   Sacrificing babies to the devil was widely assumed to be a major pastime of black magicians, probably because the pagan deity Moloch, who was equated with sorcery, required such rites: "I will set my face against that man, and cut him of from among his people, because he hathe given his children unto Molech, for to defile my Sanctuarie, and to pollute mine holy Name" (Leviticus 20.3). Typologically the sacrificed babe of the Black Mass is, of course, a parodic version of the Christ child.

457-58   contrition . . . heaven: contrition was defined by the Council of Trent (1545-63) as "sorrow of heart and detestation of sin committed, with the purpose of not sinning in future." As such, contrition is commonly held by theologians to be an internal form of repentance not merely grounded in fear of punishment but in the love of God. Prayer, as mentioned here, involves (1) submission to the divine will and (2) recognition of direct relationship with God. Repentance includes contrition and implies acts of reparation.

459-60   An attempt to invert St Paul's exhortation that we are to be fools, in worldly terms, for Christ's sake (1 Cor. 4.10).

460   makes: the singular form of the verb with a plural subject is a common feature of Marlowe's writing. It was also acceptable Elizabethan usage. The editor of B1 frequently emends to plural form.

462   As in *The Castle of Perseverance*, the ultimate temptation, which humanity cannot resist, and which signals the defeat of the Good Angel here, is avarice. The lengthy temptation sequence in *The Castle* is of great interest to the student of *Dr Faustus*. See Peter Happé (ed.), *Four Morality Plays* (Harmondsworth, 1979), pp. 143-79.
           of. [B; not in A].

462.1   [A, Exeunt; B, Ex. An.].

To God? He loves thee not:
The God thou servest in thine own appetite,
Wherein is fixed the love of Beelzebub;
To him I'll build an altar and a church
And offer lukewarm blood of new-born babes. 455

Enter GOOD ANGEL *and* EVIL [ANGEL].

GOOD ANGEL

Sweet Faustus, leave that execrable art.

FAUSTUS

Contrition, prayer, repentance: what of them?

GOOD ANGEL

O, they are means to bring thee unto heaven.

EVIL ANGEL

Rather illusions, fruits of lunacy,
That makes men foolish that do trust them most. 460

GOOD ANGEL

Sweet Faustus, think of heaven and heavenly things.

EVIL ANGEL

No Faustus, think of honour and [of] wealth.

FAUSTUS

Of Wealth!

Exeunt [ANGELS.]

464   signory of Emden: governorship of Emden, an important trading port in north-west Germany and a major trading partner with England in the sixteenth century, but hardly worth the price of one's soul.

465   Mephostophiles is to become his familiar.

469-70   Mephostophiles . . . Mephostophile: here A1 has Mephastophil*us*, followed by the Latin vocative Mephastophil*e*, keeping both forms in the second declension.

472   he lives [B; A, I live].

473-77   The legal terminology, which Mephostophiles uses to convince Faustus that his pact with the devil is binding, is spurious and inconsistent. "Buy" (473) more properly signifies a money transaction than barter; "bequeath" (475) applies to property left by will, not to a "deed of gift" (476); and "security" (477) cannot be demanded for a provision in a will or gift. Also, a will is a free and revocable act which cannot be enforced in this way; in the law codified by Justinian, which Faustus has just pushed aside as "a petty case of paltry legacies" (58) anyone attempting to coerce a testator in his favour invalidates that portion, if not the whole will. These misapplications point to the larger truth that the pact into which Faustus enters has no legal validity. Quite apart from the technical flaws in the pact, no contract is legally binding if it is immoral and no payment can be enforced even if value has been received. In folklore there is strong precedent for their being broken by the human party, to his own good and the devil's confusion. Indeed, "the devil in his dealings with men has reason to expect foul play and in most instances he says so; neither deed nor signature can protect his claims." W. S. Seiferth, "The Concept of the Devil . . . Prior to Goethe", *Monatschafte* 44 (1952), 271-89, at p. 285.

474   hazarded: the verb derives from the game of hazard, a form of dice governed by arbitrary rules. Gains and losses from such games are not legally enforcible.

479 80   As set in B; prose in A.

481   Gill cites from James Mason's somewhat later but nevertheless interesting *Anatomy of Sorcerie* (1612), p. 55: "Satan's chiefest drift & main point that he aimeth at, is the inlargement of his owne kingdom, by the eternall destruction of man in the life to come."

Why, the signory of Emden shall be mine!   465
When Mephostophiles shall stand by me,
What God can hurt thee, Faustus? Thou art safe:
Cast no more doubts! Come, Mephostophiles,
And bring glad tidings from great Lucifer.
Is't not midnight? Come, Mephostophiles: 470
Veni, veni, Mephostophile!

Enter MEPHOSTOPHILES

Now tell, what says Lucifer thy lord?

MEPHOSTOPHILES

That I shall wait on Faustus whilst [he lives].
So he will buy my service with his soul.

FAUSTUS

Already Faustus hath hazarded that for thee.

MEPHOSTOPHILES

But Faustus, thou must bequeath it solemnly   475
And write a deed of gift with thine own blood,
For that security craves great Lucifer.
If thou deny it, I will back to hell.

FAUSTUS

Stay, Mephostophiles, and tell me:
What good will my soul do thy lord?   480

MEPHOSTOPHILES

Enlarge his kingdom.

483   *Solamen miseris socios habuisse doloris*: it is a consolation to the wretched to have companions in misery. This aphorism derives from the *Sententia* of Publilius Syrus (fl. 1st century B.C.) and is quoted by Thomas à Kempis in *Vallis Liliorum* (Dr Richard Jordan).

488   There may be an allusion to Ephesians 3.20, where the faithful Christian is given "abundantly above all that we aske or thinke".

489   B1 emends text to "I'll give it him", which makes sense but loses dramatic immediacy; also, Mephostophiles has just asked for Faustus' soul for himself, though Lucifer is to be the ultimate benefactor.

490   Quite apart from common beliefs about Satanists signing pacts in their own blood, the motif has a strong dramatic force—through the stage convention of suicide by stabbing oneself as the ultimate gesture of despair. This prefigures the later moment when Mephostophiles hands Faustus a dagger (see 1337.1 and note).

491   some certain day: it may be helpful to view the play as structured around the typological diptych of the bond or pact which Faustus makes with Lucifer; viz., Day I (1-815), when the bargain is struck, and Day II (1287-1528), when the price is exacted. Between these two days there is, as it were, an intercalary day of the twenty-four years compassing Faustus' career as a necromancer.

491-93   In all forms of death other than suicide, God alone decides when a person will die (in traditional Christian theology); Mephostophiles is playing up to Faustus' presumption in wishing to displace the will of God with his own and Lucifer's.

495   proper: in the sense of being his own, but with the additional sense of proper as commendable or excellent (*OED* Proper. *a.* I. 1, II. 7, and III. 10).
         blood: the allusions to blood are insistent and a major motif in the play. As Faustus relives the original sin of Adam in his search for illegitimate knowledge, so his bond with the devil parodies God's bond with man, embodied in Christ's shedding of his own blood for man's redemption from the sin of Adam (see Romans 5.1-21 and 1 Cor. 15.20-45). In writing the bond with his own blood, Faustus rejects Christ's blood shed for his salvation. See 1484-85, and 1505.

496-97   Lucifer . . . perpetual night: a reminder that in his diabolical perversion of his original being, Lucifer is no longer the "light-bearer" of his name, but the harbinger of darkness.

497   regent: either absolute ruler or someone who rules by delegated authority (*OED* Regent. *sb.* 1 and 2.a).

FAUSTUS

Is that the reason he tempts us thus?

MEPHOSTOPHILES

Solamen miseris socios habuisse doloris.

FAUSTUS

Have you any pain that tortures others?

MEPHOSTOPHILES

As great as have the human souls of men.   485
But tell me, Faustus, shall I have thy soul?
And I will be thy slave and wait on thee
And give thee more than thou hast wit to ask.

FAUSTUS

Ay, Mephostophiles, I give it thee.

MEPHOSTOPHILES

Then stab thine arm courageously,   490
And bind thy soul, that at some certain day
Great Lucifer may claim it as his own;
And then be thou as great as Lucifer.

FAUSTUS

Lo, Mephostophiles, for love of thee
I cut mine arm and with my proper blood   495
Assure my soul to be great Lucifer's,
Chief lord and regent of perpetual night.
View here the blood that trickles from mine arm
And let it be propitious for my wish.

500-03   As set in B; prose in A.

501   deed: this term signifies a binding and legally actionable document (*OED* Deed. 4), but see 473-77 and note.

504   The chafer (portable grate) of coals with which Mephostophiles returns is an iconic stage representation of the Hell-fire of Faustus' new habitation.

506   bill: a written document, implying a legal transaction (*OED* Bill. sb^3. 1). See notes to 473-77 and 501.

507   Why streams it not: Faustus later uses the same verb to cry out for Christ's salvific blood, which "streams in the firmament" (1484).

509   is not thy soul thine own?: the biblical tradition insists that each human soul belongs not to itself but to God. A seminal passage is Luke 12.19-20: "And I will say to my soule, Soule, thou hast muche goods laid up for many years: live at ease, eate, drinke, and take thy pastime. But God said unto him, O fool, this night will they fetche away thy soule from thee." The morality plays reinforce this teaching, e.g. *Everyman*:

          Death: What, wenest thou thy lyve is gyven thee
                        And thy worldly goodes also?
          Everyman: I had wende so veryle.
          Death: Nay, nay, it was but lende thee (161-64)

MEPHOSTOPHILES

But Faustus, thou must write it in manner   500
Of a deed of gift.

FAUSTUS

Ay, so I will. But Mephostophiles,
My blood congeals and I can write no more.

MEPHOSTOPHILES

I'll fetch thee fire to dissolve it straight.

Exit.

FAUSTUS

What might the staying of my blood portend?   505
Is it unwilling I should write this bill?
Why streams it not, that I may write afresh?
'Faustus gives to thee his soul.' Ah, there it stayed!
Why shouldst thou not? is not thy soul thine own?
Then write again: 'Faustus gives to thee his soul.'   510

Enter MEPHOSTOPHILES *with a chafer of coals.*

MEPHOSTOPHILES

Here's fire. Come, Faustus, set it on.

FAUSTUS

So; now the blood begins to clear again:
Now will I make an end immediately.

MEPHOSTOPHILES

O, what will not I do to obtain his soul?

515   *Consummatum est!*: it is finished. The last words of Christ on the cross in the Vulgate version of
           John 19.30. The Geneva Bible renders this passage thus: "Now when Jesus had received the
           vinegre, he said It is finished, and bowed his head, and gave up the gost"; and adds the gloss:
           "Mans salvacion is perfected by the onlie sacrifice of Christ: & all the ceremonies of the Law are
           ended." Faustus' blasphemous parallelism is exquisitely apt. Quotation from St John's gospel,
           and in Latin, is also appropriate since the opening to the Vulgate version of this gospel was much
           invoked by magicians. See note to 168.

518   *Homo fuge!*: Flee, O man. There seems to be an allusion here to 1 Tim. 6. 11-12: "But thou, o
           man of God, flee these things, and followe after righteousness, godlines, faith, love, pacience, &
           meeknes. Fight the good fight of faith: laye holde of eternal life, whereunto thou art also called,
           & hast professed a good profession before many witnesses."
           Whither should I fly? an echo of Psalm 139.7-8, which proclaims the ubiquity of God. Interest-
           ingly, the psalm goes on to extol God's solicitude for man, so that this partial quotation parallels
           earlier ones (see 67-70 and note). See also J. H. Sims, *Dramatic Uses of the Bible in Marlowe and
           Shakespeare* (Florida, 1966), p. 25.

523   delight: give pleasure to, with connotation of enticement (*OED* Delight. *v.*).

523.1-2   The dance of the devils suggests the antimasque, i.e. the interlude within the courtly masque in
           which its own ideas and conventions are burlesqued. The *"crowns and rich apparel"* are the gim-
           crack finery of this world, for which Faustus proposes to suffer the loss of his own soul. Tinsel
           garments are used for similar symbolic purposes in another magus play, *The Tempest*.

524   show: pageant, masque, or similar display (*OED* Show. *sb¹*. 13). It was used particularly to
           describe visual rather than verbal presentation, as in the "dumb show" or mime sequence which
           was common in Elizabethan drama. There was a long-standing theological tradition that plays
           and shows are created by demons "among the other evils of idolatry, in order to draw man away
           from his lord and bind him to their own service." See Tertullian (c. 155-220 A.D.), early Chris-
           tian apologist, in his *De Spectaculis*, Cap. x.; also Milton's *Paradise Lost*, I, 718. The tradition is
           discussed by T. McAlindon, "Classical Mythology and Christian Tradition in Marlowe's *Dr
           Faustus*," *PMLA* 81 (1966), 214-23, at p. 220.

525-26   In a skilled piece of equivocation Mephostophiles both admits the limitations of magic and incites
           Faustus to greater expectations. These tricks and those to follow are not performed through
           magic as much as through the power traditionally accorded to angels.

FAUSTUS

Consummatum est! This bill is ended   515
And Faustus hath bequeathed his soul to Lucifer.
But what is this inscription on mine arm?
Homo fuge! Whither should I fly?
If unto God, he'll throw thee down to hell.
My senses are deceived, here's nothing writ —   520
I see it plain, here in this place is writ
Homo fuge! Yet shall not Faustus fly.

MEPHOSTOPHILES

I'll fetch him somewhat to delight his mind.

                                                Exit.

Enter with DEVILS, *giving crowns and rich apparel to*
FAUSTUS, *and dance, and then depart.*

FAUSTUS

Speak, Mephostophiles: what means this show?

MEPHOSTOPHILES

Nothing, Faustus, but to delight thy mind withal   525
And to show thee what magic can perform.

FAUSTUS

But may I raise up spirits when I please?

MEPHOSTOPHILES

Ay, Faustus, and do greater things than these.

FAUSTUS

Then there's enough for a thousand souls!

532   conditionally: Faustus is about to set conditions which it is beyond the capacity of Mephostophiles or Lucifer to fulfil (see note to 538).

533   All articles prescribed: more spurious legal terminology, giving only a semblance of validity (see note to 473-77)

536   Mephostophiles [B, Mephostophilis; not in A].

538   *spirit*: in Christian theology, the word denotes (1) a superhuman mode of being, not based on time, space, or bodily frame; and (2) a creature of this superhuman order, whether good or evil, angel or demon. Since God alone has the power to create or alter the essential nature of beings, the condition which Faustus seeks to impose upon Lucifer is impossible for Lucifer to fulfil.
           form and substance: medieval scholastic philosophy distinguished between two aspects of created beings. There was the *substance*, the basic substratum of things, their very essence; and there was the *form*, the material aspects of things (colour, weight, shape, and so on). A modern analogue would be to see H_2O as *substance* or essence, and to see water, ice, and steam as *forms* of it. Faustus' use of the distinction here is a piece of legalism designed to ensure that he has covered a loophole in the agreement.

542   do for: act on behalf of (*OED* Do. *v*. V. 38.a).

544-45   I.e., Mephostophiles is to be Faustus' familiar (see also 465).

549-50   by these presents: by these documents (*OED* Present. *sb¹*. II. 2.b).

550   . . . give both body and soul to Lucifer: it is not in Faustus' power to give his soul (see 509 and note) and the disposition is therefore no more effective than the corollary benefit demanded from Lucifer, i.e. that Faustus shall be a spirit (see 538 and note).

551   Prince of the East: evil was usually associated with the north, because of the frequent allusions to it as such in Jeremiah; east and west were usually associated with birth and death, because of the rising and setting of the sun and the parallel perceived between the sun and Christ (see John Donne's "Good Friday, 1613. Riding Westwards."). But Lucifer is also a name for the morning star (Venus) as seen in the east at dawn.

553   *four and twenty years* [B; A, 24]: see note to 491.

554-57   Apart from the devil's inability to enforce this part of the agreement (see note to 491-93), this provision is inconsistent with the first condition, since a spirit does not have flesh or blood.

Here, Mephostophiles, receive this scroll,   530
A deed of gift of body and of soul:
But yet conditionally that thou perform
All articles prescribed between us both.

MEPHOSTOPHILES

Faustus, I swear by hell and Lucifer
To effect all promises between us made.   535

FAUSTUS

Then hear me read them, [Mephostophiles.]
On these conditions following:
First, that Faustus may be a spirit in form and
substance;
Secondly, that Mephostophiles shall be his   540
servant, and at his command;
Thirdly, that Mephostophiles shall do for him
and bring him whatsoever;
Fourthly, that he shall be in his chamber or
house invisible;   545
Lastly, that he shall appear to the said John
Faustus at all times in what form or shape
soever he please;
I, John Faustus of Wittenberg, Doctor, by these
presents do give both body and soul to Lucifer,   550
Prince of the East, and his minister Mephosto-
philes; and furthermore grant unto them that,
four and twenty years being expired, the articles
above-written inviolate, full power to fetch or
carry the said John Faustus, body and soul,   555
flesh, blood, or goods, into their habitation
wheresoever.

By me John Faustus.

559   Mephostophiles again plays up to Faustus' love of legal terms and formality.

566-73   Mephostophiles replies to Faustus' question with great care and combines two traditional
            Christian views in his answer: hell is both a place and a state of mind. In so far as hell is a place,
            the centre or "bowels" (566) of the earth was traditionally allotted, being also in conformity with
            the classical ideas of Hades and Tartarus. In so far as hell is a state of mind, as Mephostophiles
            says, "where we are is hell" (569). Poetically, the link between the two hells is the idea of the indi-
            vidual's own body, lightly suggested here in "bowels . . . elements (566) . . . purified (572)" as a
            microcosm. The body, as microcosm, is a perfect scaled-down model of the universe and the idea
            that sin is its own punishment (which extends back from Augustine and Boethius to the Stoics)
            provides English Renaissance poets with the image of the sinner's diseased body as his own hell.
            See, for instance, the account of the Seven Deadly Sins in *The Faerie Queene*, I. iv. There is a
            good discussion of the subject in Leonard Barkan, *Nature's Work of Art: The Human Body as
            Image of the World* (New Haven, 1975). See also 314-21 and note.

570   there [B; not in A].

571   when all the world dissolves: Mephostophiles employs an image common in apocalytic literature
            to signify the final triumph of good over evil (see 2 Peter 3.3-10 and Rev. 20.7-21); the idea of
            dissolution at the end of the world also occurs in classical philosophies and becomes absorbed into
            Renaissance Christian thought.

574   Renaissance humanists took the view that the Bible revealed truth directly and that the fables of
            classical antiquity did so indirectly; the Bible, as God's revelation to his chosen people could be
            read literally, but the mythology which constituted his revelation to the Gentiles had to be inter-
            preted allegorically. Faustus inverts the humanist position here by regarding the biblical tradi-
            tion as fable. See also 300, 301 and notes.

MEPHOSTOPHILES

Speak, Faustus: do you deliver this as your deed?

FAUSTUS

Ay, take it, and the devil give thee good on't.   560

MEPHOSTOPHILES

Now, Faustus, ask what thou wilt.

FAUSTUS

First will I question with thee about hell.
Tell me, where is the place that men call hell?

MEPHOSTOPHILES

Under the heavens.

FAUSTUS

Ay, but whereabout?   565

MEPHOSTOPHILES

Within the bowels of these elements
Where we are tortured and remain for ever:
Hell hath no limits, nor is circumscribed
In one self place, for where we are is hell,
And where hell is, there must we ever be.   570
And, to conclude, when all the world dissolves
And every creature shall be purified,
All places shall be hell that is not heaven.

FAUSTUS

Come, I think hell's a fable.

577   necessity: Mephostophiles manipulates a term which has strong connotations of morality and conformity with natural law (*OED* Necessity. *sb.* 2 and 2.b). He appeals to Faustus' fallaciously argued and self-imposed doctrine of necessity (see 67–77).

580   fond: foolish; an Elizabethan usage, now archaic (*OED* Fond. *a.* 2) Lineation as in B.

587   Part of the line may be missing. In A1 "disputing" is following by "& c.", which is best rendered in modern typography by three dots. B1 has "What, sleeping, eating, walking, and disputing." On disputation, see note to 662.

587–99   In Christian tradition, marriage is not for those who are "wanton and lascivious" (588) or "a ceremonial toy" (599); in the Anglican *Book of Common Prayer* it is described as "holy Matrimony, an honourable estate, instituted of God" and in the Roman Catholic Church marriage has sacramental status. Besides, Faustus' desire for a wife is incompatible with his demand to be a spirit (538): spirits don't marry.

MEPHOSTOPHILES

Ay, think so still, till experience change thy mind.   575

FAUSTUS

Why, thinkst thou then that Faustus shall be damned?

MEPHOSTOPHILES

Ay, of necessity, for here's the scroll
Wherein thou hast given thy soul to Lucifer.

FAUSTUS

Ay, and body too; but what of that?
Thinkst thou that Faustus is so fond to imagine   580
That after this life there is any pain?
Tush, these are trifles and mere old wives' tales.

MEPHOSTOPHILES

But Faustus, I am an instance to prove the contrary,
For I am damned, and am now in hell.

FAUSTUS

How? now in Hell? Nay, and this be hell, I'll   585
willingly be damned here. What? walking, disputing . . . But leaving off this, let me have a wife, the
fairest maid in Germany, for I am wanton and
lascivious, and cannot live without a wife.

MEPHOSTOPHILES

How? A wife! I prithee, Faustus, talk not of a   590
wife.

594-95   There is apparently a slight mislineation in A, where "I'll" appears at the end of 594.

597-98   "Tut, Faustus" seems to complete the previous line. In A these words are run together with 599 as one line.

599-600   "If" is carried over into 600 in A.

601   cull: select (*OED* Cull. *v.* 1).

604   Penelope: wife of Odysseus; in the *Odyssey* she withstands the temptations of suitors during her husband's long absence.

605   Saba: the form given for the name of the Queen of Sheba in the Vulgate (1 Kings 10.1-13).

607-28   . . . this book: these lines, with the heavy reiteration of the word "book", one of the play's central symbols, may be thought of as the play's dialectical antithesis to Faustus' opening speech (29-92). There Faustus rejected the books of the traditional syllabus—Aristotle (philosophy), Galen (medicine), Justinian (law), and Jerome (theology)—in favour of the necromantic books (79) of forbidden knowledge. Now we see Faustus acquiring his new library. The book offered by Mephostophiles (607) is followed by three others whose subject matter descends through the *scala naturae* from "spirits" (616), through "planets" (620) to "plants, herbs, and trees" (624-25). The downward movement counterbalances the upward movement in the first speech from philosophy to theology. See "The Book as Symbol" in E. R. Curtius, *European Literature and the Latin Middle Ages* (New York, 1953), 302-47.

608   iterating: repetition (*OED* Iterate. *v.* 3).

FAUSTUS

Nay, sweet Mephostophiles, fetch me one, for I
will have one.

MEPHOSTOPHILES

Well, thou wilt have one. Sit there till I come:
I'll fetch thee a wife in the devil's name.   595

[*Exit*]

Enter with a DEVIL *dressed like a woman, with fireworks.*

MEPHOSTOPHILES

Tell, Faustus, how dost thou like thy wife?

FAUSTUS

A plague on her for a hot whore!

MEPHOSTOPHILES

Tut, Faustus;
Marriage is but a ceremonial toy.
If thou lovest me, think no more of it.   600
I'll cull thee out the fairest courtesans
And bring them every morning to thy bed.
She whom thine eye shall like, thy heart shall have,
Be she as chaste as was Penelope,
As wise as Saba, or as beautiful   605
As was bright Lucifer before his fall.
Hold; take this book, peruse it thoroughly:
The iterating of these lines brings gold:
The framing of this circle on the ground
Brings whirlwinds, tempests, thunder and lightning;   610
Pronounce this thrice devoutly to thyself
And men in armour shall appear to thee,

614-28   These lines are missing from the B-version, apart from the initial thanks to Mephostophiles. The imperative form of the verb in stage directions (618.1, 622.1, and 628.1) suggests that the copy used to print the A-version may have come from a prompt book or an actor's individual part; certainly, this form of stage direction does not seem primarily intended for a reader. Except in very clear instances, however, it is difficult to come to firm conclusions from stage directions.
           Jump suggests that "this book" (618) refers to the one already given by Mephostophiles (607) and that "Here they are too" (622) and "Here they be" (626) likewise refer to the same book.

620   characters: magical signs; the astrological symbols for the planets (*OED* Character. *sb*. I. 5). See also 80 and note.

621   dispositions: in its astrological sense, a disposition is the situation of a planet in a horoscope; it is supposed to affect the nature or fortunes of a person or the course of events (*OED* Disposition. II. 5.a).

Ready to execute what thou desir'st.

FAUSTUS

Thanks, Mephostophiles. Yet fain would I have
a book wherein I might behold all spells and   615
incantations, that I might raise up spirits when
I please.

MEPHOSTOPHILES

Here they are in this book.

There turn to them.

FAUSTUS

Now would I have a book where I might see all
characters and planets of the heavens, that I   620
might know their motions and dispositions.

MEPHOSTOPHILES

Here they are too.

Turn to them.

FAUSTUS

Nay, let me have one book more — and then I
have done — wherein I might see all plants,
herbs and trees that grow upon the earth.   625

MEPHOSTOPHILES

Here they be.

629 While it is possible, as some editors think, that an entirely new scene begins here and that an intervening scene has been lost, it is quite possible that this speech follows on directly from Faustus' examination of the textbook on astrology for which he has just asked (619-21). Faustus is evidently inspecting the charts and diagrams in this book. The line "When I behold the heavens . . ." echoes Psalm 8.3, which proclaims God's munificence to man, though once again Faustus leaves out the message of hope (see note to 67-70). As Faustus views the charts of the heavens, then, he is thinking both of the physical and the metaphysical; his action inevitably brings him also to St Thomas Aquinas' demonstration of the existence of God from the principles of motion and cosmic order. Mephostophiles completes the semantic bridge between the physical and metaphysical meanings of "heaven" at 633 (see note).

633 In pre-Copernican cosmology "heaven" and "the heavens" (629) are contiguous, the stars being immediately below the floor of the heaven of the blessed. See F. R. Johnson, *Astronomical Thought in Renaissance England* (Baltimore, 1937).

633-38 The glory of man is a commonplace Renaissance *topos* (see, for instance, Hamlet's meditation on man in *Hamlet* II. ii. 316f.), but Marlowe gives this perverted form of its expression very properly to a devil.

642 The Evil Angel is already invoking the first clause of the spurious contract (see 538 and note) and gaining advantage from Faustus' inattentive reading of Justinian (see 56-64 and notes). This line is a contracted syllogism: you are a spirit; God excludes spirits who have sinned from grace; therefore, God cannot pity you. The major premise is false, but Faustus wants to believe it. As to the minor premise, see note to 644.

FAUSTUS

O, thou art deceived.

MEPHOSTOPHILES

Tut, I warrant thee.

Turn to them.

FAUSTUS

When I behold the heavens, then I repent
And curse thee, wicked Mephostophiles,   630
Because thou has deprived me of those joys.

MEPHOSTOPHILES

Why, Faustus,
Thinkst thou heaven is such a glorious thing?
I tell thee: 'tis not half so fair as thou,
Or any man that breathes on earth.   635

FAUSTUS

How provest thou that?

MEPHOSTOPHILES

It was made for man: therefore man is more
excellent.

FAUSTUS

If it were made for man, 'twas made for me:
I will renounce this magic and repent.   640

Enter GOOD ANGEL *and* EVIL ANGEL.

GOOD ANGEL

Faustus, repent: yet God will pity thee.

644   The doctrine of *apocatastasis*, which teaches that all creatures capable of moral sense—i.e.
           humans, angels, and devils—will share in salvation, was attacked by St Augustine and con-
           demned by the Council of Constantinople (AD 543); but the doctrine re-emerged and found
           favour later among some Protestant groups. See 322–23 and note.

646.1   Exeunt [A; B, Exit Angels]

647   Hardness of heart, declares John Donne in one of his sermons, is a sign of the sin against the Holy
           Ghost, for which there is no forgiveness. See G. H. Cox, "Marlowe's *Dr Faustus* and 'Sin Against
           the Holy Ghost'", *HLQ* 36 (1973), 119–37). One need not look as far as the mysterious sin against
           the Holy Ghost, however, for St Thomas Aquinas says in his *Summa*: "Spiritual blindness and
           hardness of heart imply two things. One is the movement of the human mind in cleaving to evil,
           and turning away from the Divine Light; and as regards this, God is not the cause of spiritual
           blindness and hardness of heart, just as He is not the cause of sin . . . On the other hand, God, of
           his own accord, withholds His grace from those in whom He finds an obstacle: so that the cause of
           grace being withheld is not only the man who raises an obstacle to grace; but God, Who, of His
           own accord, withholds His grace." (Ia. IIae, Q.79, art. 3). Commenting on this passage in rela-
           tion to the play, M. A. O'Brien, in "Christian Belief in *Dr Faustus*", *ELH* 37 (1970), 1–11, says at
           p. 9: "Even though Faustus, as a wayfarer, retains a movable will capable of repentance, it is true
           that hardness of heart can prevent his accepting the grace of repentance."

650–54   Once again Faustus evinces despair. Suicide was regarded as the ultimate manifestation of
           despair since it involved committing mortal sin and dying in that state, with almost certain
           damnation to follow. In the morality tradition, temptation to suicide was commonly accom-
           panied by emblems of violent death. See T. W. Craik, *The Tudor Interlude* (Leicester, 1962).
           See also notes to 490 and stage direction at 1337.1.

655–56   As there was no accomplished English translation of *The Iliad* before Chapman started his (about
           five years after Marlowe's death), and as Greek was not widely known at the time, Faustus' resur-
           rection of Homer would have been even more spectacular to his contemporaries than to later
           generations. Marlowe's knowledge of the Trojan War would probably have been derived from the
           popular medieval travesty of Dictys Cretensis and Dares Phrygius, from which Caxton's *Recuyell
           of the Historyes of Troye* (1475) was also derived. Marlowe may, however, have had access to the
           lame translation by Arthur Hall (1581) from the French of Hugues Salel (1551). The *Ilias Latina*
           of Pindarus Thebanus, a Latin epitome of a thousand lines or so, was widely used as a school text
           in the sixteenth century. For the enormous popularity of quasi-Homeric material in the Eliza-
           bethan theatre, see John S. P. Tatlock, "The Siege of Troy in Elizabethan Literature, especially
           in Shakespeare and Heywood," *PMLA* 30 NS 23 (1915), 673–770.
           On the continent, Latin and vernacular editions of Homer were heavily allegorized by Christian
           humanists, who sought to justify studying the pagan Homer on the ground that he was a moralist
           whose epics contained hidden allegorical truth (see note to 574). The death of Alexander,
           Homer's name for Paris, who deserted Oenone for Helen only to return and die at Oenone's feet,
           was interpreted to signify contrition. This conventional signification invests Faustus' recollection
           with piquant irony. For a discussion of humanist allegorizing, see Don Cameron Allen, *Mysteri-
           ously Meant* (Baltimore, 1970), pp. 83–105; see also the note to 1377.

657–59   Legend held it that Amphion's music made the stones rise of their own accord to build the city of
           Thebes. This mythic event was often interpreted allegorically in the Renaissance to show the
           creative power of divinely-inspired harmony. George Sandys, the early seventeenth-century trans-
           lator of and commentator on Ovid's *Metamorphoses*, says of Amphion that he "fained . . . to
           have drawn the stones together, and built it with the musick of his harpe: in that by his wisdome
           and eloquence he brought the savage people to civility, and caused them to cohabit." The juxta-
           position of Amphion and Paris is elegant for they image, respectively, the creation and destruc-
           tion of a sophisticated city. Both Troy and Thebes are proverbially ill-omened.

660–61   basely despair: having inverted the humanist's understanding of the Amphion myth by making
           him the devil's musician, Faustus draws the inference that there is no need to despair of hell, i.e.
           to repent.

662   dispute: debate, in the manner of formal argument by disputation practised in the medieval
           schools and universities.

663   astrology: until well after Marlowe's time astronomy (the science which treats of the constitution,
           relative positions, and motions of the heavenly bodies) was not clearly distinguished from astro-

EVIL ANGEL

Thou art a spirit: God cannot pity thee.

FAUSTUS

Who buzzeth in mine ears I am a spirit?
Be I a devil, yet God may pity me;
Ay, God will pity me if I repent.   645

EVIL ANGEL

Ay, but Faustus never shall repent.

Exeunt [ANGELS.]

FAUSTUS

My heart's so hardened I cannot repent.
Scarce can I name salvation, faith, or heaven,
But fearful echoes thunders in mine ears:
'Faustus, thou art damned!' Then swords and knives,   650
Poison, guns, halters, and envenomed steel
Are laid before me to dispatch myself;
And long ere this I should have slain myself,
Had not sweet pleasure conquered deep despair.
Have not I made blind Homer sing to me   655
Of Alexander's love and Oenon's death?
And hath not he that built the walls of Thebes
With ravishing sound of his melodious harp
Made music with my Mephostophiles?
Why should I die then, or basely despair?   660
I am resolved: Faustus shall ne'er repent.
Come, Mephostophiles, let us dispute again
And argue of divine astrology.
Tell me: are there many heavens above the moon?

logy, which term has only since the late seventeenth century come to mean exclusively the study of reputed occult and non-physical influences of the stars on human affairs (*OED* Astrology and Astronomy). All Faustus' questions, with the exception of his enquiry concerning *intelligentia* (687), fall within the province of astronomy.

The transition from the subject of music (655-59) to astronomy would not have seemed abrupt in Marlowe's time: the two studies are closely related in the classical *quadrivium* (a sub-group of four out of the seven liberal arts) as taught in the Renaissance. See N.C. Carpenter, "Music in *Dr Faustus*: Two Notes", *NQ* 195 (1950), 180-81.

664-97   The discussion on astrology (astronomy) is unremarkable. In the system derived from the Greek-Egyptian astronomer Ptolemy (2nd Century AD) and which persisted beyond Marlowe's lifetime because the contradicting mathematical formulations of Copernicus had not as yet been empirically verified by Galileo, the universe consisted of transparent concentric spheres enfolded round the "centric earth" (666). Just as the heavenly spheres enfolded each other, rather like the layers of an onion, so the four sublunary elements of earth, water, air, and fire were thought to enfold each other too (667-68). Opinion on how many spheres there were above the planet earth was varied, most formulations settling for nine or ten (690-92). Faustus' irritation that his disputation with Mephostophiles has not got beyond "freshmen's suppositions" (686) is well founded.

Standard studies of the passage are those by F. R. Johnson in "Marlowe's 'Imperial Heaven'", *ELH* 12 (1945), 35-44, and in "Marlowe's Astronomy and Renaissance Skepticism", *ELH* 13 (1946), 241-54; and by Paul H. Kocher in *Christopher Marlowe* (Chapel Hill, 1946), 214-23. General guides to Renaissance cosmology are legion: three which can be recommended are Milton K. Munitz (ed.), *Theories of the Universe* (New York, 1957); Thomas P. Kuhn, *The Copernican Revolution* (Cambridge, Mass., 1957); and F. R. Johnson, *Astronomical Thought in Renaissance England* (Baltimore, 1937). There is also Arthur Koestler's vigorous discussion in *The Sleepwalkers* (London, 1959).

667   elements: the four elements of earth, water, air, and fire are described as being "folded" (668), each in the manner of an "orb" (see next note), because they were envisaged as stratified in order of decreasing density. Our land masses were seen as extrusions of earth through the surrounding element of water.

668   orb: each of the concentric hollow spheres. Each orb was believed to carry a planet on its circumference as its "intelligence" (688) or guiding force. Beyond the planets was the orb of the fixed stars.

669   As rendered in B; A, And Faustus all jointly move . . .
All the spheres move upon a single axis, which is also the axis of the earth.

670   terminine: limit; apparently an extended form of termine or in error for termining (*OED* Termine and Terminine).

671-72   The names of the pagan Gods, says Mephostophiles, are not "feigned" or misapplied in relation to the planets: in medieval and Renaissance thought the mythic and planetary entities were merged, the personalities of the gods becoming the astrological attributes of their respective planets. See Jean Seznec, *The Survival of the Pagan Gods* (Princeton, 1953). As to the "erring" or wandering of the planets, see note to 250.

674   *situ et tempore*: in direction and time.

675   four and twenty, [B; A, 24]
In the old geocentric model of the universe, all the planets and stars move round the earth in a complete circuit every twenty-four hours. Because this model was still current in Marlowe's time, the period of twenty-four years asked by Faustus would have been even more strongly associated with completion of a cycle of time than it is today (see note to 491).

676   poles of the world: the earth's axis (see note to 669).

677   poles of the Zodiac: the apparent axis governing the ecliptic, which is the plane of the sun's movement through the constellations of the Zodiac; the planets also happen to lie within this plane. The ecliptic was used to account in part for the apparently erratic or "erring" (672) behaviour of the planets.

681   double motion: within the plane of the ecliptic, each planet moves at its own speed, as well as being turned about the chief axis of the world every twenty-four hours.

Are all celestial bodies but one globe,   665
As is the substance of this centric earth?

MEPHOSTOPHILES

As are the elements, such are the spheres,
Mutually folded in each other's orb,
And jointly move upon one axle-tree,
Whose terminine is termed the world's wide pole;   670
Nor are the names of Saturn, Mars, or Jupiter
Feigned, but are erring stars.

FAUSTUS

But tell me, have they all one motion? both *situ*
et tempore?

MEPHOSTOPHILES

All jointly move from east to west in four and   675
twenty hours upon the poles of the world, but
differ in their motion upon the poles of the
Zodiac.

FAUSTUS

Tush! these slender trifles Wagner can decide:
Hath Mephostophiles no greater skill?   680
Who knows not the double motion of the planets?
The first is finished in a natural day,
The second thus, as Saturn in thirty years,
Jupiter in twelve, Mars in four; the sun, Venus
and Mercury in a year; the moon in twenty-   685
eight days. Tush! these are freshmen's supposi-
tions. But tell me, hath every sphere a dominion
or *intelligentia?*

683   The remainder of the speech is in prose.

686   freshmen: used as a title for first-year undergraduates at Cambridge; first recorded use in 1596 (*OED* Freshman. 2), but probably well established by then.
        suppositions: the medieval Latin *suppositio* was the equivalent of the Greek-derived *hypothesis*; and in medieval scholastic logic a *suppositio* is a basic, elementary, and self-evident truth. Faustus asserts, as in his allusion to Wagner (679), that these ideas are the mere exoteric appearance of astronomy; they are of no interest to the initiate who wishes to penetrate the esoteric knowledge of what would today be termed astrology.

688   *intelligentia* [B; intelligentij in A]: controlling force. It was commonly believed that angels, sometimes known as intelligences (*OED* Intelligence. *sb.* 4), imparted motion to the spheres. This animistic notion, first propounded by Plato, is recalled by John Donne in his poem "Good Friday, 1613. Riding Westwards":

>   Let man's soul be a sphere, and then, in this
>   The intelligence that moves, devotion is.

692   empyreal [imperiall, A; emperiall, B]: the empyrean or empyreal (from Greek empyros = fiery) was the highest heaven, but was commonly known as the imperial (from Latin imperium = empire), presumably through confused etymology (*OED* Empyreal. *a.* 1 and Imperial. *a.* 1).

692 93 Between these lines the B-version has this further exchange:

FAUSTUS: But is there not *coelum igneum, et cristallinum?*
MEPHOSTOPHILES: No, Faustus, they are but fables.

        F. R. Johnson takes the whole passage on astronomy, including the extra B-version material, to argue for Marlowe's intellectual position as being "that of the skeptical, empirical school among Renaissance astronomical writers, who refused to accept a system containing any sphere void of visible bodies whereby man could directly observe its motions" ("Marlowe's Astronomy and Skepticism", *ELH* 13 [1946], 241 54, at pp. 246 47). Although Johnson's conclusion is attractive to those who would like to see Marlowe as a modern thinker, its reliance on the B-version means that it must be treated with caution.

694   conjunctions: concurrence of two of the unfixed heavenly bodies, e.g. the sun and the moon, in one sign of the Zodiac.
        oppositions: the relative positions of two heavenly bodies when seen as being exactly opposite each other from the earth's surface.
        aspects: positions of the heavenly bodies in relation to each other, as viewed from the earth.
        eclipses: interceptions of light from one luminous body to another.
        These phenomena are observed in astronomy; when they are given an occult interpretation they are removed to the domain of astrology (see note to 686).

697   *Per inaequalem motum respectu totius*: through unequal motion in respect of the whole. Faustus has been asking why the system seems to be out of gear, the theory at variance with the observed facts. Mephostophiles fobs him off with a Latin tag of the sort which Faustus uses to impress and is impressed by. The question was an important one and basically reflects the impossibility of reconciling the idea that the planets had paths which were circular with the reality that their orbits were elliptical. The doctrine that the circle was the perfect figure necessitated the hypothesis of circular orbits, for only beneath the moon was created nature subject to the Fall. The hypothesis was saved by introducing a host of minor, subordinate cycles, known as epicycles. And so observation and theory were reconciled. See Arthur Koestler, *The Sleepwalkers* (London, 1959).
        The theologically acceptable conclusion, which Faustus does not begin to entertain, is that the co-existence of perfection with imperfection itself images the antithesis between God's eternity and man's fallen time. A. Kent Hieatt has brilliantly demonstrated the centrality of this paradox to the poetry of Marlowe's contemporary, Edmund Spenser, in *Short Time's Endless Monument* (New York, 1960).

MEPHOSTOPHILES

Ay.

FAUSTUS

How many heavens or spheres are there? 690

MEPHOSTOPHILES

Nine: the seven planets, the firmament, and the
empyreal heaven.

FAUSTUS

Well, resolve me in this question: why have we
not conjunctions, oppositions, aspects, eclipses,
all at one time, but in some years we have more, 695
in some less?

MEPHOSTOPHILES

Per inaequalem motum respectu totius.

FAUSTUS

Well, I am answered. Tell me, who made the world?

MEPHOSTOPHILES

I will not.

FAUSTUS

Sweet Mephostophiles, tell me. 700

MEPHOSTOPHILES

Move me not, for I will not tell thee.

FAUSTUS

Villain, have I not bound thee to tell me anything?

697   The natural culmination to a discussion of the workings of the cosmos was to posit a First Cause
          and Prime Mover, the God of St Thomas Aquinas and the scholastics.

713   An empty threat, since Mephostophiles is unable to harm anyone with enough faith to withstand
          him — compare his admission when asked to torment the Old Man (see 1362-65).

MEPHOSTOPHILES

Ay, that is not against our kingdom, but this is.
Think thou on hell, Faustus, for thou art damned. 705

FAUSTUS

Think, Faustus, upon God, that made the world.

MEPHOSTOPHILES

Remember this!

Exit.

FAUSTUS

Ay, go accursed spirit to ugly hell:
'Tis thou hast damned distressed Faustus' soul.
Is't not too late? 710

Enter GOOD ANGEL *and* EVIL [ANGEL.]

EVIL ANGEL

Too late.

GOOD ANGEL

Never too late, if Faustus can repent.

EVIL ANGEL

If thou repent, devils shall tear thee in pieces.

GOOD ANGEL

Repent, and they shall never raze thy skin.

Exeunt [ANGELS.]

715   In arguing for the superiority of the B-version, which reads "Help to save distressed Faustus'
        soul", Greg finds "Seek" in the A-version heretical in that it implies limitation to Christ's power to
        save. However, since it is not Marlowe but Faustus who is speaking, it is irrelevant to the textual
        argument whether the idea is heretical or not. Faustus challenges Christ's redemptive powers
        throughout. See 67-77 and notes, and also M. J. Warren, "*Dr Faustus*: The Old Man and the
        Text", *ELR* 11 (1981), 111-47, at p. 124.

716.1   Beelzebub does not speak in the A-version. This is the first time that the major devils allow Faustus
        to see them. They are silently and, to Faustus, invisibly present during the first conjuration scene
        (239f). The B-version's stage direction FAUSTUS *to them with this speech* at 238.1 is clearly
        wrong; Faustus' surprise and lack of recognition in the later scene further indicate that he has not
        seen Lucifer or Beelzebub before. In fact, Lucifer has to introduce himself and Beelzebub
        (720-21).

717   Lucifer takes advantage of Faustus' wilful misreading of scripture (see 67-77). An Elizabethan
        audience would have been aware not only of the misreading but also of the strong tradition in the
        morality plays wherein God's justice is tempered with mercy, e.g. *The Castle of Perseverance*,
        Mankind, and *Everyman*. The tradition is encapsulated in Psalm 85.10: "Mercie and trueth shal
        mete: righteousnes [justice] and peace shal kisse one another."

718   interest: right or title (*OED* Interest. *sb*. 1).

720   my companion prince: Beelzebub, in being described thus, exemplifies an iconographic
        tradition. It is an axiom of medieval numerology that two is the number of division, as opposed to
        unity. There are passages in the New Testament where Beelzebub is associated with self-defeating
        divisiveness (Matt 12.22-30, Mark 3.22-27, Luke 11.14-22). In the Chester mystery play of The
        Fall of Lucifer, when God temporarily vacates his throne two devils climb onto it and sit side by
        side before being discovered and thrown into hell.

725-26 The devil (= Lucifer) was reputed to have numerous sexual liaisons with female witches, as all
        the witchcraft manuals testify, and was sometimes thought to have a long-term consort. The
        latter idea comes from popular folklore rather than demonology and was dramatized in the
        medieval Dutch play *Marieken van Nijmegen*. The phrase "the devil and his dam" is proverbial.
        See *Henslowe's Diary*, p. 134.

FAUSTUS

Ah, Christ my saviour — seek to save distressed   715
Faustus' soul!

Enter LUCIFER, BEELZEBUB, *and* MEPHOSTOPHILES.

LUCIFER

Christ cannot save thy soul, for he is just;
There's none but I have interest in the same.

FAUSTUS

O, who art thou that lookst so terrible?

LUCIFER

I am Lucifer — and this is my companion   720
prince in hell.

FAUSTUS

O Faustus, they are come to fetch away thy soul.

LUCIFER

We come to tell thee thou dost injure us.
Thou talkst of Christ, contrary to thy promise.
Thou shouldst not think of God: think of the devil   725
And of his dam too.

FAUSTUS

Nor will I henceforth: pardon me in this
And Faustus vows never to look to heaven;
Never to name God, or to pray to him;
To burn his scriptures, slay his ministers;   730
And make my spirits pull his churches down.

734-35   the seven deadly sins: very common in medieval Christian thought, they originate in pre-Christian thought of the Hellenistic period. Traditional treatments of the seven deadly sins usually incorporated intense physical detail, often of a strongly iconic nature. The sins are often given genealogies and their physical appearance is the result of indulgence in the sin concerned. Attempts to balance the seven deadly sins by a dialectical opposition of seven cardinal virtues were persistent but not greatly successful. See G. R. Owst, *Literature and Pulpit in Medieval England* (1933; Oxford, 1961). Treatments of the motif before Marlowe include Chaucer's *Parson's Tale* (ed. Robinson, X [1] 387), John Gower's *Mirour de l'Omme*, William Langland's *Piers Plowman* (B-Text, Passus V-VI), and above all Edmund Spenser's *Faerie Queene* (Book I, canto iv). Among specifically dramatic precursors, see *The Castle of Perseverance.* (c. 1425) and Henry Medwall's *Nature* (c. 1490).

Pride usually occurs first in lists of the seven deadly sins, being regarded as the most deadly and the foundation of the rest. Covetousness generally follows, probably because of the church's other-worldliness in the face of growing materialism, and sometimes even displaces Pride in primacy (see *The Castle of Perseverance*). In Marlowe's pageant the sins are not in their most common order, except for the first two, but by the sixteenth century the medieval passion for hierarchy in all things, even sin, had dissipated. Marlowe's sequence must be regarded as suiting his own particular purpose.

For a comprehensive treatment of the subject, see Morton W. Bloomfield, *The Seven Deadly Sins* (East Lansing, 1952).

736-37   It was a vexed question whether Adam's innocence had lasted longer than the first day of his creation. Like Lucifer, Adam fell through pride in desiring to be god-like (Gen. 3.5-7) and Faustus replicates Adam's sin in his desire for super-human powers through the forbidden knowledge of magic.

738-39   mark this show: see note to 524. The spirit in which Faustus witnesses the pageant of the seven deadly sins, i.e. for salacious enjoyment not moral improvement, would have given grim satisfaction to those puritans of Marlowe's day who reviled the popular theatre.

741-42   names and dispositions: the seven deadly sins had acquired personalities appropriate to the vices they represented.

744   Pride: in rejecting his parents, Pride offends against the commandment to honour father and mother (Exodus 20.12); his disdain to have *any* parents means that he refuses to acknowledge his first parents, Adam and Eve. In Christian thought, the original sin of our first parents makes us totally dependent on God. Faustus has implicitly rejected his own parents "base of stock" (11) in his rise to academic eminence and his allusion to Adam (737) reveals his lack of concern for the penalty of Adam.

745   Ovid's flea: an allusion to a popular song, attributed to Ovid, but probably medieval, in which the poet says to the flea: "*Is quocumque placet; nil tibi, saeve, latet.*" See N. E. Lemaire (ed.), *Poetae Latini Minores* (Paris, 1826), vii, 275-78. This passage may be translated: "You go wherever you please; nothing is hidden from you, savage!"

751   cloth of Arras: Arras, a town in Artois, was famed for making extremely luxurious and expensive cloth, so fine that it was used for wall hangings.

LUCIFER

Do so, and we will highly gratify thee:
Faustus, we are come from hell to show thee some
pastime. Sit down, and thou shalt see all the seven
deadly sins appear in their proper shapes.

735

FAUSTUS

That sight will be as pleasing unto me as paradise
was to Adam, the first day of his creation.

LUCIFER

Talk not of paradise, nor creation, but mark this
show. Talk of the devil and nothing else: come
away.

740

Enter the SEVEN DEADLY SINS.

Now, Faustus, examine them of their several
names and dispositions.

FAUSTUS

What art thou, the first?

PRIDE

I am Pride. I disdain to have any parents. I am
like to Ovid's flea: I can creep into every corner of
a wench. Sometimes, like a periwig, I sit upon her
brow; or, like a fan of feathers, I kiss her lips.
Indeed I do! What do I not? But fie, what a scent
is here! I'll not speak another word, except the
ground were perfumed and covered with cloth of
Arras.

745

750

FAUSTUS

What art thou, the second?

753-57   Covetousness: the leather bag (754) of the avaricious man is common in the iconography of this sin. A churl (753) was in origin simply a man, but the term became applied generally to someone without rank or of ignoble character and then more specifically to the rich skinflint of Coverdale's Bible: "A nigarde shal no more be called liberal, nor the churl riche" (Isaiah 32.5).

755-56   all . . . turned to gold: in the pagan myth of the Golden Age, interpreted by Christian humanists as an indirect perception of the prelapsarian state, the lost age of perfection will return at the end of the degenerate Iron Age in which we live. Moral literature of the Renaissance frequently draws a contrast between gold as a metaphor for incorruptibility and timelessness and gold as literal cash and filthy lucre. The Renaissance distinction between exoteric (wealth-seeking) alchemy and esoteric (spiritual) alchemy is brilliantly made by Ben Jonson in the blasphemous prayer to wealth with which *Volpone* (1607) begins. See note to 151.

757   chest: the hoarder's treasure test is another common item in the iconography of this sin.

759-65   Wrath: anger is seen as being more overtly self-destructive than the other sins, wounding himself with a "case" (pair) of rapiers as he runs up and down without rational motive. Wrath is more ludicrous than horrifying. His leap out of a lion's mouth is both a parodic *parthenogenesis* and a comment on the origin of sin in bestial or sub-human conduct. The lion is often associated with Wrath: Spenser has him riding a lion (*The Faerie Queene* I. iv. 33-35).

764-65   An address to the audience is common in medieval drama, e.g. the Wakefield *Mactacio Abel* (Sacrifice of Abel), wherein Cain's servant scrutinizes the audience and declares that he sees some of his master's companions.

767-74   Envy: as black as a chimney-sweep and as evil-smelling as an oyster-seller. Envy is the progeny of filth and poverty. The particular folly of Envy here is that of the illiterate sort of Puritan, who was often portrayed as being blindly prejudiced against all learning. Such Puritans wanted the theatres closed and were therefore the subject of continual derision in drama (see note to 224).

COVETOUSNESS

I am Covetousness, begotten of an old churl in
an old leathern bag, and — might I have my
wish — I would desire that this house and all   755
the people in it were turned to gold, that I might
lock you up in my good chest. O my sweet gold!

FAUSTUS

What art thou, the third?

WRATH

I am Wrath. I had neither father nor mother: I
lept out of a lion's mouth when I was scarce half   760
an hour old, and ever since I have run up and
down the world with this case of rapiers, wounding myself when I had nobody to fight withal. I
was born in hell; and look to it, for some of you
shall be my father.   765

FAUSTUS

What art thou, the fourth?

ENVY

I am Envy, begotten of a chimney-sweeper and
an oyster-wife. I cannot read and therefore wish
all books were burnt. I am lean with seeing
others eat. O, that there would come a famine   770
through all the world, that all might die, and I
live alone! Then thou shouldst see how fat I
would be. But must thou sit and I stand? Come
down, with a vengeance!

FAUSTUS

Away, envious rascal! What art thou, the fifth?   775

776-88   Gluttony: pension (778), in a now-obsolete sense, means a sum of money left to pay the board of a
          child (*OED* Pension. *sb.* 6); bevers (779) are drinks or possibly snacks (*OED* Bevers. *sb.* 1 and 3).
          Martlemas-Beef (783) refers to cattle slaughtered for selling at Martinmas, 11 November, to pro-
          vide for the winter; Martinmas was also a fair day and therefore an occasion for considerable
          indulgence in eating and drinking. Marchbeer (786) was a strong ale or beer brewed in March
          (*OED* March. *sb²*. 2.b). The combination of these two suggests year-round festivity. Peter Pickle-
          Herring (783) was the sort of roisterer one might encounter on such occasions, though *OED* does
          not acknowledge this usage until considerably later (*OED* Pickle-herring. 2). Progeny (787) is not
          meant in the usual sense of offspring, but in the less common sense of lineage or parentage (*OED*
          Progeny. 5). Gluttony, often identified with Adam's first sin, recurs in the imagery of Marlowe's
          play: see 107, 804, 1369.

793-97   Sloth: as a scholar accustomed to a sedentary life, Faustus might well be expected to have a
          special proclivity for this sin, which was associated with melancholy, depression, and inaction — in
          short, with the rigorous life of thought and contemplation in a state of decay. Shakespeare's
          scholar prince, Hamlet, confesses to or at least suspects these weaknesses in himself. Sloth's invo-
          cation of Gluttony and Lechery indicates a traditional distinction between sins of the mind and
          sins of the flesh. Spenser employs the same grouping of fleshly sins in *The Faerie Queene*. See
          note to 1369 and cover illustration to this edition.

798   Minx: an obscure word with various connotations, all of which suit Marlowe's context: a pet dog,
          a hussy or pert girl, a wanton woman (*OED* Minx 1, 2, 2.b). *OED* lists a few rare appellations of
          "Mistress Minx", including Marlowe's.

GLUTTONY

Who, I sir? I am Gluttony. My parents are all dead and the devil a penny they have left me, but a bare pension, and that is thirty meals a day and ten bevers — a small trifle to suffice nature. O, I come of a royal parentage: my grandfather was a gammon of bacon, my grandmother a hogshead of claret-wine. My godfathers were these: Peter Pickle-Herring and Martin Martlemas-Beef. O, but my godmother: she was a jolly gentlewoman, and well-beloved in every good town and city; her name was Mistress Margery March-Beer. Now, Faustus, thou hast heard all my progeny. Wilt thou bid me to supper?

780

785

FAUSTUS

No, I'll see thee hanged! Thou wilt eat up all my victuals.

790

GLUTTONY

Then the devil choke thee!

FAUSTUS

Choke thyself, Glutton! What art thou, the sixth?

SLOTH

I am Sloth. I was begotten on a sunny bank, where I have lain ever since, and you have done me great injury to bring me from thence. Let me be carried thither again by Gluttony and Lechery. I'll not speak another word for a king's ransom.

795

FAUSTUS

What are you, Mistress Minx, the seventh and last?

799-801   Lechery: "Lechery is saying in effect that she prefers a small quantity of virility to a large extent of impotence" (Gill). In slang mutton (800) was associated with lust (*OED* Mutton. 4). The imaging of lechery in terms of gluttony is common enough (see note to 793-97) and appropriate to the predominant fantasies of Faustus. An ell (800) is a varying unit of measurement, but figuratively contrasted with the small unit of an inch, as in the proverbial: "Give him an inch and he'll take an ell." (*OED* Ell. 1.b). Stockfish (800) is dried cod, which is also a word for scrotum (*OED* Cod. sb¹. 4).

802   A1 sets this line out as being separate from Lechery's speech, but does not assign it to a speaker. The B-version gives the line to Lucifer, but since Lucifer is marked again for the next speech and since Faustus has responded in similar vein to other sins in the pageant (see 775, 789-90, and 792) this line seems to belong with Faustus.

804   The metaphor of feeding on sin reinforces the imagery of the preceding pageant scene and the ubiquitous imagery of gluttonous perversion. The B-version emends the line to the thematically weaker: "O how this sight doth delight my soul." (B731).

808   I will send for thee at midnight: an ominous anticipation of Faustus' end. This is not to be the fatal midnight, only the occasion of Faustus' first activity as an initiate in magic and witchcraft. However, the twenty-four years will pass even more quickly than the twenty-four hours of a day in stage time (see note to 491) and the only scene in the remainder of the play which specifically occurs at midnight is, in fact, the last scene. Diabolical rites traditionally take place at midnight: the witches in *Macbeth* are described as "midnight hags" (IV. i. 47).

813   chary: carefully (*OED* Chary. *a*. 8 notes Marlowe's quasi-adverbial usage). Chary has a wide range of connotations, from sorrowful to fastidious; together they reinforce the irony of Faustus' utterance, for the fatal midnight will prove that he has not been chary (careful) of his eternal life and must now be chary (sorrowful) for eternity.

LECHERY

Who, I sir? I am one that loves an inch of raw
mutton better than an ell of fried stock-fish, and   800
the first letter of my name begins with Lechery.

[FAUSTUS]

Away, to hell, to hell.

Exeunt the SINS.

LUCIFER

Now, Faustus, how dost thou like this?

FAUSTUS

O, this feeds my soul!

LUCIFER

Tut, Faustus, in hell is all manner of delight.   805

FAUSTUS

O, might I see hell and return again. How
happy were I then!

LUCIFER

Thou shalt. I will send for thee at midnight. In
mean time take this book, peruse it thoroughly,
and thou shalt turn thyself into what shape thou   810
wilt.

FAUSTUS

Great thanks, mighty Lucifer. This will I keep
as chary as my life.

815.2   *Enter* WAGNER *solus*: the B-version duplicates this speech (B558f and B777f) and for the second occasion has "Enter the Chorus" (B776.1), which confirms the present editors' view that all the choric speeches would have been spoken by Wagner in early productions; i.e. 1-28, 816-26, 931-47, 1287-94.

816-26   The chariot drawn by dragons derives from *EFB*. It is one of Marlowe's few concessions to the more sensationalist of his source's credulities. The B-version, however, greatly expands this speech with *EFB* and bombast. In the A-version, Faustus contents himself with a visit to the top of Mt Olympus, the home of the gods in Greek mythology, and the trip may be interpreted metaphorically as a journey into the *arcana* (hidden mysteries) of classical thought. In B, Faustus takes an eight-day tour of the entire universe, "From the bright circle of the horned moon,/Even to the height of *Primum Mobile*" (B785-86).

821   yoky; yoked; a rare poetic usage (*OED* Yoky. *a*).

825-26   feast . . . solemnized: in the Roman Catholic Church, the Latin term *festum*, translated as feast, is used to denote days set aside for special commemoration of an event or person; *solemnitates* are commemorative days of greater importance. Although a celebratory meal would often accompany celebration of a feast-day, the reduction of St Peter's feast to a papal orgy (886-926) would have appealed to Protestant prejudice in an English audience. St Peter, the first Pope, shares a joint feast-day with St Paul on 29 June and his imprisonment is commemorated on 1 August (Lammas Day).

827-48   Faustus is making the sort of Grand Tour which was at the time becoming fashionable to complete the education of an English gentleman. The practice was denounced by many moralists of the age; Italy, though the most magnificent embodiment of Renaissance culture, was especially vilified by Protestant Englishmen.
          The mode of Faustus' travel is unspecified, but the perspective suggests continued flight (see previous speech). In the witchcraft manuals, the ability to fly was the sign of a witch and yet witches' achievements were mainly hallucinations practised upon them by the devil. This speech hints at both, though Faustus, of course, would be unaware of the latter.

828   Trier: an attractive town on the Mosel (Moselle) River in West Germany. An administrative, commercial, and cultural centre, its importance declined at the end of the seventeenth century. It has the repository of a famous relic, the Holy Coat of Trier, Christ's seamless robe.

LUCIFER

Farewell, Faustus, and think on the devil.

FAUSTUS

Farewell, great Lucifer. Come, Mephostophiles.   815

Exeunt omnes.

Enter WAGNER *solus.*

WAGNER

Learned Faustus,
To know the secrets of astronomy,
Graven in the book of Jove's high firmament,
Did mount himself to scale Olympus' top;
Being seated in a chariot burning bright,   820
Drawn by the strength of yoky dragons' necks,
He now is gone to prove cosmography;
And, as I guess, will first arrive at Rome
To see the Pope and manner of his court,
And take some part of holy Peter's feast,   825
That to this day is highly solemnized.

Exit WAGNER.

Enter FAUSTUS *and* MEPHOSTOPHILES.

FAUSTUS

Having now, my good Mephostophiles,
Passed with delight the stately town of Trier,

835   Naples lies within the region of Campania. Some modern editors have erroneously assumed this
              juxtaposition to have been an error on Marlowe's part. There is, however, a confusion in *EFB*.

837-38   Town planning was a characteristically Renaissance preoccupation. Compare this description
              with the House of Pride in *The Faerie Queene* I. iv. In both the emphasis on the number 4 is a
              reminder of mortality: the four elements of the sublunary world made 4 the number of matter, of
              unstable fallen nature.

838   equivalent to [A, equivolence].

839   learned Maro: Publius Vergilius Maro, usually known as Virgil (70-19 BC). His reputation
              during the Middle Ages and the Renaissance was curiously ambivalent. On the one hand his
              fourth eclogue was revered as a prophecy of the birth of Christ, and Aeneas' epic journey in the
              Aeneid was allegorized as a mystical vision of the spiritual progress of man; on the other, he was
              thought to have been a magician and necromancer. The tunnel he reputedly cut (840-41) by
              magic is in fact the site of an ancient passageway. See J. W. Spargo, *Virgil the Necromancer*
              (Cambridge, Mass., 1934), 292-95.

842-44   Venice . . . which . . . aspiring top: the syntax does not make the referent of "which" at all clear;
              St Mark's in Venice does not have an aspiring top, though there is a *campanile* nearby. Perhaps
              Marlowe was more interested in symbolism than the pedantry of architectural reality. The idea of
              man's aspiring mind as a threat to the stars or gods is a common motif in Marlowe (see 20-22, 90
              and note).

850-51   privy chamber: private reception room.

853-54   Rendered as one line in A.

Environ'd round with airy mountain-tops,
With walls of flint and deep-entrenched lakes   830
Not to be won by any conquering prince,
From Paris next, coasting the realm of France,
We saw the river Main fall into Rhine,
Whose banks are set with groves of fruitful vines.
Then up to Naples, rich Campania,   835
Whose buildings fair and gorgeous to the eye,
The streets straight forth, and paved with finest brick,
Quarters the town in four equivalents.
There saw we learned Maro's golden tomb,
The way he cut an English mile in length   840
Thorough a rock of stone in one night's space.
From thence to Venice, Padua, and the rest,
In midst of which a sumptuous temple stands,
That threats the stars with her aspiring top.
Thus hitherto hath Faustus spent his time,   845
But tell me now: what resting-place is this?
Hast thou, as erst I did command,
Conducted me within the walls of Rome?

MEPHOSTOPHILES

Faustus, I have; and because we will not be
unprovided, I have taken up His Holiness' privy   850
chamber for our use.

FAUSTUS

I hope His Holiness will bid us welcome.

MEPHOSTOPHILES

Tut, 'tis no matter, man:
We'll be bold with his good cheer.

860-61   There is a further problem in syntax here (see note to 842-44) in that A lacks 859-60, which have been imported from B (836-37).

863-64   A minor topographical inaccuracy: the castle is not on the bridge itself but on the bank to which the bridge leads.

865-67   Marlowe follows *EFB* quite closely in this passage; his purpose in elaborating somewhat on *EFB* here may be to portray Rome as a worldly power rather than a spiritual power. On the iconography of the Renaissance depiction of cities, see Erwin Panofsky, *Studies in Iconology* (New York, 1964).

867   A puzzling detail: perhaps the design of the castle's defences to "match the days within one complete year" serves to identify Rome with the fallen world of Time, as does the dial on top of the House of Pride in *The Faerie Queene* (I. iv. 4), telling "the timely hours." Renaissance architects gave much thought to the symbolic function of buildings; when, in 1582, Pope Gregory signed the decree for the reform of the Julian calendar, he did so in a villa which had been specially modified to contain 365 rooms. This line is set as two in A.

868   pyramides: obelisk. Pyramides is pronounced as having four syllables, with emphasis on the second. Marlowe again uses "pyramides" as a singular form in *The Massacre of Paris*, ii. 43-46.

869   The obelisk to which Mephostophiles refers is probably the one brought back by Caligula, a century after Julius Caesar's death. Marlowe is not so much repeating the error of *EFB* as repeating the long-standing tradition to which *EFB* subscribes. There was a vogue for all things Egyptological in the later sixteenth century.

870-72   Classical Hades was separated from the upper world by the river Styx, across whose waters the souls of the newly-dead were ferried by Charon, and also contained the rivers of Acheron (woe), Cocytus (lamentation), Lethe (forgetfulness), and Phlegethon (liquid fire).

874   splendent: extremely brilliant, gorgeous, or magnificent (*OED* Splendent. 2.b).

878   bald-pate friars: in common with the monks of diverse religions, Christian monks and friars were required to shave their heads. In the Christian tradition, it was customary until as late as 1972 to leave a small fringe of hair to signify the crown of thorns worn by Christ.

879   *summum bonum*: in scholastic theology, God is *unum* (one), *bonum* (good), and *verum* (true). The compound of these attributes is the *summum bonum* (the greatest good), which is the identity of God. Mephostophiles asserts that to the average friar the greatest good is what is best to eat. Marlowe's jokes at the expense of the friars are not necessarily those of a post-Reformation Protestant: Chaucer's Pardoner uses the same imagery in denouncing those who make their bellies into their God and he denounces Gluttony as the cause of Original Sin.

880   compass: contrive or devise, usually in a bad sense (*OED* Compass. *v¹*. 2).

And now, my Faustus, that thou may'st perceive   855
What Rome containeth to delight thee with,
Know that this city stands upon seven hills
That underprops the ground work of the same:
[Just through the midst runs flowing Tiber's stream,
With winding banks that cut it in two parts,]   860
Over the which four stately bridges lean,
That makes safe passage to each part of Rome.
Upon the bridge call'd Ponte Angelo
Erected is a castle passing strong,
Within whose walls such store of ordnance are   865
And double cannons, fram'd of carved brass,
As match the days within one complete year —
Besides the gates and high pyramides
Which Julius Caesar brought from Africa.

FAUSTUS

Now, by the kingdoms of infernal rule —   870
Of Styx, Acheron, and the fiery lake
Of ever-burning Phlegethon — I swear
That I do long to see the monuments
And situation of bright splendent Rome.
Come, therefore: let's away.   875

MEPHOSTOPHILES

Nay, Faustus, stay. I know you'd fain see the Pope
And take some part of holy Peter's feast,
Where thou shalt see a troupe of bald-pate friars,
Whose *summum bonum* is in belly cheer.

FAUSTUS

Well, I am content to compass then some sport   880
And by their folly make us merriment.

882f.   From this point the remainder of the papal banquet scene is in prose. At about this point also, the
           two versions diverge: B has a much longer scene with additional characters who have no real part
           in the Faustus story. The B-version, consisting largely of knock-about farce and anti-Catholic
           jokes, continues for approximately 150 lines, whereas the A-text has less than 50 lines. The added
           B-version material does not derive from *EFB* but from John Foxe's *Acts and Monuments of
           matters happening in the Church* (1554; enlarged in 1663), more commonly known as *Foxe's
           Book of Martyrs*. The significance of the additions from Foxe, according to Constance Brown
           Kuriyama, is that they point to Rowley's authorship rather than Marlowe's. See "Dr Greg and *Dr
           Faustus*: The Supposed Originality of the 1616 Text", *ELR* 5 (1975), 171-97, at p. 191.

882   charm me that I may be invisible: to charm, in this sense, is to endow with supernatural powers
           (*OED* Charm. *v.* 2), but the practical matter is how the effect of invisibility was achieved on the
           Elizabethan stage. In the stage conventions of the age, invisibility was denoted by the wearing of a
           particular emblematic garment. *Henslowe's Diary* itemizes "a robe, for to goo invisibell" in a
           check-list of theatrical properties. Invisibility is also sometimes denoted by using the highest level
           of the three-storeyed public playhouse, as Shakespeare does for Prospero in *The Tempest*. The
           latter method cannot apply to this scene, of course, since Faustus is close at hand to snatch food
           from the banqueting table. There is an implied moment of action when Mephostophiles says "So,
           Faustus" (884) and presumably this is when he hands Faustus the symbolic garment. See *The
           Tempest* III. ii. 39 SD "Enter Ariel, invisible".

885.1-2   *sennet* [A, sonnet]. A sennet is a set of notes on a trumpet or cornet and is a conventional signal in
           Elizabethan drama for ceremonial entries and processions.

887   and you spare: if you spare; a now-archaic usage of "and" (*OED* And. c.1).

890   Here's nobody: the joke on the identity of nobody is at least as old as the Cave of Polyphemus
           episode in *The Odyssey* and persisted into Elizabethan humour. See Paul A. Jorgenson, "Much
           Ado About 'Nothing'", *SQ* 5 (1954). 287 95.

Then charm me that I may be invisible, to do
what I please, unseen of any whilst I stay in Rome.

MEPHOSTOPHILES

So, Faustus, now do what thou wilt: thou shalt not
be discerned.   885

Sound a sennet; enter the POPE *and the* CARDINAL OF
LORRAINE *to the banquet, with* FRIARS *attending.*

POPE

My lord of Lorraine, will't please you draw near.

FAUSTUS

Fall to, and the devil choke you and you spare.

POPE

How now, who's that which spake? Friars, look
about.

FRIAR

Here's nobody, if it like your Holiness.   890

POPE

My Lord, here is a dainty dish was sent me from the
Bishop of Milan.

FAUSTUS

I thank you, sir.

Snatch it.

POPE

How now, who's that which snatched the meat from

897   I'll ha't: contracted from "I'll have it"; given as "Ile hate" in A1.

900   ghost: the word was originally used in English as the equivalent of the Latin word *spiritus* and its universal modern meaning is relatively late (*OED* Ghost. *sb*. 1-3, and 8). It has been suggested that the Protestant abolition of the doctrine of Purgatory contributed to a greatly increased belief in the existence and activities of ghosts as the unquiet dead from the sixteenth century onwards. Lorraine's "ghost . . . out of Purgatory" provides the audience with two bad jokes for the price of one.

901   pardon: used here not only in its colloquial and legal senses, but more specifically in the sense of Papal indulgence (*OED* Pardon. *sb¹*. 3.a). The selling of indulgences, following the Papal Bull of 1343, led to the equation of the remission of sins with the offering of money; the controversy which resulted was one of the major causes of the Reformation.

902   dirge: a most unusual use of this word, which derives from the antiphon "*Dirige, Domine Deus* . . ." (Direct, O Lord God . . .) in the Mass for the Dead. What the friars actually chant is a litany of curses. See N. C. Carpenter, "Music in *Dr Faustus*", *NQ* 195 (1950), 180-81.

904-05   crossing . . . trick: a joke at the expense of Catholic ritual.

me? Will no man look? My Lord, this dish was   895
sent me from the Cardinal of Florence.

FAUSTUS

You say true, I'll ha't.

                                        [*Snatch it*].

POPE

What, again? My lord, I'll drink to your Grace.

FAUSTUS

I'll pledge your Grace.

                                        [*Snatch it*].

LORRAINE

My Lord, it may be some ghost newly crept out of   900
Purgatory come to beg a pardon of your Holiness.

POPE

It may be so. Friars, prepare a dirge to lay the
fury of this ghost. Once again, my Lord, fall to.

                            The POPE *crosseth himself.*

FAUSTUS

What, are you crossing of yourself?
Well, use that trick no more, I would advise you.   905

                                        Cross again.

910   bell, book, and candle: the three instruments used in the ceremony of exorcism, as prescribed in the *Rituale Romanum*, the official service book of the Roman Rite. The formula used for the cursing — *Maledicat*, the converse of *Benedicat* — comes from the ceremony of excommunication, a fate automatically earned in Canon Law for the offence of striking a clergyman. Excommunication was ratified and reconfirmed for the offence of attacking the Pope as recently as January, 1983.

912   forward and backward: Faustus mockingly associates the excommunication ceremony with his own acrostical and anagrammatical formulae (246–47).

913-14   A changes to prose here, but the rhyme "bray . . . day" suggests a continuation of the doggerel verse.

913-14   hog . . . calf . . . ass: there may have been a topical joke here. Perhaps Faustus intends to turn into animals any people who dare to use the rite of exorcism against him: compare the passage a little later, at 1026–40, where Mephostophiles threatens to do the same to Ralph, Robin, and the Vintner for vexing him. The turning of men into animals by the use of magic may be interpreted as degradation; moralist interpreters of the Circe episode in *The Odyssey* interpreted the transformation of Odysseus' companions as a mark of their depravity. See also *The Faerie Queene*, II. xii. Milton was later to use the transformation motif thus in *Comus* (1634).

916.1   See note at 614–28 on stage directions in the imperative.

919   *Maledicat dominus*: may the Lord curse [him].

923   Friar Sandelo: the friar and his colleagues are presumably Franciscans, as that was the only order of friars permitted to wear sandals. In the sixteenth century sandal was often spelt "sandell", hence the name Sandelo. The Franciscans were a particularly controversial order since it had become very difficult for them to live practically in terms of the strict rule of poverty given by their founder and it seems that some of their members lived in a style that did little to help matters. Marlowe, following *EFB*, has already had one joke at their expense in this play (274).

923-26   Although there is no formal stage direction to indicate what Faustus is up to during the ceremony, it is clear, as Gill says, that he is making a nuisance of himself. The first two maledictions concern previous actions, but the striking of Friar Sandelo (923), the disturbing of the dirge (926), and the snatching of the wine (928) are all part of the invisible Faustus' by-play.

Well, there's the second time; aware the third,
I give you fair warning.

>*Cross again, and* FAUSTUS *hits him a box of the ear,*
>*and they all run away.*

FAUSTUS

Come on, Mephostophiles, what shall we do?

MEPHOSTOPHILES

Nay, I know not: we shall be cursed with bell,
book, and candle. 910

FAUSTUS

How? bell, book, and candle; candle, book, and bell;
Forward and backward, to curse Faustus to hell.
Anon you shall hear a hog grunt, a calf bleat, and
an ass bray, because it is St Peter's holy day.

Enter all the FRIARS *to sing the dirge.*

FRIAR

Come, brethren, let's about our business with 915
good devotion.

Sing this:
Cursed be he that stole away his Holiness' meat
from the table.
>*Maledicat dominus.*
Cursed be he that struck his Holiness a blow on 920
the face.
>*Maledicat dominus.*
Cursed be he that took Friar Sandelo a blow on
the pate.

929-30   *Maledicat dominus/Et omnes sancti*: may the Lord and all the saints curse [him]. The words *Et omnes sancti* associate the cursing with the litany of saints; the triviality of the maledictions and the evident by-play during them suggest further anti-clerical satire.

930.2   *Enter* CHORUS: see note to 815.2.

931-47   No attribution is given to this speech in A.

933   stayed his course: ceased his travels.

936   gratulate: express joy at; now archaic, but quite common in sixteenth century usage (*OED* Gratulate. *v.* 2).

943-44   Emperor Charles V ruled from 1519 to 1556; the earlier part of his reign would have coincided with the last years of the historical Faustus.

946   trial: proof.

947.1   *ostler*: an old phonetic spelling for hosteler; a man who looks after horses a: an inn (*OED* Ostler).

Maledicat dominus. 925

Cursed be he that disturbeth our holy dirge.

Maledicat dominus.

Cursed be he that took away his Holiness' wine

Maledicat dominus

Et omnes sancti, Amen. 930

Beat the FRIARS *and fling fireworks among them, and so Exeunt.*

Enter CHORUS.

[CHORUS]

When Faustus had with pleasure ta'en the view
Of rarest things and royal courts of kings,
He stayed his course and so returned home,
Where such as bear his absence, but with grief,
(I mean his friends and nearest companions) 935
Did gratulate his safety with kind words
And in their conference of what befell,
Touching his journey through the world and air,
They put forth questions of astrology,
Which Faustus answered with such learned skill 940
As they admired and wond'red at his wit.
Now is his fame spread forth in every land:
Amongst the rest the emperor is one,
Carolus the fifth, at whose palace now
Faustus is feasted 'mongst his noblemen. 945
What there he did in trial of his art
I leave untold — your eyes shall see performed.

Exit.

Enter ROBIN *the ostler with a book in his hand.*

948f   Since the Chorus speech just concluded declares that a court scene is to follow (946–47), it is possible that the tavern scene was interpolated by someone other than Marlowe or his approved collaborator. Some lines which seem thematically inappropriate to the play as a whole (1032–34) tend to confirm this view; on the other hand, the comic tavern scene is thematically close in many ways to the court scene which it seems to anticipate. Certainly, there is humorous bathos in this sequence of scenes as it has come down to us, but it seems probable to the present editors that the two scenes have been accidentally reversed. Robin and Ralph may be seen to *zany* the roles of Faustus and the Emperor respectively, so their comic scene would have greater point if it were to follow rather than precede Faustus' audience with the Emperor.

950–52   The orgiastic naked dancing of the witches' sabbath seems to be what Robin has in mind. This circular, widdershins (anti-clockwise) dance, as depicted by Dürer, reverses the Renaissance image of cosmic harmony in the clockwise dance of the naked Graces, as depicted by Raphael, Botticelli, and many others.

954.1   *Enter* RALPH *calling* ROBIN: although Ralph's occupation is not stated, it becomes immediately apparent that he is a fellow-servant at the inn. Ralph is phonetically rendered as "Rafe" in A1, in conformity with Elizabethan pronunciation.

958   chafing: fuming or fretting (*OED* Chafe. *v.* 4.b).

960   blown up: an explosion was the usual comic conclusion to literary accounts of alchemical experiments from Chaucer to Ben Jonson.

961   dismembered: threatened dismemberment is a motif in the comic sub-plot as well as in the main plot (see 713, 1224–27, and 1355).
A common Renaissance image presents the human body as the universe in microcosm, so that dismemberment implies a cosmogonic reversal into chaos. The dismemberment motif is common in late medieval English drama and is a major preoccupation of the Wakefield mystery plays.

962   roaring: roistering; a good Elizabethan word to describe any person who behaves in a noisy riotous manner (*OED* Roaring. *ppl.* 2.b).

963–64   The illiterate fumblings of Robin and Ralph contrast with the learned scholarship of Faustus (see note to 948f).

966   he for his forehead: an elliptical allusion to a convention whereby a deceived husband, or cuckold, is mocked in a gesture which suggests that he wears an invisible pair of horns on his forehead.
private: following the bawdy innuendo of the previous phrase, Robin is almost certainly quibbling on genitalia as private parts, though *OED* does not cite private in this sense until as late as 1634 (*OED* private. *a.* 3.b).

967   bear: i.e. bear a child.

ROBIN

O, this is admirable! Here I ha' stolen one of
Doctor Faustus' conjuring books, and i'faith I
mean to search some circles for my own use: 950
now will I make all the maidens in our parish
dance at my pleasure stark naked before me;
and so by that means I shall see more than e'er
I felt or saw yet.

Enter RALPH *calling* ROBIN.

RALPH

Robin, prithee come away. There's a gentleman   955
tarries to have his horse, and he would have his
things rubbed and made clean. He keeps such a
chafing with my mistress about it, and she has
sent me to look thee out. Prithee, come away.

ROBIN

Keep out, keep out, or else you are blown up,   960
you are dismembered! Ralph, keep out, for I
am about a roaring piece of work.

RALPH

Come, what dost thou with that same book?
Thou canst not read.

ROBIN

Yes, my master and my mistress shall find that I   965
can read, he for his forehead, she for her private
study. She's born to bear with me, or else my art
fails.

RALPH

Why, Robin, what book is that?

970   intolerable: irresistible (*OED* Intolerable. *a*.2).

971   brimstone: medieval vernacular word for sulphur, especially used when describing its flammable character; used in early English translations of the Bible to describe the fiery substance sent by God to punish wicked men (Gen. 19.24) and the fires of hell (Rev. 19.20). (*OED* Brimstone. 1.)

975   hippocras: a drink made of wine flavoured with spices.

980-81   Playing on Nan Spit's name, Robin suggests turning and winding her as though on a spit. The extremely coarse bawdiness is inescapable. In Robin's fantasies, as in Faustus', lechery and gluttony are mingled. Faustus will seek Helen of Troy for his bed (1368-71), Robin wants the innkeeper's wife (965-68), and Ralph will have to content himself with the kitchen maid.

982   midnight: see also 340 and 808.

985   horse-bread: bread made from bran, not flour, for consumption by horses.

989.1   Robin and Ralph go off, only to return immediately: this may indicate a missing scene.

ROBIN

What book? why the most intolerable book for   970
conjuring that e'er was invented by any brimstone
devil.

RALPH

Canst thou conjure with it?

ROBIN

I can do all these things easily with it: first, I can
make thee drunk with hippocras at any tavern in   975
Europe for nothing — that's one of my conjuring
works.

RALPH

Our master parson says that's nothing.

ROBIN

True, Ralph. And more, Ralph: if thou hast any
mind to Nan Spit, our kitchen maid, then turn   980
her and wind her to thine own use, as often as
thou wilt — and at midnight!

RALPH

O brave Robin, shall I have Nan Spit, and to mine
own use? On that condition I'll feed thy devil
with horse-bread as long as he lives, of free   985
cost.

ROBIN

No more, sweet Ralph. Let's go and make clean
our boots, which lie foul upon our hands, and
then to our conjuring in the devil's name.

                                          Exeunt.

991   *Ecce signum*: behold a sign. A quasi-biblical phrase used by conjurors and stage clowns: compare
           Falstaff's use of the phrase in telling about his imaginary deeds of valour (*1 Henry IV*. II. iv.
           170). A modern equivalent would be, "Ladies and Gentlemen, before your very eyes . . .".

993.1   A vintner is an innkeeper who specializes in selling wine.

995   gull: cheat (*OED* Gull. *v*³. 1). Very common in Elizabethan parlance.
           Drawer: tapster or barman. Robin is so puffed up with the thought of his new magical powers
           that he falls to insulting his own employer by calling him "Barman".

997   Soft: an exclamation with imperative force, commanding Robin to be quiet and pay attention
           (*OED* Soft. *adv*. 8).

1000   A1 has "you are but a etc.": Greg takes the "etc" as a confession of failure of memory by the
           A-text reporter. But it may also have been (1) spoken as such (Jump), (2) an invitation to the
           actor playing Robin to *ad lib*. (Gill), or (3) a necessary piece of censorship to cover gross ob-
           scenity.

Enter ROBIN *and* RALPH *with a silver goblet.*

ROBIN

Come, Ralph, did I not tell thee we were forever   990
made by this Doctor Faustus' book? *Ecce signum,*
here's a simple purchase for horse-keepers! Our
horses shall eat no hay as long as this lasts.

Enter the VINTNER.

RALPH

But Robin, here comes the Vintner.

ROBIN

Hush, I'll gull him supernaturally. Drawer, I hope   995
all is paid, God be with you. Come, Ralph.

VINTNER

Soft, sir a word with you. I must yet have a
goblet paid from you ere you go.

ROBIN

I, a goblet, Ralph? I, a goblet? I scorn you; and
you are but a . . . I, a goblet? Search me!   1000

VINTNER

I mean so, with your favour.

ROBIN

How say you now?

VINTNER

I must say somewhat to your fellow. You, sir!

1007-08   about . . . before: Robin quibbles over the precise whereabouts of the goblet, which he now brandishes in front of him.

1015-18   What Robin reads, or pretends to read, is gibberish—a nonsensical combination of word-fragments from Latin and Greek, run together in orotund phrases. All this is reminiscent of Faustus' own conjuration speech, ending: ". . . *ipse nunc surgat, nobis dicatus, Mephostophiles!*" (254-62). In both instances Mephostophiles appears at the moment his name is invoked.

1019   The vintner is closer than Robin to real Latin, though his *O nomine domine* ("O in the name of God") is ungrammatical. This and the next two snatches of Latin are illiterate renderings of passages from set prayers in the liturgy.

RALPH

Me, sir? me, sir? Search your fill! Now sir, you may
be ashamed to burden honest men with a matter   1005
truth.

VINTNER

Well, t'one of you hath this goblet about you.

ROBIN

You lie, drawer, 'tis afore me. Sirrah you, I'll
teach ye to impeach honest men. Stand by: I'll
scour you for a goblet. Stand aside, you had best, I   1010
charge you in the name of Beelzebub. Look to the
goblet, Ralph.

VINTNER

What mean you, sirrah?

ROBIN

I'll tell you what I mean.

He reads:

Sanctobulorum Periphrasticon — nay, I'll tickle   1015
you, vintner. Look to the goblet, Ralph. *Poly-
pragmos Belseborams framanto pacostiphos tostu
Mephostophilis.*

Enter MEPHOSTOPHILES: *sets squibs at their backs: they run
about.*

VINTNER

O nomine domine, what meanst thou, Robin?
Thou hast no goblet.   1020

1021   *Peccatum peccatorum*: sin of sins.

1023   *Misericordia pro nobis*: have mercy on us.

1025.1   *Enter to them* MEPHOSTOPHILES: Mephostophiles is already on stage (1018.1) and this has
            caused some editors to think that the repetition means that there was an alternative ending to the
            scene. The sequence of events does not require this conclusion, however; all that is required is a
            distinction between the two stage directions. At the first Mephostophiles is not seen by Robin,
            Ralph and the Vintner, only perceived to be present through the fireworks he sets off behind
            them; in the second stage direction, the addition of *to them* makes it clear that he now manifests
            himself to them visually. Alternatively, the first entry need only be long enough to set off the fire-
            works. But see also next note.

1026-34   The Mephostophiles of this speech is far from the near-tragic figure of the first conjuration scene.
            Though the present scene can be justified as parodying the main plot, the descent in poetic
            grandeur may well prompt doubts about Marlowe's authorship. 1032-34 set a special problem: in
            the first conjuration scene Mephostophiles made it plain that charms and invocations could not
            force him to appear (see 86 and note), but now he admits to being "vexed with these villains'
            charms." The inconsistency suggests some tampering.

1026-27   See note to 913-14.

1038-40   It seems that the Vintner, who wasn't involved in calling up Mephostophiles anyway, has escaped,
            presumably having run off during Robin's cheeky response to Mephostophiles.

RALPH

Peccatum   peccatorum — here's thy goblet, good vintner.

ROBIN

Misericordia pro nobis — What shall I do? Good devil, forgive me now, and I'll never rob thy library more.   1025

Enter to them MEPHOSTOPHILES.

MEPHOSTOPHILES

Vanish, villains: th'one like an ape, another like a bear, the third an ass, for doing this enterprise.
Monarch of hell, under whose black survey
Great potentates do kneel with awful fear,   1030
Upon whose altars thousand souls do lie,
How am I vexed with these villains' charms!
From Constantinople am I hither come,
Only for pleasure of these damned slaves.

ROBIN

How? from Constantinople? You have had a   1035
great journey. Will you take sixpence in your
purse to pay for your supper, and be gone?

MEPHOSTOPHILES

Well, villains, for your presumption I transform thee into an ape, and thee into a dog;
and so be gone.   1040

Exit.

1046.1   In the A-text, the *Exeunt* is misplaced, coming after Ralph's last speech and before Robin's.

1046.2   The Knight has a small role as a sceptic who injudiciously seeks to discredit Dr Faustus. In the B-version, the Knight is given the name Benvolio and his part is considerably extended.

1050   rare: splendid or fine (*OED* Rare. *a.* 6.b).

1054-55   Possibly an echo from 1 Corinthians 2.9: "The things which eye hathe not sene, nether eare hathe heard . . . which God hathe prepared for them that love him", which is in turn a quotation from Isaiah 64.4. Shakespeare, through the medium of Bottom's dream, evokes the same passage in *A Midsummer Night's Dream* IV. i. 211-13.

ROBIN

How, into an ape? That's brave! I'll have fine
sport with the boys; I'll get nuts and apples
enow.

RALPH

And I must be a dog!

ROBIN

I'faith, thy head will never be out of the potage-   1045
pot.

Exeunt.

Enter EMPEROR, FAUSTUS, *and a* KNIGHT, *with* ATTENDANTS.

EMPEROR

Master Doctor Faustus, I have heard strange
report of thy knowledge in the black art — how
that none in my empire, nor in the whole world
can compare with thee for the rare effects of   1050
magic. They say thou hast a familiar spirit, by
whom thou canst accomplish what thou list. This,
therefore, is my request: that thou let me see some
proof of thy skill, that mine eyes may be witnesses
to confirm what mine ears have heard reported;   1055
and here I swear to thee, by the honour of mine
imperial crown, that, whatever thou doest, thou
shalt be no ways prejudiced or endamaged.

KNIGHT

(*Aside*) I'faith, he looks much like a conjuror.

1066-87   The Emperor's view of nobility is essentially military and genetic. His idea that mankind has declined physically and intellectually since earlier times is conventional. The Emperor is hoping to see some such courtly entertainment as the traditional masquing of the Nine Worthies (Alexander was one) brought to real life. Compare Shakespeare's masque in *Love's Labour's Lost*.

1076   From here A renders remainder of speech in verse.

1078   motion: in Elizabethan usage, commonly a puppet show (*OED* Motion. *sb*. 13.a). Hence what the Emperor is saying elliptically seems to be: "Even when I hear of his being presented in so slight a thing as a puppet show . . ." The lives of such heroes as Alexander, both historical and mythical, were commonly the subject of puppet plays, e.g. in Act V of Ben Jonson's *Bartholomew Fair*. "Motion" may also mean something like "mention", according to J. C. Maxwell, "Notes on *Dr Faustus*", *NQ* NS11 (1964), 262.

1080-87   The Emperor wishes to participate from a fairly safe distance in Faustus' essentially blasphemous activity in raising the dead (see 52-53). His insistence on this piece of necromancy to satisfy his "just desire" (1086) suggests that the Emperor himself is well advanced in spiritual depravity. The same can be said of the scholars who will shortly (in stage time) tempt Faustus to a further necromantic act in conjuring up the spirit of Helen of Troy (1295f).

FAUSTUS

My gracious sovereign, though I must confess 1060
myself far inferior to the report men have published, and nothing answerable to the honour of
your imperial Majesty, yet, for that love and duty
binds me thereunto, I am content to do whatsoever your Majesty shall command me. 1065

EMPEROR

Then, Doctor Faustus, mark what I shall say. As I
was sometime solitary set within my closet, sundry
thoughts arose about the honour of mine ancestors,
how they had won by prowess such exploits, got
such riches, subdued so many kingdoms, as we that 1070
do succeed, or they that shall hereafter possess our
throne, shall — I fear me — never attain to that
degree of high renown and great authority;
amongst which kings is Alexander the Great, chief
spectacle of the world's pre-eminence, 1075
The bright shining of whose glorious acts
Lightens the world with his reflecting beams,
As when I hear but motion made of him
It grieves my soul I never saw the man.
If, therefore, thou, by cunning of thine art, 1080
Canst raise this man from hollow vaults below,
Where lies entombed this famous conqueror,
And bring with him his beauteous paramour,
Both in their right shapes, gesture, and attire
They used to wear during their time of life, 1085
Thou shalt both satisfy my just desire
And give me cause to praise thee whilst I live.

1092-95   For once Faustus is astonishingly honest with himself and others about the limits to what magic
           can do — which makes his infatuation with the ersatz Helen of Troy all the more ironic.

1097   sign of grace: recognizing Faustus' moment of truthfulness to be unusual, the Knight alludes with
           broad irony to the long-standing doctrine of actual grace, namely "A motion of the soul bestowed
           by God *ad hoc* for the production of some good act" (*Oxford Dictionary of the Christian Church*,
           p. 587). It is this actual grace which sets the sinner on the way to salvation through repentance
           and amendment of life.

1099   lively: in a life-like way (*OED* Lively. *adv.* 4).

FAUSTUS

My gracious lord, I am ready to accomplish your
request, so far forth as by art and power of my
spirit I am able to perform.   1090

KNIGHT

(*Aside*) I'faith, that's just nothing at all.

FAUSTUS

But, if it like your Grace, it is not in my ability to
present before your eyes the true substantial
bodies of those two deceased princes, which long
since are consumed to dust.   1095

KNIGHT

(*Aside*) Ay, marry, master doctor, now there's a
sign of grace in you when you will confess the
truth.

FAUSTUS

But such spirits as can lively resemble Alexander
and his paramour shall appear before your   1100
Grace, in that manner that they best lived in, in
their most flourishing estate — which I doubt not
shall sufficiently content your imperial Majesty.

EMPEROR

Go to, master doctor, let me see them presently.

KNIGHT

Do you hear, master doctor? you bring Alexander   1105
and his paramour before the Emperor!

1108-10   An allusion to one of the most famous of classical myths, narrated by Ovid, *Metamorphoses* III, 140-250. Actaeon, grandson of Cadmus, accidentally caught sight of Diana, goddess of chastity, when she was bathing naked. As a punishment, the irate goddess changed him into a stag, whereupon he was pursued and killed by his own hounds. Ovid's seminal account concludes with the question of how just or unjust the goddess was to inflict such a heavy punishment for such an offence. The myth, enormously popular with Renaissance moralists, always carried ambivalent undertones. Shakespeare, in the opening lines of *Twelfth Night*, follows the English emblem writer Whitney and sees Actaeon as the symbol of a violent man destroyed by his own desires. Emblem writers saw him variously as an image of the search after forbidden knowledge or of the arbitrariness of fate; there was even an interpretation which saw Actaeon as Christ transformed into man and unwittingly destroyed by men who did not recognize their god. See Jean Seznee, *The Survival of the Pagan Gods* (Princeton, 1953), p. 93. Here Faustus jokes by diverting the myth into a matter of horns, which are the conventional image for the cuckold (see note to 966).

1112   and: if (*OED* And. *c*. 1); cf. 887.

1119-20   The Emperor is wrong, as most sixteenth- and seventeenth-century accounts of magic and witchcraft indicate: such spectacles are generally regarded as hallucinations. See, for instance, Reginald Scot, *The Discoverie of Witchcraft* (London, 1584).

FAUSTUS

How then, sir?

KNIGHT

I'faith, that's as true as Diana turned me to a
stag.

FAUSTUS

No sir, but when Actaeon died he left the horns   1110
for you. Mephostophiles, be gone!

Exit MEPHOSTOPHILES.

KNIGHT

Nay, and you go to conjuring, I'll be gone.

Exit KNIGHT.

FAUSTUS

I'll meet with you anon for interrupting me so.
Here they are, my gracious lord.

Enter MEPHOSTOPHILES *with* ALEXANDER *and his* PARAMOUR.

EMPEROR

Master doctor, I heard this lady while she lived   1115
had a wart or mole in her neck. How shall I
know whether it be so or no?

FAUSTUS

Your highness may boldly go and see.

EMPEROR

Sure these are no spirits, but the true substantial

1123.1   In *EFB* the horns are fortuitously placed on the Knight's head in a moment of fun; here the incident is modified, becoming part of a confrontation between scholar and soldier. See N. C. Carpenter, "*Miles* versus *Clericus* in Marlowe's *Faustus*", *NQ* 197 (1952), 91-93, and note to 1143.

1125   bachelor: the Emperor plays upon the word as (1) a designation in knighthood, and (2) an unmarried man. The Emperor may also have in mind the meaning of (3) scholarly status, as in *baccalaureus artium* or Bachelor of Arts.

1126   wife . . . horns: see note to 966.

1129   Compare *2 Tamburlaine* III. ii. 89: "Fenc'd with the concave of a monstrous rock." Either Marlowe is having a joke at his own expense or, if he did not write the scene, someone else is recalling a Marlovian-sounding phrase.

1130   gentleman: a person of sufficiently high birth to entitle him to a coat of arms; also, in a more general sense, a person of superior position in society (*OED* Gentleman. 1 and 4).

1131   Villain: originally a low-born rustic, as opposed to gentleman; both words were still redolent of class distinction in Marlowe's time, but by then "villain" could also mean, as it does exclusively now, an unprincipled scoundrel (*OED* Villain. *sb*. 1).

1132   no haste but good: a well-known proverb, making the point that there's no point in hurrying unless it is to good effect (see Tilley, H199).

1135   met with: been revenged upon; the same usage occurs in *Much Ado About Nothing* I. i. 47.

1137   penance: possibly an anti-Catholic jest, since the Church of England did not, by this time, recognise penance as a sacrament.

bodies of those two deceased princes.   1120

Exit ALEXANDER [*and his* PARAMOUR].

FAUSTUS

Will't please your highness now to send for the
knight that was so pleasant with me here of late?

EMPEROR

One of you call him forth.

Enter the KNIGHT *with a pair of horns on his head.*

How now, sir knight? Why, I had thought thou
hadst been a bachelor, but now I see thou hast a   1125
wife, that not only gives thee horns but makes
thee wear them! Feel on thy head!

KNIGHT

Thou damned wretch and execrable dog,
Bred in the concave of some monstrous rock,
How dar'st thou thus abuse a gentleman?   1130
Villain, I say, undo what thou has done.

FAUSTUS

O, not so fast, sir! there's no haste but good.
Are you remembered how you crossed me in
my conference with the Emperor? I think I
have met with you for it.   1135

EMPEROR

Good master doctor, at my entreaty, release
him: he hath done penance sufficient.

1142-43   sir knight . . . speak well of scholars: see note to 1123.1. So concludes the confrontation between scholar and soldier, ending as it usually does in literary accounts, in victory to the scholar.

1147.1   *Exit* EMPEROR: this stage direction takes no account of the Knight or the Attendants brought in at 1046.2. Two explanations are possible: (1) Elizabethan stage directions are often haphazard where there is no need for absolute precision, and in this instance it seems plain enough that the Knight and Attendants can be expected to go off as they came in, i.e. in the wake of the Emperor; (2) some material may be missing. In our opinion the former is more probable. The fact that two further episodes centring on Benvolio (the name given in B to the Knight of the A-version) follow at this point in B does not justify the conclusion of Greg and Jump that material has been *omitted* from A rather than *added* to B. See Introduction.

          However energetically one upholds the integrity of A, the fact remains that to the modern reader the transition from the scene at court with the Emperor to the journey with Mephostophiles across country will seem abrupt. It need not be a problem for the modern theatre director or his audience: the morality tradition so evident elsewhere in *Dr Faustus* allows for such transition by operating within unspecified locale that can be altered in an instant with the removal of a single prop, e.g. a throne for the Emperor. In this tradition the fortunes of the protagonist are paramount and other characters simply fade out once their purpose is served.

1148-49   Though set in prose in A, these two lines are almost certainly blank verse, like those which follow.

1149   silent foot: a common image in sundial mottoes of the period.

1150   The imagery derives from the Greek myth of the three Fates, wherein Clotho spun the thread of life, Lachesis measured it, and Atropos cut it.

          vital life: since *vita* in Latin means life, the phrase is tautologous but used for rhetorical effect.

1151   The line is elliptical; the full meaning would be something like: "Calls for the reward which my behaviour in recent years merits." The idea of death as a debt owed to nature is a Renaissance commonplace, but its meaning is intensified for Faustus by his recollection that the prescribed period of twenty-four years is nearly over.

1153   The return to Wittenberg, Faustus' starting point, anticipates the conclusion.

1155   This fair and pleasant green: the scene has changed from imperial palace to open countryside and the action from stately audience to private journey, all within a few lines. See notes to 948 and 1147.1.

1156.1   A horse-courser was a horse dealer, a profession which then enjoyed the sort of reputation accorded to the second-hand car dealers of today. In the horse-courser episode one may discern a motif common in the medieval *fabliau* whereby someone qualified to perpetrate a particular kind of dishonesty is deceived through the tricks of his own trade.

FAUSTUS

My gracious lord, not so much for the injury he
offered me here in your presence as to delight you
with some mirth, hath Faustus worthily requited   1140
this injurious knight; which being all I desire, I am
content to release him of his horns. And, sir knight,
hereafter speak well of scholars. Mephostophiles,
transform him straight. Now, my good lord, having
done my duty, I humbly take my leave.   1145

EMPEROR

Farewell, master doctor; yet, ere you go, expect
from me a bounteous reward.

                                        Exit EMPEROR.

FAUSTUS

Now, Mephostophiles, the restless course
That time doth run with calm and silent foot,
Shortening my days and thread of vital life,   1150
Calls for the payment of my latest years.
Therefore, sweet Mephostophiles,
Let us make haste to Wittenberg.

MEPHOSTOPHILES

What, will you go on horseback or on foot?

FAUSTUS

Nay, till I am past this fair and pleasant green,   1155
I'll walk on foot.

Enter a HORSE-COURSER.

1158   Fustian: the horse-courser's appellation for Faustus is probably ignorant rather than intentionally insulting, but either way it is apt and suggests that Faustus is degenerating into a word-spinning trickster. Meanings of fustian include high-sounding words, bombast, rant, jargon, made-up language, and gibberish (*OED* Fustian. 2).

1158   Mass: expletive oath, short for "By the Mass."

1165-70   The short passage wherein the horse-courser asks Mephostophiles to intercede for him with Dr Faustus contains in embryo a comic device later to be used to great effect by Ben Jonson in *Volpone* and *The Alchemist*: partners in crime pretend not to be working in collusion and one of them supposedly intercedes with the other on behalf of a third party who is, in fact, their shared victim.

1168-69   . . . he has a great charge, neither wife nor child: he has a great burden of responsibility without a wife or family to comfort him (*OED* Charge. *sb*. II. 8).

1172   ride him not into the water. The motif of disenchantment upon immersion in water is common to many folk cultures. See, for instance, Stith Thompson, D766.1, D766.1.1, and D789.5.

1174   drink of all waters: go anywhere (Gill); as in *Twelfth Night* IV. ii. 57. The expression may also be pseudo-biblical: see Ex. 15.23, Prov. 5.15, and Jer. 2.18.

HORSE-COURSER

I have been all this day seeking one Master
Fustian. Mass, see where he is. God save you,
master doctor.

FAUSTUS

What, horse-courser! you are well met. 1160

HORSE-COURSER

Do you hear, sir? I have brought you forty
dollars for your horse.

FAUSTUS

I cannot sell him so. If thou likest him for fifty,
take him.

HORSE-COURSER

Alas, sir, I have no more. 1165
[To MEPHOSTOPHILES] I pray you, speak for me.

MEPHOSTOPHILES

I pray you let him have him: he is an honest
fellow and he has a great charge, neither wife nor
child.

FAUSTUS

Well, come give me your money. My boy will 1170
deliver him to you. But I must tell you one thing
before you have him: ride him not into the water
at any hand.

HORSE-COURSER

Why, sir, will he not drink of all waters?

FAUSTUS

O yes, he will drink of all waters, but ride him 1175

1180-81   Despite its popularity as a refrain, *OED* does not give an obscene meaning for hey-ding-ding, but see ding, v. 1-4. For eel, see Eric Partridge, *Shakespeare's Bawdy* (London: Routledge and Kegan Paul, 3rd ed., 1968), p. 98.

1182   good-bye [A, God buy]; the phrase from which "good-bye" is contracted was "God-be with you", and "good" became a substitute for "God" by association with other leave-taking formulae, e.g. "good-night" (*OED* Good-bye).

1184   if I bring his water: diagnosis by analysis of urine was common.

1189   fatal time: in two senses, being (1) the time that will be fatal to his soul, i.e. the moment of death; and (2) the time when the pact with the devil must be honoured.

1191   confound: allay (*OED* Confound. *v.* 1).

1193   conceit: frame of mind (*OED* Conceit. *sb.* c); this meaning has long been obsolete.

1193.1   The imperative stage direction once again suggests an instruction to an actor rather than a commentary on the action for the reader. See Note to 614-28 and 1147.1). As to the chair, many of the morality plays required no more in the way of stage properties than a *sedes* or chair and possibly a table.
           The stage direction recalls Dürer's engraving, "The Temptation of the Scholar", which chiefly depicts false *otium*, or leisure degenerated into sloth. See cover illustration.

1195   Dr Lopus: one Dr Lopez was private physician to the Queen until charged with complicity in a plot to poison her. He was executed in June 1594 and enjoyed a brief posthumous notoriety. The allusion is important to us because it supports some views of the text, namely: (1) that the A-text is a report of an actual performance, the allusion intruding into the syntax of the passage in the manner of an *ad lib* that has been faithfully recorded; (2) that the performance thus reported would have been given soon after the scandal broke for so brief and unexplained an *ad lib* to have remained topical; and (3) that the reporter jotted down all that he heard without exercising editorial discretion and thereby left for posterity a very accurate rendition of what he heard and saw. See also Introduction.

1196   purgation . . . purged: the emetic which Dr Faustus has prescribed has been for cleansing the horse-dealer through evacuation of money.

not into the water; ride him over hedge or ditch,
or where thou wilt, but not into the water.

HORSE-COURSER

Well, sir, now am I made man for ever, I'll not
leave my horse for forty. If he had but the quality
of hey-ding-ding, hey-ding-ding, I'd make a   1180
brave living on him; he has a buttock as slick as
an eel. Well, good-bye, sir, your boy will deliver
him me. But hark ye, sir, if my horse be sick or ill
at ease, if I bring his water to you, you'll tell me
what it is?   1185

Exit HORSE-COURSER.

FAUSTUS

Away, you villain! What, dost think I am a horse-
doctor? What art thou, Faustus, but a man con-
demned to die?
Thy fatal time doth draw to final end;
Despair doth drive distrust unto my thoughts.   1190
Confound these passions with a quiet sleep:
Tush, Christ did call the thief upon the cross;
Then rest thee, Faustus, quiet in conceit.

Sleep in his chair.

Enter HORSE-COURSER *all wet, crying.*

HORSE-COURSER

Alas, alas, Doctor Fustian, quotha — mass,
Doctor Lopus was never such a Doctor — has   1195
given me a purgation, has purged me of forty
dollars! I shall never see them more. But yet, like

1205   a bottle of hay: from the French *botte*, meaning bundle. The phrase still exists in British dialect use (*OED* Bottle. *sb³*. 1).

1208   snipper-snapper: insignificant young fellow.

1209   hey-pass: an exclamation used by jugglers or stage conjurors in commanding articles to move; hence an appellation for the juggler himself or, as here, his assistant (*OED* Hey-pass).

1213-14   glass-windows: Faustus' spectacles. Glass windows were still very rare in sixteenth century domestic architecture, so the horse-courser is alluding to Faustus' expensive pretensions, satisfied at his (the horse-courser's) expense.

1215   Faustus' sleep is disturbed almost immediately (1193f). Sleeplessness is often associated with an uneasy conscience in the drama of the period. See, for instance, *Macbeth* II. ii. 34-42.)

an ass as I was, I would not be ruled by him, for
he bade me I should ride him into no water. Now
I, thinking my horse had had some rare quality 1200
that he would not have had me known of, I, like
a venturous youth, rid him into the deep pond at
the town's end. I was no sooner in the middle of
the pond but my horse vanished away and I sat
upon a bottle of hay, never so near drowning in 1205
my life. But I'll seek out my doctor and have my
forty dollars again — or I'll make it the dearest
horse! O, yonder is his snipper-snapper. Do you
hear? you, hey-pass, where's your master?

MEPHOSTOPHILES

Why sir, what would you? you cannot speak with him. 1210

HORSE-COURSER

But I will speak with him.

MEPHOSTOPHILES

Why, he's fast asleep. Come some other time.

HORSE-COURSER

I'll speak with him now, or I'll break his glass-
windows about his ears.

MEPHOSTOPHILES

I tell thee, he has not slept this eight nights. 1215

HORSE-COURSER

And he have not slept this eight weeks, I'll speak
with him.

1223.1   *Hallow*: shout.

1223   So, ho, ho!: huntsman's cry to direct hounds to the hare (Gill).

1224.1   A knockabout incident reminiscent of folk drama and such modern descendents as Punch and Judy. On a more serious level, a parodic and comic variation on the dismemberment motif (see note to 961). Severed heads and limbs were common stage props at the time. See *Henslowe's Diary* p. 318.

MEPHOSTOPHILES

See where he is, fast asleep.

HORSE-COURSER

Ay, this is he. God save ye, master doctor, master
doctor, master Doctor Fustian. Forty dollars,   1220
forty dollars for a bottle of hay!

MEPHOSTOPHILES

Why, thou seest he hears thee not.

HORSE-COURSER

Hallow in his ear: So, ho, ho! so, ho, ho! No,
will you not wake? I'll make you wake ere I go!

Pull him by the leg, and pull it away.

Alas, I am undone! What shall I do?   1225

FAUSTUS

O my leg, my leg! Help, Mephostophiles! call the
officers! My leg, my leg.

MEPHOSTOPHILES

Come, villain, to the constable.

HORSE-COURSER

O Lord, sir, let me go, and I'll give you forty
dollars more.   1230

MEPHOSTOPHILES

Where be they?

1232   hostelry [A, oastrie]: ostry is an obsolete variant of hostry.

1240   Duke of Vanholt: given as Anholt in *EFB*.

1244.2 The phrase "to them" indicates that Faustus and Mephostophiles re-enter immediately, probably at another entrance to indicate that the locale has changed, and that the Duke and Duchess join them after a brief pause.

HORSE-COURSER

I have none about me. Come to my hostelry and
I'll give them you.

MEPHOSTOPHILES

Be gone, quickly!

HORSE-COURSER *runs away.*

FAUSTUS

What, is he gone? Farewell he! Faustus has his leg   1235
again and the horse-courser, I take it, a bottle of
hay for his labour. Well, this trick shall cost him
forty dollars more.

Enter WAGNER.

How now, Wagner? what's the news with thee?

WAGNER

Sir, the Duke of Vanholt doth earnestly entreat   1240
your company.

FAUSTUS

The Duke of Vanholt! an honourable gentleman,
to whom I must be no niggard of my cunning.
Come Mephostophiles, let's away to him.

Exeunt.

Enter to them the DUKE *and the* DUCHESS. *The* DUKE
speaks.

1253   pleasure: please.

1257   a dish of ripe grapes: a traditional icon in Nativity scenes for the blood of the Christ-child, in anticipation of the sacrificial act which will enable later generations to transubstantiate wine into Christ's blood during the Mass. There may be some authorial irony in the pregnant Duchess' craving for grapes "in the dead time of winter" (1256 and 1265-66).

DUKE

Believe me, master doctor, this merriment hath   1245
much pleased me.

FAUSTUS

My gracious lord, I am glad it contents you so
well; but it may be, madam, you take no delight
in this. I have heard that great-bellied women do
long for some dainties or other. What is it,   1250
madam? Tell me, and you shall have it.

DUCHESS

Thanks, good master doctor, and, for I see your
courteous intent to pleasure me, I will not hide
from you the thing my heart desires; and were it
now summer, as it is January and the dead time   1255
of the winter, I would desire no better meat than
a dish of ripe grapes.

FAUSTUS

Alas, madam, that's nothing. Mephostophiles,
be gone.

Exit MEPHOSTOPHILES.

Were it a greater thing than this, so it would   1260
content you, you should have it.

Enter MEPHOSTOPHILES *with the grapes.*

Here they be, madam. Wilt please you taste on
them?

1268-72   Faustus wrongly identifies the climatic difference between northern and southern hemispheres with the distance between east and west, but there may be an allusion to the *colures* of the Ptolemaic scheme. See Heninger, pp. 40 and 198. Saba (Sheba) is the modern Yemen, formerly renowned for its spices; see *Paradise Lost* IV. 162-63.

1279-86   reward . . . reward: the offers of reward and Faustus' obsequiousness in this scene reduce him to the level of an entertainer performing at Royal Command.

DUCHESS

Believe me, master doctor, this makes me wonder
above the rest — that, being in the dead time of 1265
winter and in the month of January, how you
should come by these grapes.

FAUSTUS

If it like your Grace, the year is divided into two
circles over the whole world; that, when it is here
winter with us, in the contrary circle it is sum- 1270
mer with them, as in India, Saba, and farther
countries in the east; and, by means of a swift
spirit that I have, I had them brought hither, as
ye see. How do you like them, madam? be they
good? 1275

DUCHESS

Believe me, master doctor, they be the best
grapes that e'er I tasted in my life before.

FAUSTUS

I am glad they content you so, madam.

DUKE

Come, madam, let us in, where you must well
reward this learned man for the great kindness 1280
he hath showed to you.

DUCHESS

And so I will, my lord, and whilst I live
Rest beholding for this courtesy.

FAUSTUS

I humbly thank your Grace.

1287-94   Wagner acts again as choric commentator (see note to 815.2), and for the last time. In *EFB*, however, Wagner does not fade out at this point but becomes successor to Faustus' magical powers.

The mention of banquetting and carousing shortly before death may be the first of several parodic inversions of Christ's passion (from Latin *passio* = suffering). See Joseph Longo, "Marlowe's *Dr Faustus*: Allegorical Parody in Act V", *Greyfriar* 15 (1974), 38-49.

1295-96   conference about fair ladies: as an exercise in virtuosity, the subject of the most beautiful lady in the ancient world (or the worthiest hero) was common in academic debates.

1304-05   your friendship is unfeigned: in classical, medieval and Renaissance thought, friendship was essentially a mutually improving relationship, based upon moral rectitude. Here, however, the scholar has just incited Faustus to an action that is contrary to Christian morality, i.e. calling up spirits, and which will further jeopardise his soul. See John Conley, "The Doctrine of Friendship in *Everyman*", *Speculum* 44 (1969), 374-82.

DUKE

Come, master doctor, follow us and receive your   1285
reward.

Exeunt.

Enter WAGNER *solus.*

WAGNER

I think my master means to die shortly,
For he hath given to me all his goods;
And yet, methinks, if that death were near,
He would not banquet, and carouse, and swill   1290
Amongst the students — as even now he doth —
Who are at supper with such belly-cheer
As Wagner ne'er beheld in all his life.
See where they come: belike the feast is ended.

Enter FAUSTUS *with two or three* SCHOLARS.

FIRST SCHOLAR

Master Doctor Faustus, since our conference   1295
about fair ladies, which was the beautifullest in all
the world, we have determined with ourselves that
Helen of Greece was the admirablest lady that
ever lived. Therefore, master doctor, if you will do
us that favour, as to let us see that peerless dame   1300
of Greece whom all the world admires for majesty,
we should think ourselves much beholding unto
you.

FAUSTUS

Gentlemen, for that I know your friendship is

1308   Sir Paris: the scholars speak of Paris—the Trojan prince who caused the Trojan War by
          persuading Helen to leave her husband, the Greek King Menelaus, and return with him to
          Troy—as though he were a knight from the world of medieval chivalry and romance. Such
          medievalisation of classical myth was common: see Jean Seznec, *The Survival of the Pagan Gods*
          (Princeton, 1953), at pp. 11–36.

1310   Dardania: Troy, sometimes known eponymously after its legendary founder, Dardanus.

1311.1   HELEN *passeth over over the stage*: this form of words is quite common and seems to signify
          movement across the stage by use of extraordinary places of entry and exit: see Allardyce Nicoll,
          "Passing over the Stage", *Shakespeare Survey* 12 (1959), 47–55.

1314   then [A, tho]: "tho", now archaic, is a demonstrative adverb meaning "at that time" (*OED* Tho.
          adv. 1. 1).

1318.1   The Old Man enters at the moment when the impressionable scholars have just expressed
          admiration for Faustus' soul-endangering act of necromancy. In the morality tradition, forces of
          good and evil counsel vie for the protagonist's attention, as in the opposition between the Good
          and Evil Angels; in a less abstract and more immediately human way, the scholars represent evil
          in the form of meretricious flattery while the Old Man tells Faustus bluntly that he is in danger,
          but not beyond hope of redemption. See B. Langston's essay on "*Dr Faustus* and the *Ars Mori-
          endi* Tradition", in A. Williams (ed.), *A Tribute to George Coffin Taylor: Studies and Essays,
          Chiefly Elizabethan, by his Students and Friends* (Chapel Hill, 1952), 148–67. For detailed
          discussion of the Old Man figure in relation to wider medieval traditions, see T. S. R. Boase,
          Death in the Middle Ages (London, 1972).
          Aspects of this scene are also discussed by Michael J. Warren, "*Dr Faustus*: The Old Man and the
          Text", *ELR* 11 (1981), 111–47.

1322f   J. H. Sims, in *Dramatic Uses of Biblical Allusion in Marlowe and Shakespeare* (Gainsville, 1966),
          says that "Almost everything the Old Man says to Faustus is traceable to Bible texts" (p. 4).
          In some instances it is a question of common biblical cadence rather than significant allusions:
          e.g. in the first two lines "I might prevail" (Num. 22.6, 1 Sam. 17.9); "guide thy steps" (2 Sam.
          22.37, Ps. 18.36, Jer. 10.23); and "the way of life" (Ps. 16.11, Prov. 10.17, John 14.6, Acts 2.28).

unfeigned and Faustus' custom is not to deny the 1305
just requests of those that wish him well, you shall
behold that peerless dame of Greece, no otherwise for pomp and majesty than when Sir Paris
crossed the seas with her and brought the spoils to
rich Dardania. Be silent, then, for danger is in 1310
words.

Music sounds, and HELEN *passeth over the stage.*

SECOND SCHOLAR

Too simple is my wit to tell her praise,
Whom all the world admires for majesty.

THIRD SCHOLAR

No marvel then the angry Greeks pursued
With ten years' war the rape of such a queen, 1315
Whose heavenly beauty passeth all compare.

FIRST SCHOLAR

Since we have seen the pride of nature's works
And only paragon of excellence,

Enter an OLD MAN.

Let us depart, and for this glorious deed
Happy and blessed be Faustus evermore. 1320

FAUSTUS

Gentlemen, farewell; the same I wish to you.

Exeunt SCHOLARS.

OLD MAN

Ah, Doctor Faustus, that I might prevail,
To guide thy steps unto the way of life,

1326-30   Medieval *memento mori* (remember death) literature constantly stresses the corruption and putrefaction of man's mortal body in contrast to the incorruptibility of the soul. A characteristic version is the story of the angel who visits an anchorite to enlist his help in burying a putrefying corpse: the holy man stops his nostrils at the stench, while the angel is impassive; but, as they return to the anchorite's cell, the angel stops his nostrils at the sight of a handsome youth. See Barbara Tuchman, *A Distant Mirror* (New York, 1978).

1330   flagitious: extremely wicked (*OED* Flagitious. *a.* 2). The word is rare before the seventeenth century, but had been used by Wyclif in his 1382 translation of 2 Macc. 7.34.

1331-33   While the idea that sinners are saved by Christ's atonement on the cross is common to most Christian thought, the degree of insistence on Christ's mercy (1332) and the image of grace being infused (1340-42) suggest a Protestant emphasis. The wording of 1333 is very close to Rev. 1.5, where Christ is said to have "washed us from our sinnes in his blood."

1335   despair and die: in the *ars moriendi* (art of dying) tradition, there were usually five temptations to afflict the dying man, one of them being the sin against hope or sin of despair. Temptation to despair was often advanced by brooding on sins committed. The dying man could be rescued from this temptation, however, by the apparition of saints whose salvation testified to divine mercy, e.g. Peter, Paul, Mary Magdalen, and the Good Thief: they would urge him not to despair and would aver that a single moment of true contrition would suffice for his salvation.
Damned thou art: misapplying Calvin's doctrine of predestination, Faustus falls into presumption and despair. At this moment, as Mephostophiles prepares to hand him the dagger (see note to 1337.1), Faustus shows unrepentance, obstinacy, and resistance to truth. Shortly, in envy and malice, he will seek to torment the benevolent Old Man, who reminds him of God's mercy. The function of the Old Man is, in part, as the saving apparition of a saintly being; but in popular Renaissance understanding Faustus may already be beyond salvation through having committed the unforgivable sin against the Holy Ghost (see Matt. 12.31) since unrepentance, obstinacy, and resistance to truth are signs of this sin. See G. H. Cox, "Marlowe's Dr Faustus and 'Sin Against the Holy Ghost'", *HLQ* 36 (1973), 119-37.

1336   Hell calls . . . with a roaring voice: the mouth of hell is frequently represented as the jaws of a beast in medieval iconography and medieval drama. The voice of evil roars like a lion (though God does too!) through the Old Testament, especially in Job and Jeremiah.

1337   Presumably, Mephostophiles has just re-entered. In Tudor drama, the handing of a dagger as an invitation to suicide is a well-established convention to indicate despair: see T. W. Craik, *The Tudor Interlude* (Leicester, 1952). The same motif occurs in the non-dramatic literature of the time, most strikingly in *The Faerie Queene*, I. ix. 33-54, where Despair assails the Redcross Knight: "He to him raught a dagger sharp and keen/And gave it him in hand . . ." See Elaine C. Bowe, "Doctrines and Images of Despair in Christopher Marlowe's *Doctor Faustus* and Edmund Spenser's *The Faerie Queene*" DAI 29 (1969), 2206A.

1340-42   The imagery of angels variously pouring benediction and wrath is pervasive in the apocalyptic vision of Revelation (5.8, 15.7, 16.1-17, 17.1, 21.9). This imagery also became incorporated into the iconography of martyrdom as rendered by the painters of the Italian Renaissance.

By which sweet path thou mayst attain the goal
That shall conduct thee to celestial rest.   1325
Break heart, drop blood, and mingle it with tears,
Tears falling from repentant heaviness
Of thy most vile and loathsome filthiness,
The stench whereof corrupts the inward soul
With such flagitious crimes of heinous sins   1330
As no commiseration may expel
But mercy, Faustus, of thy Saviour sweet,
Whose blood alone must wash away thy guilt.

FAUSTUS

Where art thou, Faustus? wretch, what hast thou done?
Damned art thou, Faustus, damned: despair and die!   1335
Hell calls for right, and with a roaring voice
Says 'Faustus, come; thine hour is come . . .'

MEPHOSTOPHILES *gives him a dagger.*

And Faustus will come to do thee right.

OLD MAN

Ah! stay, good Faustus, stay thy desperate steps:
I see an angel hovers o'er thy head   1340
And with a vial full of precious grace
Offers to pour the same into thy soul.
Then call for mercy, and avoid despair!

FAUSTUS

Ah, my sweet friend, I feel thy words
To comfort my distressed soul: 1345
Leave me awhile to ponder on my sins.

1348.1   There is no stage direction to indicate the Old Man's departure in A.

1349-52   The formal antitheses of the *ars moriendi* and the morality play traditions are very strong here, reinforced by the rhetorical figure of *parison* (clauses of corresponding structure) in 1350.

1352   snare: a trap for animals in the form of a running noose, and hence suggestive of the hangman's rope offered along with other engines of death by figures representing despair (see 650-54 and note).

1353   I arrest thy soul: now that Faustus feels close to death, Mephostophiles makes a show of power. He becomes like the angel of death in the Dance of Death tradition, arresting sinners and taking them to judgement: see John Lydgate, *The Dance of Death* (Ellesmere MS 287, 369, 373, and 567). Hamlet also recalls this tradition as he speaks of death as "this fell sergeant, strict in his arrest" (V. ii. 322). In the Dance of Death tradition, Death is God's minister who calls sinners to account, cutting short their lives for their own good (see *Everyman* 40-50, 63); but in Marlowe's play, Mephostophiles is an impostor who invites Faustus to the wrongful death of suicide.

1355   The threat is exaggerated, for, as Mephostophiles will shortly concede, he can only afflict and even then without success against one who has faith in God (1365-67).

1358-59   Faustus insists on his obligation to the Devil, even though he has had ample opportunity to reflect. As a theologian he might have realized that his compact was no more valid as a pseudo-religious "vow" (1359) than as a contract (see note to 473-77). In traditional moral theology a vow had to be made or confirmed freely and without threat to be valid, and had to tend towards some future good.

1361   greater danger: the only greater danger is damnation, which Mephostophiles hopes to ensure.

1362   that base and crooked age: the Old Man. After the twenty-four years of his career as necromancer, Faustus himself is now old. The Old Man who is to be saved becomes a visual antithesis to the old man who is about to be damned—Faustus himself.

OLD MAN

I go, sweet Faustus, but with heavy cheer,
Fearing the ruin of thy hopeless soul.

[*Exit* OLD MAN.]

FAUSTUS

Accursed Faustus, where is mercy now?
I do repent, and yet I do despair: 1350
Hell strives with grace for conquest in my breast.
What shall I do to shun the snares of death?

MEPHOSTOPHILES

Thou traitor, Faustus, I arrest thy soul
For disobedience to my sovereign lord.
Revolt, or I'll in piecemeal tear thy flesh.   1355

FAUSTUS

Sweet Mephostophiles, entreat thy lord
To pardon my unjust presumption,
And with my blood again I will confirm
My former vow I made to Lucifer.

MEPHOSTOPHILES

Do it then quickly, with unfeigned heart,   1360
Lest greater danger do attend thy drift.

FAUSTUS

Torment, sweet friend, that base and crooked age
That durst dissuade me from thy Lucifer,
With greatest torments that our hell affords.

1369   glut . . . desire: once again gluttony and lechery merge, lulling Faustus into the distractions of sloth, the sin which provokes despair (see notes to 793–97, 799–801).

1370–71   paramour . . . Helen: commentators have disagreed as to whether in the following episode Faustus commits an unpardonable sin of demoniality in having sexual intercourse with a *succubus* (devil in female form) or whether such a sin was thought to exist. The writers on witchcraft agree that this sin does occur but that it may be pardoned. Commentators on the issue in relation to *Dr Faustus* have taken their evidence from less authoritative sources. See Michael J. Warren "*Dr Faustus*: The Old Man and the Text" *ELR* 11 (1981), 111–47, at p. 138.

          Ignoring the remaining way of escape which Mephostophiles himself has confirmed (1365–67), Faustus' request for Helen as a distraction from his spiritual plight has specific significance: Helen represented, according to medieval moralised reading of Homer, the destructiveness of sensuality unchecked by moral restraint. Renaissance commentaries extended the significance to an earlier phase in the myth, where Paris awarded the golden apple contested by three goddesses to Venus and in return was promised her closest earthly manifestation—Helen. Hence, this tale of an apple and its destructive outcome was viewed as a pagan glimmering of the biblical fall of man. See Don Cameron Allen, *Image and Meaning*, revised edition (Baltimore, 1968).

1373–74   vow . . . oath: see note to 1358–59.

1377–96   Though this is one of the most poignant dramatic speeches ever written, exquisitely expressing a yearning for the lost world of heroic Greece, its matter is at odds with its manner. Marlowe has created in it a microcosm of the play itself—full of vain aspiration based upon deluded vision and dependent upon a passion that can express itself only in terms of destruction. Perhaps it should be understood as a piece of overwrought bombast.

1377   Was this the face . . .?: no, it wasn't. See note to 1092–95.

          a thousand ships: Homer does not number the ships of the Greek fleet. It is possible that Marlowe is alluding to Homer at one or two removes, through Lucian or Seneca: see A. H. Gilbert, "A thousand ships", *MLN* 66 (1951), 477–78.

1379   make me immortal: the embrace of the false Helen only confirms Faustus in his mortality and heightens the likelihood of his damnation. In the remainder of the speech, classical epic is transformed into medieval romance. (See note to 1308.)

          The transformation hints at the sexual amorality of the chivalric romance and the pathos of an ageing scholar attempting to become a man of action in his last days.

1380   sucks: given that what Faustus sees is not Helen but a *succubus*, Marlowe is here using the rhetorical figure of *syllepsis* (using one word while suggesting two meanings) for ironic resonance.

1382   Here will I . . .: the expression recurs as "I will" in 1384, 1386, and 1388, hinting at Faustus' self-destructive wilfulness in seeking out the impossible; Marlowe uses the rhetorical device of *parison* (corresponding structure in a sequence of clauses, pointed up by the same verbal formula).

1383.1   The silent, but visually telling, re-entry of the Old Man at the moment when Faustus declares that "all is dross that is not Helena" is a reminder of other values.

1384–85   Earlier in his career Faustus had promised to do great things for Germany and its schools through his magic; now, in the cause of self-gratification, he wishes to destroy even the university that made him.

1386   weak Menelaus: husband of Helen, he was far from weak. He would have defeated Paris in single combat (*Iliad*, iii), but for the intervention of the goddess Aphrodite on behalf of her favourite, Paris (see note to 1370–71).

1388   Though Achilles slew Hector, the Trojan champion, Paris managed to wound Achilles in the heel; this was Achilles' undoing, for one heel was the only part of his body which had not been charmed into invulnerability when he was dipped, as an infant, into the River Styx by his mother, Thetis.

MEPHOSTOPHILES

His faith is great: I cannot touch his soul;   1365
But what I may afflict his body with
I will attempt, which is but little worth.

FAUSTUS

One thing, good servant, let me crave of thee:
To glut the longing of my heart's desire,
That I may have unto my paramour   1370
That heavenly Helen which I saw of late,
Whose sweet embracings may extinguish clean
These thoughts that do dissuade me from my vow,
And keep mine oath I made to Lucifer.

MEPHOSTOPHILES

Faustus, this — or what else thou shalt desire —   1375
Shall be performed in twinkling of an eye.

Enter HELEN.

FAUSTUS

Was this the face that launched a thousand ships
And burnt the topless towers of Ilium?
Sweet Helen, make me immortal with a kiss.
Her lips sucks forth my soul: see where it flies!   1380
Come, Helen, come give me my soul again.
Here will I dwell, for heaven be in these lips,
And all is dross that is not Helena.

Enter OLD MAN.

I will be Paris, and for love of thee
Instead of Troy shall Wittenberg be sacked;   1385
And I will combat with weak Menelaus,
And wear thy colours on my plumed crest;
Yea, I will wound Achilles in the heel

1392-93   The story of Semele follows immediately upon that of Actaeon in *Metamorphoses* III, and shares
with it the common theme of a mere mortal's presumptuousness in knowing, or seeking to know,
the hidden nature of a divine being. Semele, mistress of Jupiter, monarch of the gods, implored
him to manifest himself to her in his full divine form; she perished in the resultant conflagration.

1394-95   Arethusa was a nymph of Elis who bathed in the waters of the river Alpheus and thereby inflamed
his lust. She fled from him and he pursued her underground course to Sicily, where she was transformed into a spring. The myth of Alpheus and Arethusa was usually ponderously allegorised as a
version of the soul's pursuit of truth. George Sandys, writing in 1632, remarks in his commentary
on *Metamorphoses* V that "Alpheus drew his pedigree from the Sun," presumably drawing on
Fulgentius, who allegorises Alpheus in this myth as "veritas lux" (= the light of truth).

1397-1405 The Old Man's admonition, given with the brusque earnestness of one who is himself close to
death, is in keeping with the tradition of the wise old counsellor in the morality play, a tradition
which Shakespeare was shortly to reaffirm in the figure of John of Gaunt in *Richard II*, and again
later in the figure of the Earl of Kent in *King Lear*. See also note to 1318.1.

1398   The Old Man talks of Faustus excluding grace as his own act of will. The Old Man's speech is in
accord with moderate Anglicanism of the late sixteenth century, which had moved away from its
sterner Calvinist tendencies. Calvin taught that grace was irresistible to God's chosen, but that it
was never offered to the reprobate.

1400   sift: make trial of (*OED* Sift. *v.* 2.a). This rather unusual usage occurs in Christ's last words to
Peter, as rendered in the Coverdale Bible of 1535: "Satan hath desyred after you, that he might
sifte you even as wheate" (Luke 22.31). This allusion is a reminder that Marlowe did not only
know or have recourse to the Geneva Bible, which has "winnow" instead of sift.

1401   There may also be an allusion here to 1 Peter 1.7, where the apostle talks of faith being tried by
fire.

1403   heavens smiles: another example of the singular form of the verb following a plural subject (see
note to 460).

1405.2   In the B-version, a scene of gloating devils follows at this point. They rejoice that they have him
in their power and they are joined by the Evil Angel, who describes the torture-house of hell in
terms of pitch-forks and boiling lead (B1895-1919, 1995-2034). The added material in the B-
version puts Faustus beyond redemption before his death and prepares for the final scene of the
B-version (B2093-2122) wherein Faustus' dismembered body is discovered.

And then return to Helen for a kiss.
O, thou art fairer than the evening air,   1390
Clad in the beauty of a thousand stars;
Brighter art thou than flaming Jupiter
When he appeared to hapless Semele,
More lovely than the monarch of the sky
In wanton Arethusa's azured arms —   1395
And none but thou shalt be my paramour.

Exeunt.

OLD MAN

Accursed Faustus, miserable man,
That from thy soul exclud'st the grace of heaven
And fliest the throne of his tribunal seat!

Enter the DEVILS.

Satan begins to sift me with his pride: 1400
As in this furnace, God shall try my faith;
My faith, vile hell, shall triumph over thee.
Ambitious fiends, see how the heavens smiles
At your repulse and laughs your state to scorn.
Hence hell! for hence I fly unto my God.   1405

Exeunt.

Enter FAUSTUS *with the* SCHOLARS.

FAUSTUS

Ah, gentlemen!

1408   chamber-fellow: a companion; a usage deriving from the practice of sharing a room or rooms at university or the Inns of Court (*OED* Chamber-fellow).

1410f   For the first time in the play, the *psychomachia* (internal conflict) is presented subjectively — psychologically in the modern sense — and not in terms of externalised allegorical representations, to the extent that what Faustus perceives here and at 1441 is not perceived by others. In this development, Marlowe affirms the witchcraft writers' view that the devil works upon and deceives his own followers through delusion and hallucination.

1416   a surfeit of deadly sin: the culmination to the imagery of appetite in the play; Faustus' response to the pageant of the seven deadly sins was "This feeds my soul." (804.)

1420-22   Once again, Faustus' despair is dependent upon perverse pride. Now he uses the anathematised doctrine of *apocatastasis* (see 644) not for its own heretical sake, but simply to aver that his capacity for sin exceeds even the devil's. His reference to the devil's great sin of tempting Adam and Eve to their fall is yet another reminder that Faustus himself has replicated original sin in his search for forbidden knowledge. See note to 18-26. The motif of despair as pride in one of its more perverse manifestations is quite common in medieval and Renaissance writing; Skelton gave it notable dramatic treatment in *Magnyfycence* (ed. Happé; Harmondsworth, 1979), 2300f.

FIRST SCHOLAR

What ails Faustus?

FAUSTUS

Ah, my sweet chamber fellow! Had I lived with
thee, then had I lived still, but now I die
eternally. Look: comes he not? comes he not?   1410

SECOND SCHOLAR

What means Faustus?

THIRD SCHOLAR

Belike he is grown into some sickness by being
over-solitary.

FIRST SCHOLAR

If it be so, we'll have physicians to cure him.
'Tis but a surfeit, never fear, man.   1415

FAUSTUS

A surfeit of deadly sin that hath damned both
body and soul.

SECOND SCHOLAR

Yet, Faustus, look up to heaven: remember
God's mercies are infinite.

FAUSTUS

But Faustus' offence can ne'er be pardoned.   1420
The serpent that tempted Eve may be saved,
but not Faustus. Ah, gentlemen, hear me with
patience and tremble not at my speeches,

1425-27   Faustus rejects the humanistic tradition rather than his abuse of it.

1426-34   At the outset, Faustus sought his "world of profit and delight" (82) in defiance of the specific
           warning given in Mark 8.36: "For what shal it profite a man, thugh he shulde winne the whole
           worlde, if he lose his soule?" He now returns to the same passage from scripture in a changed state
           of mind, but without hope of salvation through repentance. Instead, he uses it to justify his
           despair.

1438   One of the alleged signs of a witch was his/her inability to shed tears: "No not so much as their
           eyes are able to shed teares (thretten and torture them as ye please) while first they repent (God
           not permitting them to dissemble their obstinacie in so horrible a crime)"—James I,
           Daemonologie, p. 81.

though my heart pants and quivers to remember
that I have been a student here these thirty years.   1425
O, would I had never seen Wittenberg, never read
book! And what wonders I have done all Germany
can witness, yea all the world; for which Faustus
hath lost both Germany and the world, yea, heaven
itself — Heaven the seat of God, the throne of the   1430
blessed, the kingdom of joy — and must remain in
hell for ever; hell, ah, hell for ever! Sweet friends,
what shall become of Faustus, being in hell for
ever?

THIRD SCHOLAR

Yet, Faustus, call on God.   1435

FAUSTUS

On God, whom Faustus hath abjured? on God,
whom Faustus hath blasphemed? Ah, my God, I
could weep, but the devil draws in my tears. Gush
forth blood, instead of tears, yea, life and soul! O,
he stays my tongue! I would lift up my hands, but   1440
see — they hold them, they hold them!

ALL

Who, Faustus?

FAUSTUS

Lucifer and Mephostophiles.
Ah, gentlemen! I gave them my soul for my cunning.

ALL

God forbid!   1445

1447   Vain: unprofitable, worthless (*OED* Vain. *a.* 1); the sense employed in the famous aphorism of Ecclesiastes: "Vanitie of vanities, saith the Preacher, vanieies of vanieies, all is vanity." (1.2.)

four-and-twenty [B; A, 24].

1449   bill: see notes to 473–77, 501, and 506.

1458–70   This episode in following Wagner's choric commentary on Faustus' last supper with his students before his impending death, extends the ironic comparison with Christ's last supper into the next stage of his Passion — the agony in the garden. Here Christ asks three apostles to watch and pray while he prepares himself spiritually for the events to come. In the play, Faustus is seen with three students, he reflects upon the necessity of what must follow (1449-50), and he asks the three to pray for him (1463-65). See note to 1287-94.

1458   save [B; not in A].

FAUSTUS

God forbade it indeed, but Faustus hath done it:
for vain pleasure of four-and-twenty years hath
Faustus lost eternal joy and felicity. I writ them a
bill with mine own blood: the date is expired, the
time will come, and he will fetch me.   1450

FIRST SCHOLAR

Why did not Faustus tell us of this before, that
divines might have prayed for thee?

FAUSTUS

Oft have I thought to have done so, but the devil
threatened to tear me in pieces if I named God,
to fetch both body and soul if I once gave ear to   1455
divinity; and now 'tis too late: gentlemen away,
lest you perish with me.

SECOND SCHOLAR

O, what shall we do to [save] Faustus?

FAUSTUS

Talk not of me, but save yourselves and depart.

THIRD SCHOLAR

God will strengthen me: I will stay with Faustus.   1460

FIRST SCHOLAR

Tempt not God, sweet friend, but let us into the
next room and there pray for him.

1470.1   In the B-version, the scene continues with a triumphant speech by Mephostophiles and concludes with another visitation of the Good and Evil Angels, in which the Evil Angel gloats on the horrors of hell in turgid rhymed verse (see note to 1405.2).

1470.2   The striking of the clock initiates the single remaining hour of Faustus' life, and it is passed in a monologue of just under sixty lines. The phrase 'the eleventh hour' has widespread currency, of course, because of the parable of the labourers in the vineyard (Matthew 20, 1-16), which indicates the possibility of last-minute salvation, and which immediately precedes Christ's announcement of his own sacrifice (20.17-19). Marlowe may also be using the commonplace idea of the twelve ages of man, based upon the parallel between the individual life and the months of the year, and, hence, the houses of the zodiac. In Augustine and the Church Fathers, eleven is the number of error and transgression, as it goes beyond ten, the divine *tetraktys*, envisaged as the image of perfection, and is therefore an image of excess.

1477-79   The sentiment is akin to Augustine's famous prayer, "Give me chastity and continence, but not yet" (*Confessions*, VIII, 7).

1480   *O lente, lente currite noctis equi*: Run slowly, O horses of the night. A quotation from Ovid's erotic elegy in *Amores* I (13, 37-38) where the poet, in the arms of his mistress, composes an ode to Aurora, goddess of sunrise, imploring her to imagine that she is in bed with a lover, and reluctant to rise. Marlowe's own translation reads, "But heldst thou in thine armes some Cephalus; Then wouldst thou cry, stay night and runne not thus." (The Mason Text, reprinted in a Scolar Press facsimile, 1973, n.p.) So Faustus concludes his appeal to the heavens with a quotation from a pornographic poem. Ovid's elegy was widely admired by Renaissance poets, and much imitated.

FAUSTUS

Ay, pray for me, pray for me; and what noise
soever ye hear, come not unto me, for nothing
can rescue me.   1465

SECOND SCHOLAR

Pray thou, and we will pray that God may have
mercy upon thee.

FAUSTUS

Gentlemen, farewell. If I live till morning, I'll
visit you; if not, Faustus is gone to hell.

ALL

Faustus, farewell.   1470

Exeunt SCHOLARS.

The clock strikes eleven.

FAUSTUS

Ah, Faustus —
Now hast thou but one bare hour to live,
And then thou must be damned perpetually.
Stand still, you ever-moving spheres of heaven,
That time may cease, and midnight never come.   1475
Fair nature's eye, rise, rise again, and make
Perpetual day; or let this hour be but a year,
A month, a week, a natural day,
That Faustus may repent and save his soul.
O lente, lente currite noctis equi!   1480
The stars move still, time runs, the clock will strike,
The devil will come, and Faustus must be damned.

1483-87   Faustus, whose quest for forbidden knowledge has re-enacted the sin of the First Adam, now appeals to the redemptive blood of the Second Adam, Christ, in an attempt to establish a personal relationship between fallen man and his saviour. The imagery here, as elsewhere in the final passage, should be compared with that of the contract at 475f. Faustus' pact with the devil is a parodic version of God's covenant with man: see 515.

1483   Probably suggested by the conventional emblem of a man with a winged arm and a weighted arm: see Whitney's *A Choice of Emblemes*, p. 152, reproduced on p. xlix of the present edition, figure 7. "One hande with winges, woulde flie unto the starres,/And raise mee up to winne immortall fame . . . th'other still is bounde,/With heavie stone, which houldes it to the grounde." A version of this emblem (Alciati, ed. 1567, emblem 64), appears on the title page of the 1604 edition of *Doctor Faustus*, where it serves as the device of the printer Valentine Simmes.

1486   Calvin says that those in despair "do finde no rest, from being vexed and tossed with a terrible whirle-winde, from feeling themselves to be torne in peeces by God being angirly bent against them." (*Institution of the Christian Religion*, as quoted by Kocher, p. 113).

1487-70   Invoking the name of Lucifer, Faustus loses the vision of Christ. It is replaced by a vision of the stern Jehovah of the Old Testament, with the avenging, weapon-wielding arm of medieval illumination and Renaissance pietistic engraving.

1491-92   This image of inescapable judgment is reminiscent of Jewish apocalyptic writing. See Luke 23.30: "Then shal they beginne to say to the mountaines, Fall on us; and to the hills, Cover us." See also Hosea 10.8 and Revelation 6.16: ". . . And said to the mountaines and rockes, Fall on us, and hide us from the presence of him that sitteth on the throne, and from the wrath of the Lambe."

1493-1501 There may be an ironic and complex allusion here to the fall of Lucifer as recounted in Isaiah 14. 12-16. See J. P. Brockbank, "Damned Perpetually," in *Dr Faustus: a Casebook* (London, 1969), pp. 174-75.

1495-96   Faustus is alluding to his horoscope, and to the disposition of the stars at his nativity: he asserts that he was predestined to be damned. Generally speaking, the proponents of natural astrology upheld the concept of Free Will, and man's accountability for his own actions, by saying that the stars which reign at one's nativity may provide one with particular character traits, but Free Will remains unimpaired. See Don Cameron Allen, *The Star-Crossed Renaissance* (Durham, N.C.: 1941).

1501.1   *The watch* . . . In the obsolete sense of a dial or clock-face (*OED* watch. *sb.* 20), and not the modern sense of a small pocket chronometer. Cf. *Richard II*, V. v. 49-58.

1507   . . . a thousand years: Not an empty hyperbole. Ten was the number of completion, and of the circle, as were its multiplicates one hundred, one thousand and so forth. Ben Jonson's "Epistle to Elizabeth Countess of Rutland" concludes its hundred lines with "a vow as new, and ominous as the years,/Before his swift and circled race be run". See Donne's ten-line poem, "The Computation".

1508   The belief that hell would ultimately pass away originates with Origen; for a detailed discussion, see D. P. Walker, *The Decline of Hell: Seventeenth-Century Discussions of Eternal Torment* (London, 1964), passim, and especially pp. 59-70. See also notes to 322-23, 644, and 1420-22.

1512   *Metempsychosis* [A, *Metem su cossis*; B, *Metemsycosis*]. The A-text gives a good phonetic rendering of what would have been heard in the theatre. Scansion and lineation are a traditional problem here; we agree with Simpson in lineation and scansion, viz.,

Ah, Pýthagóras *métempsýchosis!*

1512-14   The doctrine of the transmigration of souls in Western thought is usually associated with the sixth century BC Greek philosopher, Pythagoras of Samos. He is also associated with number symbolism.

1513-16   These lines are ironic when viewed as the culmination of lines 90-92.

1514-15   Lineation as in B; rendered as one line in A.

O, I'll leap up to my God! who pulls me down?
See, see where Christ's blood streams in the firmament;
One drop would save my soul, half a drop. Ah, my
Christ!
Ah, rend not my heart for naming of my Christ —   1485
Yet will I call on him — oh, spare me Lucifer!
Where is it now? 'Tis gone.
And see where God stretcheth out his arm
And bends his ireful brows.   1490
Mountains and hills, come, come, and fall on me
And hide me from the heavy wrath of God.
No, no! then will I headlong run into the earth.
Earth, gape! O no, it will not harbour me.
You stars that reigned at my nativity,   1495
Whose influence hath allotted death and hell,
Now draw up Faustus like a foggy mist
Into the entrails of yon labouring cloud,
That when you vomit forth into the air
My limbs may issue from your smoky mouths,   1500
So that my soul may but ascend to heaven.

The watch strikes.

Ah! half the hour is past:
'Twill all be past anon.
O God, if thou wilt not have mercy on my soul,
Yet for Christ's sake, whose blood hath ransomed me,   1505
Impose some end to my incessant pain.
Let Faustus live in hell a thousand years,
A hundred thousand, and at last be saved.
O, no end is limited to damned souls.
Why wert thou not a creature wanting soul?   1510
Or, why is this immortal that thou hast?
Ah, Pythagoras' *metempsychosis!* were that true,
This soul should fly from me and I be changed
Unto some brutish beast:

1518   At one level, these parents are Adam and Eve, but the line also suggests the curses of Job at 3.3 and 3.11.

1523-24   An idea current among non-Christian Arab philosophers of the Middle Ages was of the spiritual universe as an ocean from which each individual human soul is a droplet temporarily detached during life, returning to the ocean of the world-soul on death and therefore becoming indistinguishable and undifferentiated. Cf. Andrew Marvell's poem "On a Drop of Dew."

1528   The Renaissance magus traditionally renounces his craft *in extremis*. See Andrew V. Ettin, "Magic into Art: the Magician's Renunciation of Magic in English Renaissance Drama," *TSLL* 19 (1977), 268-93.

1528.1   Between Faustus' last words and the Epilogue the B-text intrudes a scene in which scholars collect together Faustus' scattered remains and give them a decent burial. This scene distorts Marlowe's conclusion, which strongly suggests that the devil's final and finest trick upon Faustus is to induce his suicide. There is reference to the gathering of Faustus' mangled remains in *EFB*, but this is one of the many pieces of sensationalist credulity which Marlowe omits from his play.

1529-30   Some critics suggest that the homiletic epilogue derives from the *Mirror for Magistrates* and that the first two lines are directly indebted to Thomas Churchyard's contribution on "Shore's Wife" in the *Mirror*. See A. Thaler, "Churchyard and Marlowe," *MLN* 38 (1923), 89-92. More significant, perhaps, is the suggestion that the two lines recall Christ's parable of the vine, as related in John 15.4-7: see M. O'Brien, "Christian Relief in *Dr Faustus*," *ELH* 37 (1970), 1-11. But the moral significance of pruning is a commonplace in the emblem tradition, where the gnarled or twisted bough which is lopped and burned, and the straight bough which flourishes, are often graphically represented. See Henkel and Schöne, cols. 152-164.

1530   The laurel has many meanings in Renaissance iconography, most of which are connected with fame, poetic eminence, or worldly success. The meaning here, however, is probably related to the popular idea that the laurel was difficult to burn. In Ripa's *Iconologia* (Rome, 1613), the burning of the laurel is an image of the purification of those who have offended God; Whitney (p. 67) prints verses comparing the laurel with a clear conscience, and the virtuous "are like unto the Laurell tree,/The others, like the blasted boughes that die." The imagery hence suggests the depth of Faustus' fall from what he should have been, and refers us, indirectly, back to the novel and specialised nature of the play's subject matter as described in the Chorus' initial lines.

All beasts are happy, for when they die   1515
Their souls are soon dissolved in elements,
But mine must live still to be plagued in hell.
Cursed be the parents that engendered me!
No, Faustus, curse thyself, curse Lucifer
That hath deprived thee of the joys of heaven.   1520

The clock striketh twelve.

O, it strikes! it strikes! now, body, turn to air,
Or Lucifer will bear thee quick to hell.

Thunder and lightning.

O soul, be changed into little water drops
And fall into the ocean, ne'er be found.
My God! my God! look not so fierce on me!   1525

Enter DEVILS

Adders and serpents, let me breathe awhile!
Ugly hell, gape not! come not Lucifer!
I'll burn my books — ah, Mephostophiles!

                                   Exeunt with him.

Enter CHORUS.

CHORUS

Cut is the branch that might have grown full straight,
And burned is Apollo's laurel bough   1530
That sometime grew within this learned man.

1536.1   *Terminat hora diem, terminat author opus.* "The hour has concluded the day, the writer has finished his task." The hour has concluded the last day of Faustus' life. His last twenty-four hours also complete his allotted span of twenty-four years as magician. Editors have found no classical source for the line, and have inclined to the view that it was added by the printer of the A-text and thence included in subsequent editions. Its gnomic nature suggests, perhaps, affinities with the motto of the traditional emblem. Its source is almost certainly quite demotic, as it is virtually identical with many of the lugubrious *memento mori* inscriptions which garnished sundials in the sixteenth and seventeenth centuries, and which invited the onlooker to view his own impending death in the concluding hours of the day whose course he was scrutinising. *Nulla hora sine linea.* See H. K. F. Eden and Eleanor Lloyd (eds), *The Book of Sundials* (London: Bell, 3rd ed., 1890).

    The emblem which concludes the text of the 1604 edition, a framed device of Justice striking a bushel of corn, with the motto "Such as I make. Such will I take," is the personal device of the printer, Valentine Simmes. For this device, and for the device cited above at 1483, see Ronald B. McKerrow, *Printers' and Publishers' Devices in England and Scotland, 1485–1640* (London: The Bibliographical Society, 1949), entries 142 and 313.

Faustus is gone: regard his hellish fall,
Whose fiendful fortune may exhort the wise
Only to wonder at unlawful things,
Whose deepness doth entice such forward wits   1535
To practise more than heavenly power permits.

Terminat hora diem, terminat author opus.